T0215657

Software
Quality Assurance

Integrating Testing, Security, and Audit

Internal Audit and IT Audit

Series Editor: Dan Swanson

Software Quality Assurance

Integrating Testing, Security, and Audit

Abu Sayed Mahfuz

CRC Press
Taylor & Francis Group
Boca Raton   London   New York

CRC Press is an imprint of the
Taylor & Francis Group, an **informa** business
AN AUERBACH BOOK

CRC Press
Taylor & Francis Group
6000 Broken Sound Parkway NW, Suite 300
Boca Raton, FL 33487-2742

First issued in paperback 2021

© 2016 by Taylor & Francis Group, LLC
CRC Press is an imprint of Taylor & Francis Group, an Informa business

No claim to original U.S. Government works

Printed on acid-free paper
Version Date: 20151124

ISBN-13: 978-1-4987-3553-7 (hbk)
ISBN-13: 978-0-367-56797-2 (pbk)

Library of Congress Cataloging-in-Publication Data

Names: Mahfuz, Abu Sayed, author.
Title: Software quality assurance : integrating testing, security, and audit / author, Abu
    Sayed Mahfuz.
Description: Boca Raton : Taylor & Francis, 2015. | Includes bibliographical references
    and index.
Identifiers: LCCN 2015045370 | ISBN 9781498735537 (alk. paper)
Subjects: LCSH: Computer software--Quality control. | Computer software--Testing.
Classification: LCC QA76.76.Q35 M34 2015 | DDC 005.3028/7--dc23
LC record available at http://lccn.loc.gov/2015045370

Visit the Taylor & Francis Web site at
http://www.taylorandfrancis.com

and the CRC Press Web site at
http://www.crcpress.com

Contents

V

SECTION II TESTING

Section III Challenges

Preface

Twelve years ago in my master's degree class, when I was introduced to software quality, information security, and audit courses, honestly speaking, I was not able to comprehend the in-depth meaning, importance, and necessity of it as much as I did a few years later when I started working as a software quality specialist in the real world.

Software quality and cybersecurity are comparatively well known in the IT field; however, I am a little dissatisfied when it is given less importance or taken lightly. This is one of the motivations behind writing this book.

The advocacy of this book is the high value of software quality, security, and reliability, which are the integral characteristics of it. Audit, inspection, and testing are the methodological processes to reach this goal.

We cannot complete the meaning of software quality without including security, reliability, inspection, and audit, which is the ultimate perspective of this book.

This book offers 11 chapters in 4 sections.

As the very high-level overview: Section I, which includes Chapters 1 and 2, addresses the basic concepts of software quality and software life cycle.

Section II, which contains Chapters 3–5, is about testing, the definition, planning and designing of tests, and after testing is complete, how to prepare test result and reports.

Section III includes Chapters 6–8, which basically deal with challenges, incidents, defects, and risk management.

Section IV includes Chapters 9–11 and discusses recommendations about the best characteristics of software quality such as information security, audit and software reliability, and process management.

Content Overview

Chapter 1 "Quality Concept and Perspectives" contains four parts that discuss software quality concepts, quality characteristics, validation and verification, reviews and audits. Most of the theoretical part of this chapter is based on IEEE Standards such as IEEE 9126, 1012, COBIT, and CMMI.

Chapter 2 "Management and Process" includes three major parts concerned with software management, software life cycle, and life cycle process.

Software management includes information governance, information technology governance, overall strategic management, and data governance; it also includes IEEE 12207 as the expert models for software management. Part 2, "Software Life Cycle Models" includes three major models: spiral, agile, and waterfall. Part 3 discusses the life cycle processes and highlights the primary life cycle process and supporting life cycle processes.

Chapter 3 "Testing: Concept and Definition" includes three major parts: "Testing in the Software Life Cycle," "Software Testing Life Cycle," and "Kinds/Types of Testing." This chapter also addresses how testing is an integral part of overall software development and the whole development process. The chapter further discusses the whole testing process and its life cycle.

Chapter 4 "Testing: Plan and Design" includes four major parts: Part 1 discusses test plan and strategy, Part 2 addresses test approach and stages, Part 3 addresses test design factors, and Part 4 introduces test case specification and design.

The four parts introduce definition of testing and a real-time practical plan and how the plan should be designed. "Test Approach and Stages" introduces step-by-step process of test design, requirement analysis, preparing test data, test scheduling, test estimation, and so on. Part 3 "Test Design Factors" discusses the test design process and factors involved in test designing, and Part 4 "Test Case Specification and Design" introduces the test case design process and it also introduces sample test case.

Chapter 5 "Test: Execution and Reporting" includes three major parts; it fundamentally introduces test execution and the result reporting process—basically what a tester or test lead needs to do before starting test execution and during test execution and how to report after completing the test execution, including requirement traceability matrices, defect reports, and so on.

Chapter 6 "Incident Management" includes five major parts. This chapter defines incident, accident and failure, roots and sources of any incident that may occur, and also discusses initial documentation and classification of any incident.

This chapter also discusses the need and the process of an investigation and how to handle an incident. Part 4 provides a sample form for how to document an issue. Finally, Part 5, on security incidents discusses reporting and responding to security incidents.

Chapter 7 is concerned with defect management, what is a defect, why defects happen, and how to prevent them.

There are three parts in this chapter. Part 1 addresses the definition and analysis of defects; Part 2 addresses the defect management process and methodology; and Part 3 addresses root cause analysis, introducing the practical methodologies of how to manage and how to prevent defects in the future.

Chapter 8 is concerned with risk, vulnerability, and threat management. The three parts of this chapter and two appendices address conceptual aspects and identification of risks, vulnerability, and threats. Part 1 addresses risk, its identification, assessment, risk response, and mitigation. Part 2 addresses the combination of overall vulnerability with risk and threat. Part 3 provides mostly evaluations and solutions from the OCTAVE perspective.

Chapter 9 addresses information security in three parts. Part 1 provides the definition and the importance of information security and discusses the different aspects of security issues, what needs to be secured and from what. It also provides some examples of security issues. Part 2 discusses the methodologies and strategies of information security based on ISO standards, COBIT, and OCTAVE. Part 3 provides an example of a security policy document.

Chapter 10 discusses the information audit in three parts. Part 1 addresses the basic definition and planning aspects of an information audit, different dimensions of audit planning, and details of an IT audit. Part 2 addresses the key considerations for IT audit processes and procedures. Part 3 discusses the audit and information security aspects, and it indicates what an auditor needs to focus on to ensure the information security assurance is audited.

Chapter 11 contains two parts. Part 1 discusses the definition and measurement and metrics of reliability based on standards and quality metrics methodology (CMM) models. Part 2 discusses ISO 15504 standard, CMMs, PSP, and TSP. This chapter also has an appendix that contains a software process improvement sample document.

Acknowledgments

First, I thank Professor Dan Shoemaker, who introduced me to the whole idea of software quality and audit 13 years ago in 2003, in my master's degree class at the University of Detroit Mercy, and also for his recent encouragement in authoring this book. My heartfelt prayer and salute goes to the soul of my late father Mowlana Tofael Ahmad who left a huge legacy to me in knowledge, dignity, and principle; and to my late mother Mushfika Begum for her unparalleled love, care, and unconditional support. May God please be with you.

I must acknowledge my wife Mehona for her great support and patience with me, my son Saleh and (while authoring) 1-year-old daughter Rahma, from whom I have taken precious time to author this book. Rahma means blessings, and she truly brought blessings into my life with her birth. I certainly owe you both more time, and you truly deserve it.

I am thankful to Dan Swanson, for his consistent guidance and advice on this book; thanks to my friend Shuzon Reza, senior system analyst at Bank of America, for taking the time to review this book and for his valuable feedback. Certainly my appreciation goes to CRC Press, Taylor & Francis Group for their desire to publish this book.

Author

Abu Sayed Mahfuz, ITIL, MIS, MA, has over 15 years of experience in the business and information technology profession, including database management, technology manager, software quality lead and technology instruction in such prestigious companies as Hewlett Packard, Fannie Mae, Ford Motor Company, and the University of Michigan Health Systems.

Mahfuz is a distinguished trainer and speaker and also an author of four other published books. For more than 8 years, Mahfuz has contributed to the design of software quality strategies, quality plans, reports, and test cases. He has presented papers on software quality assurance at several academic seminars including at some universities abroad. Mahfuz has authored hundreds of articles on different aspects of software including quality and management.

He is a subject matter expert and specializes in software quality strategy, analysis, planing, and reporting. He is also involved in cybersecurity and internal audits.

Mahfuz earned his master's degree in computer and information systems from the University of Detroit Mercy and earned two other master's degrees from Malaysia and Bangladesh. He also earned ITIL Foundation certification and several software quality-, cybersecurity-, and phishing-related internal certifications from Hewlett Packard.

SECTION I
CONCEPT

1

QUALITY CONCEPT
AND PERSPECTIVES

Introduction

This chapter as the title implies deals with the conceptual aspects of software quality. There are four parts in this chapter: Part 1 defines the basic concepts of quality, the importance and necessity of software quality, and the integration of test, security, and audit as a primary part of quality.

Part 2 of this chapter introduces the characteristics of software quality, based on IEEE 9126 Standard, control objectives for information and related technology (COBIT), and capability maturity model integration (CMMI). This section also tries to find the connection among these three major standards when they meet each other.

Part 3 discusses the validation and verification, based on IEEE Standard 1012 and IEEE Standard for Software Verification and Validation.

Part 4 discusses the types and processes of review and audit.

Part 1: Software Quality Concept

Defining Software Quality

Total quality management is a journey, not a destination.

Thomas Berry

Software quality is NOT ONLY TESTING! Testing is just a part of it. Software quality is mostly compared or paralleled with the testing or activities of testing. However, software quality is NOT ONLY TESTING! It is wider and more comprehensive than testing or generic terms of quality assurance.

When we talk about software quality, we are basically talking about multiple dimensions and a wider area.

The perspective of quality differs among people and from object to object. It can also differ by time and space perspectives, especially in the performance, and a quality perspective depends on a person's experiences. It may differ in the business management and user's perspective. Quality does not necessarily mean the same thing to a customer as it does to a developer.

Quality also has multiple levels, such as levels of reliability, security, and risk management.

Commercial value of quality has a different meaning to a seller than it does to the users. For sellers, profit is the key factor of value, whereas for users, user friendliness is the most important value.

The perceptions of quality differ among different stakeholders, clients, developers, users, managers, even to software quality specialists, testers, and executives. There are also differences of opinion about the perceptions of quality among quality specialists and academic specialists. Certain characteristics of a software may be acceptable to some quality specialists but may not be acceptable to other specialists.

William A. Foster, an American Marine, who received the Medal of Honor said,

> Quality is never an accident; it is always the result of high intention, sincere effort, intelligent direction and skillful execution; it represents the wise choice of many alternatives.

Quality is not cheap or simple. And, it is not easy, simple, or cheap to achieve quality. Quality means the best, excellence. Quality cannot be achieved accidentally. Quality needs to be achieved through the right plan, dedication, and the best service.

The IEEE Standard 610, which is the Glossary of Software Engineering Technology, defines a software quality assurance as the following:

1. A planned and systematic pattern of all actions necessary to provide adequate confidence that an item or product conforms to established technical requirements.
2. A set of activities designed to evaluate the process by which products are developed or manufactured.*

---

* IEEE Std 610.12-1990 (Revision and redesignation of IEEE Std 792–1983), p. 60.

Integrating Test, Security, and Audit

So if we say, software quality is not just testing, then what is it?

Well, Henry Ford, the founder of Ford Motor Company, said it well, "Quality means doing it right when no one is looking."

In fact, Henry Ford placed it as every stakeholder's personal responsibility, ethics, and ownership of the process.

Let us be a little more specific from Henry Ford's view about the definition of software quality, which means a developer, a project manager, or a tester will take the ownership and responsibility in the process of the production, to produce the best product and to do his or her best job. That is what Henry Ford probably meant to say.

In this book, it is advocated that the testing, information security, and audit are integral parts of software quality that also includes reliability, risk management, incident management, defect management, and return on investment.

Software quality goes beyond testing and more than functionality or even more than incident management or risk management. Quality certainly covers these aspects but extends further to nonfunctional quality. The following illustration gives an overall idea about our proposal of software quality and its integration with security and audit. Figure 1.1 basically shows the central point of our theme. As the combination of software testing, security assurance and audit are the foundational pillars of software quality assurance; however, managing

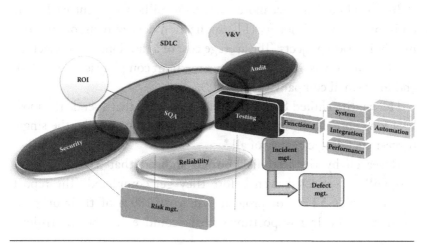

Figure 1.1 Software quality, information security, audit, risk management, and defect management as they are related to each other.

every incident, either small or big, seems serious or simple and must be considered important and well managed. Managing and documenting all defects professionally may help to achieve reliability in the software.

As per risk management, it should not be limited to visual or obvious dimensions of software risks. Risk management should also include genius and serious thought process, for example, what could be a possible risk for this product 20 years later, or what kind of risk the user may face using this product even in the middle of an ocean.

Why Is Software Quality Important?

Well, why not? Quality is important everywhere, isn't it?

American confectioner, philanthropist, and founder of The Hershey Chocolate Company, Milton Hershey said, "Give them quality. That's the best kind of advertising."

John Lasseter, another successful businessman, American animator, film director, screenwriter, producer, and the chief creative officer at Pixar, Walt Disney Animation Studios, and Disney Toon Studios said, "Quality is the best business plan."

In the modern technological world, technology and software are among the most widely used products in human history, certainly, it is a great success; however, it has also one of the highest failure rates of any product in human history due to lack of quality.

In the United States, more than $250 billion is spent each year on information technology (IT) application development of approximately 175,000 projects. The average cost of a development project for a large company is $2,322,000, for a medium company is $1,331,000, and for a small company is $434,000.

Hence, the United States will be the country that spends the most by a long shot, and—in a sign of the times—apps will be the single biggest spending category of all.*

Research by the Standish Group showed that 31.1% of projects will be canceled even before they get completed. The report also indicates 52.7% of projects will cost 189% of their original estimates. The lost opportunity costs could easily be in trillions

---

* See, http://techcrunch.com/2013/07/1s5/forrester-2-1-trillion-will-go-into-it-spend-in-2013-apps-and-the-u-s-lead-the-charge/

of dollars. One example given by the Standish Group report is Denver's failure to produce reliable software to handle baggage at the new Denver airport that is costing the city $1.1 million per day.

Additionally, only 16.2% of software projects are completed on time and on budget. In large-sized companies, only 9% of their projects come on time and on budget.*

In the United States, more than 200 million people use computers every day either for business or for fun.

Over 200 million people use devices that contain embedded software such as smart phones, home appliances, and entertainment devices.

In the United States, about 15 million companies use computers and software for their business purpose.

On the basis of a report, the software deployed in the United States is provided by about 77,186 software companies and another 10,000 U.S. companies create devices with embedded software.

A huge number of companies that produce devices with embedded software have moved to China, Taiwan, Japan, India, and other offshore countries.†

The quality of software is important, because poor quality can and will affect each citizen personally in unpleasant ways. The Home Depot credit card incident in 2014 impacted our lives, which is certainly a software security and quality issue. If there is a problem with IRS software, a miscalculation can affect millions of people.

Early in 2010, hundreds of computers were shut down and many businesses including hospitals were disrupted when the McAfee antivirus application mistakenly identified part of Microsoft Windows as a virus and stopped it from loading.

What Is the Benefit of Software Quality in Business?

As John Lasseter said, "Quality is the best business plan." That is what we mean when we say, "Quality costs nothing," which means

---

* The Standish Group 1995. *The Standish Group Report CHAOS©*. Reprinted here for sole academic purposes.
† Capers Jone and Olivier Bonsignour. *The Economics of Software Quality*, Addison-Wesley, 2011, p. 34.

the returns for the quality product are high. Everyone appreciates best quality. Also quality provides:

- The potential for an increased profitability
- Consumers expect and deserve quality in return for the money they pay
- Quality builds up the brand and makes the product more profitable

The winner of the quality game gets the attention and the sales.

- Better quality leads to
  - Increased production
  - Lower warranty costs
  - Lower marketing costs
  - Fewer surprises

- Positive customer experiences delight the consumer and lead to additional sales.

Lack of Quality Is the Reason for Failure

Although discussion on the details for failure is not focused, certainly, failure is the quality issue, and we also would like to share fundamental causes that relate to the quality factors or could be helpful for a software quality specialist.

Failure Factors

There is a famous saying about the importance of planning "If you fail to plan you plan to fail."

Certainly, planning plays the most important role in the success and failure of a project; either in a project level or in a testing level or any other part of software quality, if there is a lack of plan or it is an issue.

In many cases, the fundamental cause of project failure or challenges is due to time and cost overruns, as well as percentage of features delivered. According to a CHAOS research from 2004 to 2012, in 2012, 74% of the projects failed or challenged due to time overruns, 59% due to cost, and 69% due to features.

Project size also plays a role in the failure of projects. Projects of larger size are more challenged or mostly fail; however, smaller projects are less challenged and succeeds in more than 75% of cases. Obviously, smaller projects have better control than the larger projects.

Many times lack of performing careful analysis causes project failure. Rushing or trying to finish earlier also causes quality issues.

Albert Einstein said, "If you can't explain it simply, you don't understand it well enough."

Complexity is one of the causes of failing projects; failing to split the project into smaller tasks also causes software quality issues or project failure. Complexity can also be caused by the size of the project; if the project is too big, there is a huge possibility that the project may become complex and complicated.

In fact, one of the objectives of planning is to reduce the complexity of the project and make it simple.

According to a case study by the FBI, lack of training, experience, and micromanagement contributed to specification problems. Requirements were continually added to the system even as it was falling behind schedule and caused project failure.*

According to another case study by NASA, in testing, system test leakage or lack of requirement understanding causes project failure or quality issues.†

Studies also show similar problems as failure factors, as follows:

1. Poor project planning
2. Inadequate documentation of project requirements
3. Insufficient understanding of the business
4. Lack of support and involvement from senior management
5. No written quality plan or no effective implementation of the plan

Another study (1998) by the Standish Group found that the most common causes of project failure were management-based considerations, which includes:

---

* Andrew Short. Reasons for software failures. https://indico.cern.ch/event/276139/
  contribution/49/attachments/500995/691988/Reasons_for_software_failures.pdf.
† Ibid.

1. Incomplete requirements
2. Lack of user involvement
3. Lack of resources, unrealistic expectations
4. Lack of executive support
5. Changing requirements

Part 2: Software Quality Characteristics

As we have seen in Part 1, quality may have different meanings to different stakeholders.

IEEE 1061 has provided an outline of the methodology to be specified in the International Organization for Standardization (ISO)/International Electrotechnical Commission (IEC) 9126 Standard—software product quality characteristics.*

What Is the Business Benefit of Quality Characteristics?

Software quality characteristics, which is basically defined in ISO 9126, help to eliminate any possible misunderstanding between the purchaser and the supplier.

The purchaser is able to understand clearly and communicate his or her requirements for the product to be developed.

The supplier is able to understand the requirement and is able to assess with confidence whether it is possible to provide the product with the right level of software quality. Well, certainly there should be common rules or standards or criteria which can be followed, and ISO and IEC have set these standards for quality.

Standard for Quality Characteristics ISO/IEC 9126   Before ISO/IEC 9126, the ISO 9000 family addresses various aspects of quality management and contains some of ISO's best known standards. The standards provide guidance and tools for companies and organizations who want to ensure that their products and services consistently meet customer's requirements, and that quality is consistently improved. ISO 9001 Standard is concerned with the quality assurance processes such as the development, supply, installation, and maintenance of

---

* ISO/IEC 9126. First edition 1991-12-15.

computer software. The standard ISO/IEC 9126 is used for the quality of software product that has to be used in conjunction with the ISO/IEC 14598 for the evaluation of software products.

Standards in the ISO 9000 family include

- ISO 9001:2008—sets out the requirements of a quality management system
- ISO 9000:2005—covers the basic concepts and language
- ISO 9004:2009—focuses on how to make a quality management system more efficient and effective
- ISO 19011:2011—sets out guidance on internal and external audits of quality management systems

Other standards related to or that can be used in conjunction with ISO/IEC 9126 and ISO/IEC 14598 are as follows:

- ISO/IEC 12119—Quality requirements for software packages
- ISO/IEC 12207—Software life cycle processes
- ISO/IEC 14143—Software measurement
- ISO/IEC 15271—Guide for ISO/IEC 12207
- ISO/IEC 15504—Software process assessment (also known as Spice)
- ISO/IEC 15939—Software measurement process

Quality Characteristics

The six characteristics proposed by the ISO 9126 quality model (Figure 1.2) are

1. Functionality
2. Reliability
3. Usability
4. Efficiency
5. Maintainability
6. Portability

These characteristics are then decomposed into subcharacteristics and metrics. Each one of these six characteristics also suggests subcharacteristics of software quality model displayed in Table 1.1.

Figure 1.2   Quality characteristics at a glance based on ISO/IEC 9126.

Table 1.1   Subitems of Quality Characteristics Laid Down Based on ISO Standard

QUALITY CHARACTERISTICS	
FUNCTIONALITY	Suitability
	Accuracy
	Interoperability
	Security
	Functionality compliance
RELIABILITY	Maturity
	Fault tolerance
	Recoverability
	Reliability compliance
USABILITY	Understandability
	Learnability
	Operability
	Usability compliance
EFFICIENCY	Time behavior
	Resource behavior
	Efficiency compliance
MAINTAINABILITY	Analyzability
	Changeability
	Stability
	Testability
	Maintainability compliance
PORTABILITY	Adaptability
	Installability
	Coexistence/conformance
	Replaceability
	Portability compliance

Detailed Descriptions of Quality Characteristics

ISO 9126 Standard defines quality characteristics as follows:

Functionality

Functionality is composed of the following attributes:

Suitability   The software attribute that bears on the presence and appropriateness of a set of functions for specified tasks.

Accuracy   The software attribute that bears on the provision of right or agreed results or effects.

Interoperability   The software attribute that bears on its ability to interact with specified systems.

Security   The software attribute that bears on its ability to prevent unauthorized access, whether accidental or deliberate, to programs and data.

Functionality Compliance   The software attribute that makes the software adhere to application-related standards or conventions or regulations in laws and similar prescriptions.

Reliability

Reliability is composed of the following attributes:

Maturity   The software attribute that bears on the frequency of failure by faults in the software.

Fault Tolerance   The software attribute that bears on its ability to maintain a specified level of performance in cases of software faults or of infringement of its specified interface.

Recoverability   The software attribute that bears on the capability to reestablish its level of performance and recovers the data directly affected in case of a failure and on the time and effort needed for it.

Reliability Compliance   It will make the software comply to standards, laws, and regulations relating to reliability.

Usability

Usability is composed of the following attributes:

Understandability   The software attribute that bears on the users' effort for recognizing the logical concept and its applicability.

Learnability   The software attribute that bears on the users' effort for learning its application (e.g., operation control, input, and output).

Operability   The software attribute that bears on the users' effort for operation and operation control.

Usability Compliance   It will make the software comply to standards, laws, and regulations relating to usability.

Efficiency

Efficiency is composed of the following attributes:

Time Behavior   The software attribute that bears on response and processing times and on throughput rates in performing its function.

Resource Behavior   The software attribute that bears on the amount of resources used and the duration of such use in performing its function.

Efficiency Compliance   It is to help clients deliver regulatory compliance programs and streamline compliance architectures for efficiency.

Maintainability

Maintainability is composed of the following attributes:

Analyzability   The software attribute that bears on the effort needed for the diagnosis of deficiencies or the causes of failures or for the identification of parts to be modified.

Changeability   The software attribute that bears on the effort needed for modification, fault removal, or environmental change.

Stability   The software attribute that bears on the risk of unexpected effect of modifications.

Testability   The software attribute that bears on the effort needed for validating the modified software.

Maintainability Compliance   It will make the software comply to standards, laws, and regulations relating to maintainability.

Portability

Portability is composed of the following attributes:

Adaptability   The software attribute that bears on the opportunity for its adaptation to different specified environments without applying other actions or means than those provided for this purpose for the software considered.

*Installability**   The software attribute that bears on the effort needed to install the software in a specified environment.

Coexistence/Conformance   The software attribute that makes the software adhere to standards or conventions relating to portability.

Portability Compliance   It will make the software comply to standards, laws, and regulations relating to portability.

Control Objectives for Information and Related Technology (COBIT)

Introduction

COBIT is a framework created by Information Systems Audit and Control Association for IT management and IT governance.

It produces a very efficient and effective form of assurance by requiring that the security solution originate from a coherent set of auditable control statements.

COBIT is designed to meet multiple requirements. It allows an organization to assess the business risks and assign control objectives to a common set of IT functions.

By definition, an IT control objective is a precise statement of the desired result or purpose to be achieved by implementing control procedures within a particular activity. COBIT dictates best practice in the accounting and control of IT assets.

These best practices optimize IT governance and represent expert consensus.

These are presented in a logical structure within a domain and process framework.

---

* Replaceability: The software attribute that bears on the opportunity and effort of using it in the place of other specified software in the same environment. Replaceability may include attributes of both installability and adaptability. The concept has been introduced as a subcharacteristic of its own because of its importance.

Thus, COBIT establishes a reference model that can be used to judge whether management activities are complete and correct.

To achieve those ends, COBIT dictates explicit

- organizational structure
- control policies
- practices and procedures

COBIT is primarily oriented toward the practical application in conventional IT business.

The five principles of COBIT (Figure 1.3) are as follows:

1. Meeting stakeholder needs
2. Covering the enterprise end-to-end
3. Applying a single integrated framework
4. Enabling a holistic approach
5. Separating governance from management

Meta-Requirements

COBIT used existing reference models to establish the following generic business requirements:

1. Quality requirements
   - Quality
   - Cost
   - Delivery
2. Security requirements
   - Confidentiality
   - Integrity
   - Availability

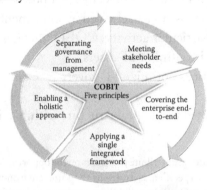

Figure 1.3   Five principles of control objectives for information and related technology (COBIT).

3. Fiduciary requirements
   - Effectiveness and efficiency of operations
   - Reliability of information
   - Compliance with laws and regulations

These aforementioned three meta-requirements can be factored into seven distinct end qualities (Figure 1.4) as follows:

1. Effective
2. Available
3. Efficient
4. Compliant
5. Confidential
6. Reliable
7. Having integrity

These are the universally desirable characteristics.

Capability Maturity Model Integration (CMMI)

CMMI, Version 1.1, has defined the quality and process performance attributes (Figure 1.5) as follows:*

1. Functionality
2. Reliability
3. Usability

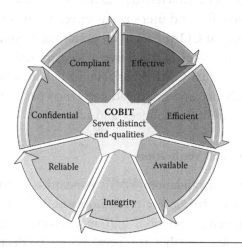

Figure 1.4 Seven distinct end qualities of COBIT.

---

* Capability Maturity Model® Integration (CMMISM), Version 1.1, p. 427.

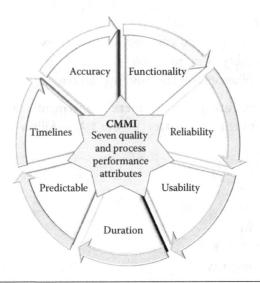

Figure 1.5   Seven qualities and process performance attributes of CMMI.

4. Duration
5. Predictability
6. Timelines
7. Accuracy

Quality Characteristics, COBIT, and CMMI

The software quality characteristics, as defined in IEEE 9126, mostly focus on functionality and user's perspective, whereas the seven distinct end qualities of COBIT focus on performance and security perspectives and consistency of the software (Figure 1.6).

It is remarkable that CMMI basically include functional perspective and performance and even load and stress perspective as added duration, predictability, timeliness, and accuracy.

Part 3: Validation and Verification

The verification and validation (V&V) standard is a process standard that addresses all software life cycle processes, including acquisition, supply, development, operation, and maintenance. Software V&V processes determine whether the development products conform to the requirements of that activity and whether the software satisfies its intended use and user needs. This determination includes analysis,

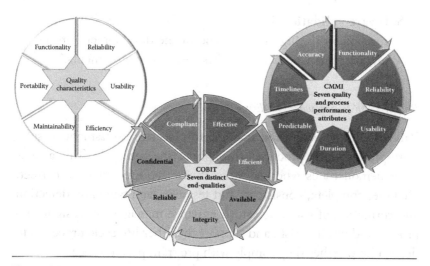

Figure 1.6   Common areas and relationship in three major quality characteristics of ISO 9126, COBIT, and CMMI.

evaluation, review, inspection, assessment, and testing of software products and processes.

Although "verification" and "validation" at first seem quite similar in CMMI models, on closer inspection, you can see that each addresses different issues. Verification confirms that work products properly reflect the requirements specified for them. In other words, verification ensures that "you built it right. And validation confirms that the product, as provided, will fulfill its intended use. In other words, validation ensures that 'you built the right thing'."*

In other words,

Verification: Are we building the product right? (This is static method for verifying design and code.)

Validation: Are we building the right product? (This is dynamic process for checking and testing the real product.) Software validation always involves executing the code.

According to IEEE Standard glossary,

Software verification is the process of evaluating a system or component to determine whether the products of a given development phase satisfy the conditions imposed at the start of that phase.†

---

* Ibid, p. 26.
† The IEEE Standard 610, Glossary of Software Engineering Technology, p. 81.

Software validation is the process of evaluating a system or component during or at the end of the development process to determine whether it satisfies specified requirements.*

Role of V&V in Software Quality

Validation and verification provide an objective assessment of software products and processes throughout the life cycle. This assessment demonstrates whether the software requirements are correct, accurate, complete, consistent, and testable, facilitate early detection and correction of software errors, enhance management insight into process and product risk, and support the other life cycle processes to determine whether they comply with program performance.

Software V&V Processes

The V&V processes shall address all those life cycle processes used by the project. The V&V effort shall conform to the task descriptions, inputs, and outputs.

Some V&V activities and tasks include analysis, evaluations, and tests. The V&V effort performs these tasks to develop the supporting basis of evidence showing whether the software product satisfies its requirements.

V&V Task Reports   The V&V effort shall document V&V task results and status. Task reports include

1. Anomaly evaluation
2. Concept documentation evaluation
3. Configuration management assessment
4. Contract verification
5. Criticality analysis
6. Evaluation of new constraints
7. Hardware/software/user requirements allocation analysis
8. Hazard analysis
9. Installation checkout

---

* Ibid, p. 80.

10. Installation configuration audit
11. Interface analysis
12. Migration assessment
13. Operating procedures evaluation
14. Proposed change assessment
15. Recommendations
16. Retirement assessment
17. Review results
18. Risk analysis
19. Security analysis
20. Software design evaluation
21. Software requirements evaluation
22. Source code and source code documentation evaluation
23. System requirements review
24. Test results
25. Traceability analysis

V&V Activity Summary Reports An activity summary report shall summarize the results of V&V tasks performed for the following V&V life cycle activities:

1. Acquisition support
2. Planning
3. Concept
4. Requirements
5. Design
6. Implementation
7. Test
8. Installation and checkout
9. Operation
10. Maintenance

V&V Anomaly Reports The V&V effort shall document in an anomaly report each anomaly that it detects.

The V&V final report shall be issued at the end of the installation and checkout activity or at the conclusion of the V&V effort.

Testing: Application   This is the most important part of the validation process. The stakeholders describe a valid set of requirements, the developers provide solution specification, and the test team provides test specification and test cases.

They must ensure that whatever test requirements, cases, and specifications they define truly reflect the conditions for the intended situation.

That definition process also includes determination of the procedures to be used to analyze the test results.

These tests are always defined in advance by an individual test plan, developed as part of the project management process.

Unit Testing Plan   IEEE Standard 1008 describes the following three phases of the unit testing process:

1. Test planning
2. Creation of the test set
3. Measurement of the test unit

Each contains a hierarchy of activities and tasks.
The focus is on specifying a minimum set of tasks for each activity.

Determine Features to Be Tested   The specific unit testing process is defined in this phase including determination of the following:

1. Inputs (requirements and design documentation)
2. Tasks
3. Identification and clarification of requirements
4. Identification of nonfunctional items to test
5. Selection of features to test (procedures, states, transitions, and data)
6. Outputs (elements to be included and unit requirements)

Design the Test Set   This is the place where the actual technical work is assigned including

- Inputs (exactly what will be tested)
- Tasks

- Architecture of the test set (e.g., a hierarchically decomposed set of test objectives)
- Explicit test procedures (from the requirements set and objectives)
- Define the test cases including
  - Control flows
  - Anticipated data transformation outcomes
- Design outputs (e.g,. test design and test case specifications)

Implement the Test Plan Implement planning and input test case specifications.

Implement tasks are as follows:

- Obtain test data
- Obtain any special resources
- Obtain test items (manuals, procedures, and data)
- Implement outputs (test data, resources, and array of test items)

Execute the Test Procedures As planned,

- Utilize the input specifications
- Execute the tasks
- Run tests
- Determine results (including recording failures and identification of source)
- Record test outcomes as output including failure analysis

Part 4: Reviews and Audit

Reporting is the primary outcome of the V&V process as it supports software quality assurance, software configuration management, and general project management.

Reviews establish the basis for the software verification component of the IEEE 1028. It defines five types of software review and provides detailed procedures for executing each of these review types.

The five types of reviews are as follows:

1. Management review
2. Technical reviews
3. Inspections
4. Walkthroughs
5. Audits

Management Reviews

The following are a few definitions of the management review:

Management review is a review by an organization's top management or other manager level viewers with a goal of assessing the organizations success at achieving objectives established for the business system thus ensuring its continued suitability, adequacy, and effectiveness.

Management review typically includes analysis of customer satisfaction/customer feedback, cost of poor quality performance trends within the business, achievement of objectives defined in the business plan, results of internal audits status of corrective and preventative actions, and follow-up from previous reviews.

It could be the regular evaluation of whether management systems are performing as intended and producing the desired results as efficiently as possible. Management reviews help to fill the gap between day-to-day work activities and periodic formal audits.

Some state that management review is similar to a doctor giving a routine physical examination—even when no overt signs of illness are present.

The aim of a management review is to observe progress, to regulate the plans and schedules, and to be able to value the effectiveness of management approaches.

Management reviews support decisions about corrective actions, changes in the allocation of resources, or changes to the scope of the project.

Management reviews identify consistency with and deviations from plans or adequacies and inadequacies of management procedures.

According to IEEE Standard for Software Reviews and Audits,* management reviews monitor the management process including

- Plans
- Schedules
- Requirements
- Approaches (for the purpose of assessing fitness)

They support decisions about corrective actions allocation of resources and scoping.

Application   Management reviews are carried out for the purpose of supporting the management personnel having direct responsibility for the system. They are meant to discover and report variations from plans and/or defined procedures. They primarily focus on planning and/or corrective action artifacts.

Focus   Management reviews are carried out for management personnel, which involves the following (potential) management roles:

- Decision maker
- Review leader
- Recorder
- Management staff
- Technical staff
- Customer (or user) representative

Input   Management reviews can consider the following items:

- Statements of objectives
- The software product
- The project management plan
- Status (relative to plans) checks
- Anomalies
- Procedures

Resources, status reports, and (pertinent) regulations also have to be considered.

When to Conduct a Management Review   Management reviews should be scheduled as part of initial project planning. These are usually tied to

---

* IEEE Standard for Software Reviews and Audits, IEEE Std1028™-2008 (Revision of IEEE Std 1028–1997), pp. 6–11.

milestones and terminal phases. This does not exclude ad hoc management reviews, which can be scheduled and held for the following purposes:

- Software quality management
- Functional management
- The customer

Review Procedures

Planning Planning for review procedures is composed of the following:

- Resourcing and funding assurance
- Scheduling
- Reporting and feedback procedure definition
- Formulation of team and assurance of competent personnel
- Assignment of roles and responsibilities
- Distribution of materials
- Training and orientation

Preparation and Execution Preparation and execution for review procedures are composed of the following:

- Initial analysis by reviewers
- Documentation and classification of anomalies
- Objective review
- Evaluation of software against objectives
- Evaluation of project status
- Review of anomalies with producer
- Generation and documentation of action items
- Risk assessment and recommendations

Technical Reviews

Technical review is a form of peer review in which "a team of qualified reviewers examines the correctness of the software product for its intended use and identifies inconsistencies from specifications and standards. Technical reviews may also provide recommendations for replacements." (IEEE Std 1028™-2008, revision of IEEE Std 1028–1997).

The objective of a technical review is to evaluate a software product to verify its correctness, and it provides the management with evidence to confirm the technical status of the project.

Technical reviews evaluate the software product including the following:

- Software requirements specification
- Software design description
- Software test documentation
- Software user documentation
- Maintenance manual
- System build procedures
- Installation procedures
- Release notes
- Specifications
- Software development process descriptions
- Software architectural descriptions*

Responsibilities Technical reviews are carried out for technical and technical management personnel. However, it involves potential management roles such as decision maker, review leader, recorder, technical staff, technical managers, and customer technical staff.

Input The technical reviews team can prepare a statement of objectives for the technical review, what is intended to achieve from this review, name and details of the software being examined and reviewed, the project management plan, and can also consider items such as anomalies, defects, and procedures.

Inspections

Different names could be used for the term inspection. Some call it software inspection, which also could extend to the design and its documentation. Some call it code inspection, which relates more to the source code. Software testing is also a kind of inspection.

However, it must not be confused with the so called "code review" or "walkthrough," which is usually done in a single meeting lasting for a couple of hours. A proper code inspection may take

---

* Ibid.

several days and needs the help of tools to browse the symbols in order to find the places where they are used. Proper inspections can be applied for almost all work products in the software life cycle.

The purpose of the inspection is to detect and identify software anomalies. They also

- Verify whether the product meets its specification
- Verify whether the product meets quality requirements and conforms to regulations and standards
- Produce a list of deviations from standards and specifications
- Collect software engineering data
- Use the software engineering data to improve the inspection process

The inspection leader shall be responsible for planning and organizing tasks pertaining to the inspection. He or she should finalize the parts/components of the software product to be inspected, then he or she should be responsible for the planning and preparation so that the inspection is conducted in an orderly manner and meets its objectives, should ensure that the inspection data is collected, and should issue the inspection output.

Inspectors shall identify and describe anomalies in the software product. Inspectors shall be chosen based on their expertise and should be represented by different groups such as business requirements, design, test, and so on.

Responsibilities   All the participants in the review are inspectors, but the producer should not be the leader or recorder. This involves the following (potential) roles:

- Inspection leader
- Recorder
- Reader
- Producer
- Inspector

The inspection team should prepare a statement of objectives for the inspection, mention the name and details of the product being examined, and document all inspection procedures, inspection reporting forms, and current anomalies or issues.

Inspection Rules and Procedures

The roles and responsibilities of everyone shall be assigned by the inspection leader. The inspection leader shall answer questions about any checklists and the role assigned and all necessary information should be provided.

Each inspection team member shall examine the software product and other inputs prior to the review meeting. Anomalies detected during this examination shall be documented and sent to the inspection leader. The inspection leader should classify anomalies. If the inspection leader determines that the extent or seriousness of the anomalies is warranted, the inspection leader may cancel the inspection, requesting a later inspection when the software product meets the minimal entry criteria and is reasonably defect free. The inspection leader should forward the anomalies to the author of the software product for disposition.

The inspection leader or reader shall specify a suitable order in which the software product will be inspected (such as sequential, hierarchical, data flow, control flow, bottom-up, or top-down).

The inspection leader shall verify that inspectors are prepared for the inspection. The inspection leader shall reschedule the meeting if the inspectors are not adequately prepared. The inspection leader should gather individual preparation times and record the total in the inspection documentation.

At the end of the inspection meeting, the inspection leader shall have the anomaly list reviewed with the team to ensure its completeness and accuracy. The inspection leader shall allow time to discuss every anomaly when disagreement occurred. The inspection leader shall not allow the discussion to focus on resolving the anomaly but on clarifying what constitutes the anomaly. If a disagreement as to the existence or severity of an anomaly cannot be quickly resolved during the meeting, that disagreement shall be documented in the anomaly report.

Walkthroughs

A walkthrough or walk-through is a form of software peer review "in which a designer or programmer leads members of the development team and other interested parties through a software product and the participants ask questions and make comments about possible errors, violation of development standards, and other problems." (IEEE Standard for Software Reviews and Audits, IEEE Std 1028™-2008 [Revision of IEEE Std 1028–1997]).

As indicated by the IEEE Standard 1028, a software design document or code, test case specifications, and a variety of other technical documentation may also be walked through. However, it should be noted that a walkthrough is different than an inspection.

The purpose of a walkthrough is to evaluate a software product. A walkthrough could also serve the purpose of educating an audience regarding a software product. The major objectives are to find anomalies, to improve the software product, to consider alternative implementations to valuate conformance to standards and specifications, and to evaluate the usability and accessibility of the software product. It also intends to include exchange of techniques, style variations, and training of the participants.

Responsibilities   Responsibilities involve the following (potential) roles:

- Walkthrough leader
- Recorder
- Producer
- Team member

The walkthrough team should prepare a statement of objectives for the walkthrough, mention the name and details of the product being walked through—document all walkthrough procedures—standards that are in effect for that primary process.

For a review to be considered a systematic walkthrough, a team of at least two members (including the author) should be assembled. Roles may be shared among the team members. The walkthrough leader or the author may serve as the recorder. The walkthrough leader may be the author.

Individuals holding management positions over any member of the walkthrough team shall not participate in the walkthrough.

The walkthrough leader shall conduct the walkthrough, shall handle the administrative tasks pertaining to the walkthrough, and ensure that the walkthrough is conducted in an orderly manner. The walkthrough leader shall prepare the statement of objectives to guide the team through the walkthrough. The walkthrough leader should ensure that the team members are fully prepared for each discussion item and should issue the walkthrough output.

Each walkthrough team member shall examine the software product and other review inputs prior to the review meeting. Anomalies detected during this examination shall be documented and sent to the walkthrough leader. The walkthrough leader should classify anomalies to ensure that walkthrough meeting time is used effectively. The walkthrough leader should forward the anomalies to the author of the software product for disposition.

The walkthrough leader shall describe the roles and responsibilities or everyone. The walkthrough leader shall state the purpose of the walkthrough and should act as a facilitator to confirm that everyone has a chance to express their opinion. The leader also should ensure that all voices are heard. The walkthrough leader should remind the team members to comment only on the software product and not its author.

The team members raise their specific questions, opinions, or observations when the author completes the presentation. The walkthrough leader coordinates discussion and guides the meeting to a decision-making stage or identified action for each item. The recorder notes all recommendations and required actions.

The output of the walkthrough shall be documented, which includes the detailed information about the project being walked through with the name and position of the walkthrough team. Statement of the objective that has to be accomplished by this walkthrough has to be prepared and also see whether they are being achieved. The details of each anomaly such as name, ID, location, and detailed description of the anomaly are collected, and there should be a recommendation for each anomaly.

Walkthrough data should be used to improve the walkthrough process itself.

Frequently occurring anomalies can be used to produce walkthrough checklists.

Process considerations such as preparation time and number of participants should also be considered to improve the efficiency of the walkthrough process.

Audits

Information audit is a comprehensive item, and a specific definition for the information audit cannot be universally agreed upon
among the scholars; however, IEEE Standard 610 defines information audit as

> An independent examination of a work product or set of work products
> to assess compliance with specifications, standards, contractual agree-
> ments, or other criteria.*

Another definition that is offered by ASLIB is that "Information
Audit is a systematic examination of information use, resources and
flows, with a verification by reference to both people and existing documents, in order to establish the extent to which they are contributing
to an organization's objectives."

Since information audit is huge and has a wider scope, a full chapter is dedicated to information audit; the details of the information
audit will be discussed in Chapter 9 of this book.

We will have a brief discussion on information audit as it is a part
of reviews and reports.

The purpose of a software audit is to provide an independent evaluation of conformance of software products and processes to applicable regulations, standards, guidelines, plans, specifications, and
procedures.

The audit team should consist of a lead auditor, a recorder, one or
more auditor(s), an initiator, and an auditing organization.

Auditors shall prepare for the audit by concentrating on the audit
plan, products, rules and regulations, standards, guidelines, plan compliance, contracts, reports and other documentations, source codes,
and deliverables.

The auditors should have all the evidences, examining documents,
and witnessing processes. The auditors should conduct all the examination activities that are defined in the audit plan. They shall undertake
additional investigative activities if they consider such activities are
required to define the full extent of conformance or nonconformance.

---

* IEEE Std 610.12-1990 (Revision and redesignation of IEEE Std7SZ.1983). IEEE
  Standard Glossary of Software Engineering Terminology, p. 11.

Auditors shall document the observations of nonconformance and exemplary conformance. An observation is a statement of the fact found during an audit that is substantiated by objective evidence. Examples of nonconformance are as follows:

The output of the audit is that the audit report should contain the purpose and scope of the audit, name and details of audited organization, including location, liaison staff, and management, details of the software products or processes audited, applicable rules and regulations, standards, guidelines, manuals and all documentations, plans, specifications, and procedures used for the evaluation criteria.

In addition, recommendations shall be provided to the audited organization or the initiator.

2

MANAGEMENT AND PROCESS

Introduction

This chapter, as the title indicates, is focused primarily on test management topics. Part 1 discusses software management, which includes information governance (IG), information technology (IT) governance, overall strategic management, and data governance (DG), and it also includes IEEE 12207 as the expert models for software management. Part 2 discusses software life cycle and its models, which includes three major software models such as spiral, agile, and waterfall. Part 3 discusses the life cycle processes, which highlight the primary life cycle process and supporting life cycle processes.

Part 1: Software Management

Software Management

Software management consists of the following three major components:

1. Information governance
2. Making the process systematic
3. IT process alignment

Information Governance

When we talk about IG, we may also need to understand a few other terms. Some may get confused between IG and the IT governance. Certainly, they are two different things, but they are related. However, another term that should also be discussed in the topic is DG, as all three terms are similar industry terms.

Information Governance, IT Governance, and Data Governance

Basically, the IG processes are at a higher level than IT governance and are much higher than DG, but both data and IT governance can be (and should be) a part of an overall IG program (Figure 2.1).

They are all a subset of corporate governance. DG is a part of broader IT governance, which is also a part of even broader IG.

IT Governance

IT governance is to ensure that IT creates business value and contributes toward meeting business objectives, and the alignment of IT with the business is essential.

The IT governance is primarily the actual software development and maintenance activities of the IT department or function, and IT governance efforts focus on making IT efficient and effective.

Data Governance

DG involves processes and controls to ensure that information at the data level is accurate and not redundant.

DG focuses on information quality at the lowest or root level so that subsequent reports, analyses, and conclusions are based on clean, reliable, trusted data (or records) in database tables.

IG–EG and Strategic Planning

Information governance (IG) in the perspective of enterprise governance (EG) and strategic planning ensures that information is utilized to support decision making for the organization. IG addresses all information, whether it is generated internally or externally to the organization,

Figure 2.1   Information technology (IT) governance, strategic management, and data governance (DG) can be (and should be) a part of an overall information governance (IG) program.

regardless of its state or location such as marketing, finance, HR, and so on. The IG process helps define the information throughout its life cycle. IG ensures that tools are available and in order (Figure 2.2).

Strategic planning is an important element of IT governance and is the alignment of IT with the business. Strategic plan should be addressed in terms of an external aspects and internal aspects, both business and the company infrastructure.

Strategic plan should also include operational integration with the organizational infrastructure and processes and IT infrastructure and processes.

Making the Process Systematic

Another important component of software management is making the process systematic, which basically includes the following:

1. Purposefully planned, designed, and enterprise wide strategic integration framework
2. Implementing a strategic concept

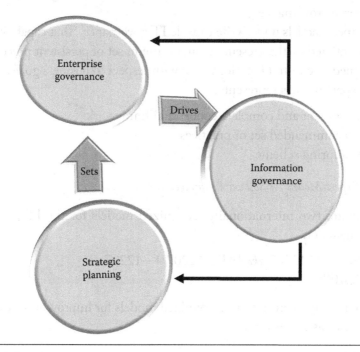

Figure 2.2 Enterprise governance drive information governance and strategic planning sets enterprise governance and they connect each other.

IT Process Alignment

IT process alignment includes the following:

1. Optimum alignment is achieved when IT strategy is referenced to and directly underwrites the business strategy.
2. Role of the best practice frameworks in underwriting both aspects of that endeavor, integrating approaches alignment and governance.
3. Overall enterprise governance.
4. IT governance assures stakeholders that the business will be profitable and productive.

It embodies the strategic and tactical means to monitor and assess business performance toward those goals, and it provides the assurance that issues vital to business success will be effectively identified and dealt with IG.

The specific purpose of an IT governance infrastructure is to codify the rules for how the IT function will operate within the overall enterprise governance system. This views IT as an integral aspect of corporate governance.

Expert models underwrite capable IT governance. That capability is substantiated by the presence of an optimum set of persistent processes designed to ensure IT performance with respect to business goals.

Expert models represent

A coherent and complete conceptual framework
A recommended set of practices
A tailoring scheme

The Expert Models for Software Management

There are two internationally recognized models for the IT process management:

ISO/IEC 12207 *aka* IEEE 12207.0—12207.2
COBIT

Generally, there are five recognized models for improving software processes as follows:

TSP
PSP

The CMM software
ISO 9000
CMMI

ISO 12207/IEEE 12207.0

Worldwide, the only model for software process definition is the 12207 domain of standards.

12207 was designed to serve as an explicit conceptual model for

- Creating a comprehensive management scheme
- Structuring a requirement management process
- Managing configurations and the change process
- Managing data control and documentation activity

Serves as a Model for

- Managing software procurement
- Managing integration activities
- Managing verification and validation (V&V) and IV&V
- Managing all forms of support activity
- Managing organizational interfaces

Integration of IEEE 12207 and SESC

The Systems Engineering Services Corporation (SESC) and IEEE 12207 fully integrate the following software management principles and standards.

Acquisition

Software acquisition—IEEE 1062
System engineering process—IEEE 1220
System requirement specification IEEE—1233

Development

Developing SW life cycle process IEEE 1074
SW requirement specification IEEE 830

SW design descriptions IEEE 1016 and 1016.1
SW test plan outline IEEE 829
SW unit testing 1008
SW safety plans IEEE 1228

Operation

Software maintenance: IEEE 1219

Supporting Documentation

Quality assurance: IEEE standards: SQA Plans 730, 730.1, SQ
   Metrics Methodology 1061
Configuration management: SW CM Plans 828, 1042
Verification and validation: 1012
Joint review: SW reviews and audits 1028
Problem resolution: Classification for SW anomalies: 1044 and
   1044.1
SW project management plan 1058
Measure to produce reliable SW 982.1 and 982.2
SW productivity metrics 1045

Part 2: Software Life Cycle Models

What Is Software Life Cycle?

In concept, software life cycle is the same as any other concepts of life cycle.

In software engineering, software life cycle is basically the beginning to the end of the software development.

It also could be defined as a system development methodology, software development life cycle, or software development process.

The IEEE Standard 610, Glossary of Software Engineering Technology, defines a software life cycle as follows:

> The period of time that begins when a software product is conceived and ends when the software is no longer available for use. The software life cycle typically includes a Zzconcept phase, requirement phase, design

phase, implementation phase, test phase, installation and checkout phase, operation and maintenance phase, and sometimes, retirement phase. (These phases may overlap or be performed iteratively.)[*]

There are several models for software development life cycle. We will discuss some of these models. However, whichever model you follow in software development, some process has to go through. First thing to know is what is required? What needs to be developed? Based on that requirement, the developer will design and develop, then it needs to be validated and tested to verify if it is working as required, and then it is delivered to the user or the customer. In the IEEE standard, this process is defined as

1. Requirement gathering and analysis
2. Design
3. Implementation or coding
4. Testing
5. Deployment
6. Maintenance

Life Cycle Models

There are several methodologies or life cycle development models that fit within the 12207 framework.

Boehm's Spiral This model was first described by Barry Boehm in his 1986 paper "A Spiral Model of Software Development and Enhancement." In 1988, Boehm published a similar paper to a wider audience. These papers introduce a diagram that has been reproduced in many subsequent publications discussing the spiral model (Figure 2.3).[†]

Agile Methodology In recent time, agile methodology has become so familiar and it requires some more attention and explanation as to what it is and what it means.

---

[*] IEEE Std 610.12-1990, *Revision and Redesignation of IEEE Std* 792-1983, p. 68.

[†] Ron Patton. Software development lifecycle models. In: *Software Testing*, SAMS Publishing, Indianapolis, IN.

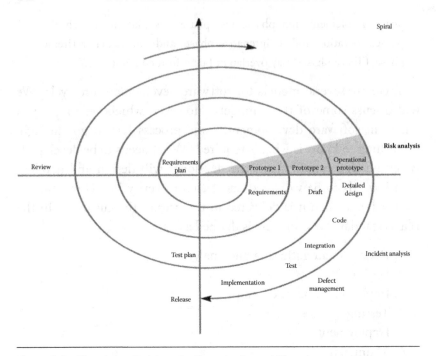

Figure 2.3   The spiral methodology of software development life cycle.

What Is Agile? What Does It Mean?   According to Merriam-Webster's dictionary, agile is defined as "able to move quickly and easily." Another meaning is given as quick, smart, and clever.

- Ability to move with quick easy grace (an agile dancer)
- Having a quick resourceful and adaptable character (an agile mind)

Google gives the definition as

- Able to move quickly and easily, such as "Ruth was as agile as a monkey."
- Able to think and understand quickly.

The main characteristic of agile is that the agile methods replace high-level design with frequent redesign, and that it is characterized by the division of tasks into short phases of work and frequent reassessment and adaptation of plans (Figure 2.4).

The keywords for agile method are "frequent redesign" and "tasks into short phases." In Chapter 1, we have learned that one of the reasons for project failure is the project being too big. In fact, Agile

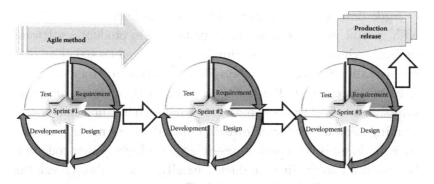

Figure 2.4   An agile methodology of software development life cycle.

can resolve that problem. Agile works the other way, each portion of requirement could be considered as one project by itself. It has its own requirement phase, design and development phase, and test phase.

Agile Principles

The Agile manifesto is based on the following 12 principles:

1. Customer satisfaction by rapid delivery of useful software
2. Welcome changing requirements, even late in development
3. Working software is delivered frequently (weeks rather than months)
4. Close, daily cooperation between business people and developers
5. Projects are built around motivated individuals who should be trusted
6. Face-to-face conversation is the best form of communication (colocation)
7. Working software is the principal measure of progress
8. Sustainable development that is able to maintain a constant pace
9. Continuous attention to the technical excellence and good design
10. Simplicity—the art of maximizing the amount of work not done—is essential
11. Self-organizing teams
12. Regular adaptation to changing circumstances

Agile development includes a number of different methodologies with specific guidance as to the steps to take to produce a software project, such as extreme programming, scrum, and crystal clear. The commonality between all of the agile methods is that they are iterative and incremental. The iterations in the agile methods are typically shorter—2–4 weeks in most cases, and each iteration ends with a working software product. However, unlike the spiral model, the software produced is not a prototype—it is always high-quality code that is expanded into the final product. Basically, agile methods break the product into small incremental builds. These builds are provided in the iterations (Figure 2.5).

Spiral model and agile model look similar; however, there is a little difference. The spiral model is an example of iterative development. A typical iteration will be somewhere between 6 months and 2 years and will include all aspects of the life cycle—requirements analysis, risk analysis, planning, design, and architecture and then a release of either a prototype (which is either evolved or thrown away, depending on the specific methods chosen by the project team) or a working software. These steps are repeated until the project is either ended or finished.*

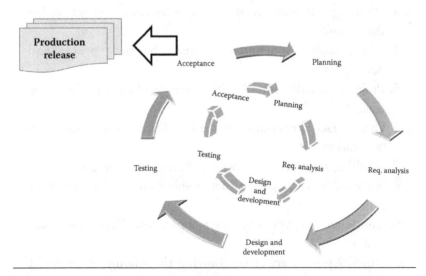

Figure 2.5   Another example of agile methodology of software development life cycle.

* Rex Black. *Managing the Testing Process*, Wiley Publishing, Inc., p. 411.

Figure 2.6 An Example of Kanban Storyboard in Agile Methodology of Software Development Life Cycle

KANBAN STORY BOARD

PRIORITIZED	IN DEV	IN-TEST	ACCEPTED
US10—Abu	US22—James	US-43—Normal	US-40
Login page	E-mail link	Customer care page	
US11—Abu	US-13	US-15	US-18
Login verification	Contact page	Report link	
US11—Abu	US-13	US-15	US-18
Login verification	Contact page	Report link	

The agile model works through the user's story. The user writes a short description of what he wants, and a small phase of the life cycle is based on that (Figure 2.6).

Waterfall The waterfall model is a sequential design process that is used in software development processes, where the progress is seen as flowing steadily downward (like a waterfall) through the phases of conception, initiation, analysis, design, construction, testing, production/implementation, and maintenance.

The IEEE Standard 610, Glossary of Software Engineering Technology, defines a waterfall model as a model of the software development process in which the constituent activities, typically a concept phase, requirements phase, design phase, implementation phase, test phase, and installation and checkout phase are performed in that order, possibly with overlap but with little or no iteration, which is in contrast with incremental development, rapid prototyping, and spiral model (Figure 2.7).*

Part 3: Life Cycle Processes

Software life cycle processes (Figure 2.8) has two levels:

1. Primary life cycle process
2. Supporting life cycle process

---

* IEEE Std 610.12-1990, *Software Life Cycle*.

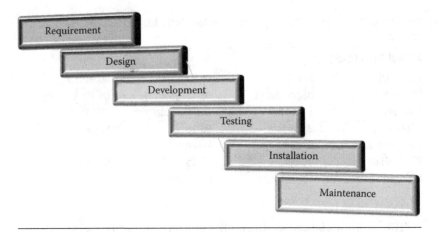

Figure 2.7 An example of waterfall methodology of software development life cycle.

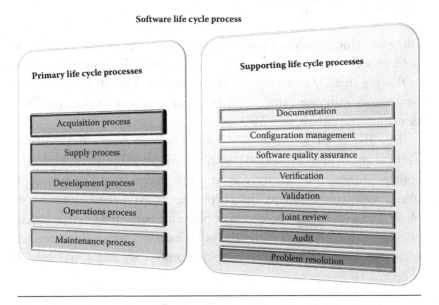

Figure 2.8 Primary and supporting life cycle processes of software life cycle process.

Primary Life Cycle Process

The primary life cycle process consists of the following five components (Figure 2.9):[*]

1. Acquisition process
2. Supply process

---

[*] IEEE 12207, *Personal IEEE Standard Study and Professor Dan Shoemakers Classnotes.*

3. Operation process
4. Development process
5. Maintenance process

Acquisition Process The acquisition process consists of the following five tasks:

1. Initiation
2. Request for proposals (RFP)
3. Contract preparation
4. Supplier monitoring
5. Acceptance and completion

Initiation Initiation describes a concept or need to acquire, defines and analyzes system requirements, analyzing risk and cost benefit, and defines acceptance and evaluation criteria.

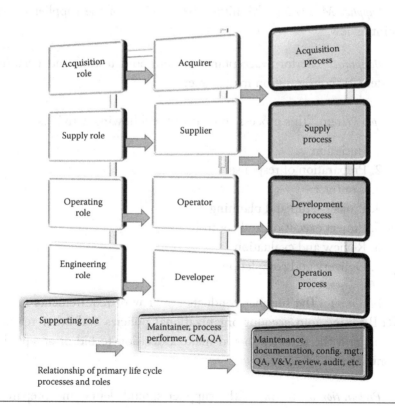

Relationship of primary life cycle processes and roles

Figure 2.9 Primary process and its role in software life cycle process.

Request for Proposal Documenting the acquisition requirement defines contract milestones and assures acquisition participants to know the requirements.

The acquisition documentation should include the following:

1. System requirements
2. Scope statement
3. Instructions for bidders
4. List of software products
5. Terms and conditions
6. Control of subcontracts
7. Technical constraints

Contract Preparation Establishes a procedure for supplier selection, prepare and negotiate a contract, and institute a process for change control.

Supplier Monitoring Monitors the activities of the supplier under joint review.

Acceptance Perform acceptance reviews and testing and perform systematic configuration management.

Supply Process This process consists of the following activities:

1. Initiation
2. Preparation of response
3. Contract
4. Project setup and planning
5. Project execution and control
6. Review and evaluation
7. Delivery and completion

Initiation The supplier conducts a review of requirements in the RFP taking into account organizational policies and other regulations, and the supplier should make a decision to bid or accept the contract.

Preparation of Response The supplier should define and prepare a proposal in response to the RFP.

Contract The supplier shall negotiate and enter into a contract with the acquirer organization to provide the software product or service. The supplier may request modification(s) to the contract as part of the change control mechanism.

Project Setup and Planning The supplier should review the acquisition requirements because it is necessary to

- Define the framework and quality
- Define scheme for managing and assuring the project
- Define or select a life cycle model
- Define resource needs appropriate to the scheme
- Perform risk analysis and tradeoffs
- Write project plan

Project Execution and Control The supplier should implement and execute the project management plan as well as the following:

- Execute the project management plan
- Monitor and control the project
- Manage and control subcontractors
- Interface with independent V&V
- Interface with specified parties

Review and Evaluation The supplier should coordinate contract reviews activities, interfaces, and communication with the acquirer's organization to

- Coordinate contract review process
- Conduct/support all specified reviews
- Perform V&V processes as specified
- Make all reports available
- Facilitate customer access to subcontractors

Delivery and Completion The supplier shall

- Deliver the software as specified
- Provide assistance in support of delivered product

Development Process The development process contains the activities for requirements analysis, design, coding, integration, testing, and installation and acceptance related to software products.

According to IEEE 12207.2, this development process consists of the following activities and output on the activities:*

1. Process implementation and the output will be development plans and models
2. System requirements analysis and the output will be system requirement
3. System architectural design and the output will be system architecture
4. Hardware, software, and manual operations
5. Software requirements analysis and the output will be software requirement
6. Software architectural design and the output will be software architecture
7. Software detailed design and the output will be software detail design
8. Software coding and testing and the output will be software code/database
9. Software integration and the output will be integrated software
10. Software qualification testing and the output will be design and code
11. System integration and the output will be integrated software
12. System qualification testing and the output will be design and code
13. Software installation and the output will be installation plan installed software
14. Software acceptance support and the output will be deliverable software

Operations Process   The operator role includes four activities. According to IEEE 12207.2, this operation process consists of the following activities and outputs on the activities:†

1. Implementation process: The output will be the operation plan and operation procedure

---

* IEEE/EIA 12207.2-1997, *A Joint Guide Developed by IE EE and EIA*, p. 21.
† Ibid., p. 36.

2. Operational testing process: The output will be the released operational software
3. System operation: The output will be the system functions performed
4. User support: The output will be the user requests and problem resolutions

Maintenance Process The maintainer role includes the following six activities:

1. Implementation process: The output will be maintenance plans/procedures.
   The activities consists of the following tasks:
   a. Develop and document a plan
   b. Establish a problem reporting procedure
   c. Interface with configuration management

2. Problem and modification analysis: The output will be problem analysis and modification solution.
   The activities consist of the following tasks:
   a. Perform problem analyses on trouble reports
   b. Replicate or verify the problem
   c. Consider options for performing the modification
   d. Document these options
   e. Obtain approval for the selected modification

3. Modification implementation: The output will be a modified software.
   The activities consist of the following tasks:
   a. The maintainer shall determine which units need to be modified.
   b. Enter development and perform the required modification, testing, and assurance procedures.

4. Review and acceptance: The output will be review results.
   The maintainer shall
   a. Perform reviews as specified in the change plan
   b. Obtain final approvals

5. Migration: The output will be migration plans/reports, migrated system.

a. A migration plan will be developed and approved.
b. Notifications will be performed and all documentation archived.
c. Postoperation reviews will be carried out and reported.
d. Required data will be assured accessible.

6. Retirement: The output will be retirement plans and archives.
a. A retirement plan will be developed and approved.
b. Early notifications will be carried out.
c. Notifications will be performed and all documentations are archived at the time of retirement.
d. Required data will be assured accessible.

Supporting Life Cycle Processes

The supporting life cycle processes defines the eight supporting life cycle processes, which are mentioned earlier, the details are given as follows:

Documentation Process   The documentation process is basically keeping record of information and data produced by a life cycle process or activity.

Documentation process consists of four activities:

1. Implementation process
2. Design and development process
3. Production process
4. Maintenance process

Configuration Management Process   The configuration management process is administrative and technical procedure to identify and control changes and releases and report the status.

The configuration management process consists of the following six major activities:

1. Implementation
2. Configuration identification
3. Configuration control
4. Status accounting

5. Configuration evaluation (promotion)
6. Release management

Quality Assurance Process   The quality assurance process makes sure that the software products and processes follow the specified requirements and comply with the plans.

Quality assurance may make use of the results of other supporting processes, such as verification, validation, joint reviews, audits, and problem resolution.

The software quality assurance process consists of the following four major activities:

1. Implementation
   a. A plan for conducting quality assurance should be developed, documented, implemented, and maintained.
   b. Scheduled and ongoing quality assurance activities and tasks shall be executed.
   c. Register quality assurance activities and tasks are made available to the acquirer.

2. Product assurance
   a. All plans required by the contract are documented, comply with the contract, are consistent, and are executed.
   b. Software products and related documentation comply with the contract and adhere to the plans.
   c. On delivery, products shall be assured to have fully satisfied contractual requirements and are acceptable.

3. Process assurance
   a. Software life cycle processes employed for the project comply with the contract and follow the plans.
   b. Comply with the internal software engineering practices, development and test environment, and libraries.
   c. Acquirer and other parties are given required support in accordance with the contracts, negotiations, and plans.
   d. Software product and process measurements are in accordance with the established standards and procedures.
   e. Staff has skill and knowledge needed to meet the project requirements and receive necessary training.

4. Assurance of quality systems

Verification Process   The verification process is to verify whether the software products fulfill the requirements.

The software verification process consists of the following two things:

Implementation   Determine whether project warrants verification.

- If verification is warranted, a verification process shall be established.
- If independent verification is warranted, a qualified organization shall be selected.
- Activities and products requiring verification shall be determined.
- A verification plan shall be developed.
- The verification plan shall be implemented, and the results of the activities were made available to the acquirer.

Verify All or Some of These Items   Contract verification.

- Process verification
- Requirement verification
- Design verification
- Code verification
- Documentation verification
- Integration verification

Validation Process   The validation process is a process to determine whether the requirements and the product fulfill its intended application.

The software validation process consists of the following two things:

- Process implementation
- Execution and analysis of test result

Process Implementation   Determine whether the project warrants a validation effort.
- Establish a validation process to validate the system or software product.

- Identify and select a qualified organization responsible for performing the validation.
- Develop a validation plan.
- Implement the validation plan.

Execution and Analysis of Test Results   Ensure that test requirements, cases, and specifications reflect the requirements.

- Conduct tests.
- Validate whether the software product satisfies its intended use.
- Test the software product as appropriate in selected areas of the target environment.

Joint Review Process   The joint review process is for evaluating the status and products of an activity of a project as appropriate. Joint reviews are at both project management and technical levels and are held throughout the life of the contract. This process may be employed by any two parties, where one party (reviewing party) reviews another party (reviewed party).

Joint review process consists of the following three activities:

1. Implementation
2. Project management reviews
3. Technical reviews

Audit Process   The audit process is a process for determining compliance with the requirements, plans, and contracts as appropriate. This process may be employed by any two parties, where one party (auditing party) audits the software products or activities of another party (audited party).

Audit process consists of the following two activities:

1. Implementation process
2. Audit process

Implementation Process   Implementation process consists of the following tasks:

- Audits shall be held at predetermined milestones as specified in the contract.

- Auditing personnel shall not have any direct responsibility for the software products and activities they audit.
- All resources required to conduct the audits shall be agreed by the parties. These resources include supporting personnel, location, facilities, hardware, software, and tools.
- The parties should agree on the following items at each audit: Agenda, software products (and results of an activity) to be reviewed, audit scope and procedures, and entry and exit criteria for the audit.
- Problems detected during the audits shall be recorded and entered into the problem resolution process.
- After completing an audit, the audit results shall be documented and provided to the audited party.
- The audited party shall acknowledge to the auditing party any problems found in the audit and related problem resolutions planned.
- The parties shall agree on the outcome of the audit and any action item, responsibilities, and closure criteria.

Audit Process Tasks

The audit process consists of the following tasks:

- Audits shall be held at predetermined milestones as specified in the project plans.
- Auditing personnel shall not have direct responsibility for all aspects of the audit.
- Resources required to conduct the audits shall be provided by the parties.
- Parties must agree on the agenda, products, scope, procedures, and entry and exit criteria.
- Problems detected shall be recorded and entered into problem resolution process.
- After completing an audit, results shall be documented and provided to the audited party.
- Parties shall agree on outcomes and any action item responsibilities and closure criteria.
- Audits shall be conducted to ensure audit criteria.

SECTION II
TESTING

3

TESTING: CONCEPT AND DEFINITION

Introduction

This chapter, as the name indicates, introduces the basic relationship between software and testing and how testing is an integral part of overall software development. Part 1 discusses how testing is integrated into the whole development process. Part 2 discusses the whole testing process and its life cycle. Part 3 defines the major types of testing.

Part 1: Testing in the Software Life Cycle

What Is Software Testing?

Testing is oriented toward "detection" primarily of the defects and anomalies that fall under the general category of a software "bug." Functionally, testing involves operation of a system or application under controlled conditions.

The controlled conditions should include both positive and negative conditions.

Testing should intentionally attempt to make things go wrong to determine if things happen when they should not or things do not happen when they should.

The IEEE Standard 610, Glossary of Software Engineering Technology, defines testing as "The process of operating a system or component under specified conditions, observing or recording the results, and making an evaluation of some aspects of the system or component."

IEEE Standard 829-1983 defines testing as "The process of analyzing a software item to detect the differences between existing and required conditions (that is, bugs) and to evaluate the features of the software items."*

Each project in software development should be following a life cycle model.

Where is the place for testing in a software life cycle? The simple answer is "it is part of it." There can be no software development life cycle (SDLC) without testing. However, when and how should testing be done? The general V-model plays an especially important role to answer this question. In the following V-model, the whole life cycle of a software development is clearly displayed; the sequence of the development is based on the requirement and specification. The first stage in the software life cycle is the high-level designing and the second is the final build. Once the final build is completed, the first step is the unit test usually done by the developer, and the next step is the system integration test, or SIT. After the SIT test, it goes to the system test; after system test is done, it goes to user acceptance test, or UAT.

In Figure 3.1, it is also displayed that there is a thin connection arrow right to left and left to right that means there is a thin but very important connection between development and unit test and design and SIT test, specification and system test and requirement and UAT test.

Requirements

Identification and Specification

The needs and requirements of the customer are gathered, specified, and finally approved. Thus, the purpose of the system and the desired characteristics and features are defined and identified (Figure 3.1).

Specification

Requirement specification is discussed in Part 3 of Chapter 4.

Functional System Development

The requirements are mapped onto functions and dialogues of the new system.

---

* IEEE Std 610.12-1990 (Revision and redesignation of IEEE Std 792-1983).

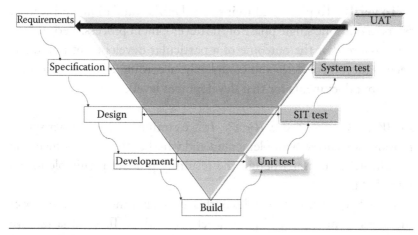

Figure 3.1   The V-model that displays the whole process from requirement to user acceptance test.

Technical System Design

The implementation of the system is designed. This includes the definition of interfaces to the system environment and the decomposition of the system into smaller understandable system architecture. Each subsystem can then be developed independently.

Component Specification

Each subsystem, including its task, behavior, inner structure, and interfaces to other subsystems, is defined.

Coding

Coding consists of the process of designing, writing, unit testing, debugging/troubleshooting, and maintaining the source code.

Testing

Are We Building the Right System?   During validation, the tester judges whether a product (or a part of the product) solves its task, and therefore, whether this product is suitable for its intended use.

To validate: To affirm, to declare as valid, to check if something is valid. In addition to validation testing, the V-model also requires verification testing.

To verify: To prove and to inspect. Unlike validation, verification refers to only one single phase of the development process. Verification shall assure that the outcome of a particular development phase has been achieved correctly and completely, according to its specification (the input documents for that development level).

Are We Building the System Right?   It is examined as to whether specifications are correctly implemented and whether the product meets its specification but not whether the resulting product is suitable for its intended use.

In reality, every test includes both aspects, but the validation aspect increases from lower to higher levels of testing. To summarize, we again list the most important characteristics and ideas behind the general V-model.*

Part 2: Software Testing Life Cycle

Software testing life cycle (STLC) process is an integral part of the SDLC. The overall aspect of STLC phase deals with testing and rectifying any error code generating within the program under various test conditions.

STLC is basically testing phases in the SDLC. As we have stated earlier, testing is a part of SDLC, in the same way, STLC is also part of SDLC. In other words, when we talk about STLC, we may say we are talking about only the testing.

Similar to SDLC, STLC has its own phases as follows:

> *Requirement analysis*   Even though requirement analysis is part of whole SDLC; however, it is a major part of testing life cycle.
>
> *Test planning*   Preparing the test strategy and planning (test planning is described in Chapter 3).

---

* Andreas Spillner, Tilo Linz, Hans Schaefer, and Rocky Nook. *Software Testing Foundations: A Study Guide for the Certified Tester Exam*, 2007, p. 42.

Test case development Creating the testing environment and writing the test cases (test planning is mentioned in Chapter 4).

Test execution Test executing and reporting are mentioned in Chapter 5.

Result analysis Analysis result and bug report (result analysis is described in Chapter 5).

Defect analysis and fix Analyze bugs and application errors (defect analysis and its management are described in Chapter 7).

Test result analysis and reporting This is a postconditional process that involves collecting data from the end users (test execution is discussed in Chapter 5).

SDLC and STLC

As we can see, SDLC and STLC have some common features but they are different to each other in several ways. The following are some explanations to make it clearer.

1. STLC is a part of SDLC. We cannot have STLC running independently.
2. STLC is limited to testing, and the SDLC is a greater scope with more inputs and executions.
3. STLC is the very important part of the SDLC. A software release cannot happen without running it through STLC process (Figure 3.2).

SDLC consists of the following (Figure 3.3):

- Requirement analysis
- Design
- Development
- Testing
- Installation
- Maintenance

Figure 3.2   Place of test in software development life cycle.

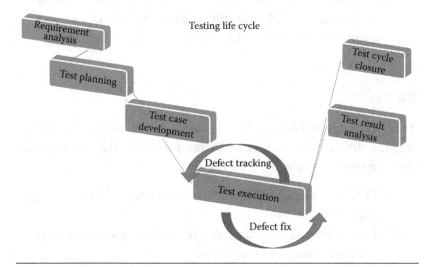

Figure 3.3   The testing life cycle.

STLC consists of the following:

- Requirement analysis
- Test planning
- Test case development
- Test execution (defect tracking and fixing)
- Test result analysis
- Test cycle closure*

---

* Andreas Spillner, Tilo Linz, Hans Schaefer, and Rocky Nook. *Software Testing Foundations: A Study Guide for the Certified Tester Exam*, 2007.

Part 3: Kinds/Types of Testing

What kinds of testing are there?

There are numerous forms of testing all with a slightly different purpose and focus.

We are going to examine and discuss the most common approaches, for instance, "hand testing" versus the use of tools and automated CASE style testing equipment.

They are also implemented with varying degrees of rigor depending on the integrity level required for the software product being tested.

Black Box Testing

Black box testing verifies the functionality of an application—not necessarily having specific knowledge of the application's code/internal structure. Black box tests are normally based on requirements and the functionality specified in them. Their purpose is to confirm that a given input reliably produces the anticipated output condition. This testing process is performed by quality assurance (QA) teams.

White Box Testing

White box testing is based on the knowledge of the internal logic of an application's code and includes tests such as coverage of code statements, branches, paths, and conditions. This testing process is generally performed by software developers by using a targeted set of prearranged test cases.

The purpose of white box testing is to confirm internal integrity and logic of the artifact and code.

Unit Testing

The unit test is a method in which a programmer tests whether individual units of source code are fit for use. This testing process is usually conducted by the development team or programmer and not by testers as it requires detailed knowledge of the internal design and code. This is the most "micro" scale level of the testing process. It is not always easily done unless the application has a well-designed architecture with tight code and may require developing automated tools.

Integration Testing

Integration testing is a phase in software testing in which individual software modules are combined and tested as a group. This kind of test is an important part of the traditional life cycle because it applies to the integration aspect of the system or software development process. It amounts to the testing of the combined parts of an application to determine if they function together correctly. This testing process is usually conducted by testing teams. The "parts" can be code modules, individual applications, and (more importantly) client and server applications on a network.

Incremental Integration Testing

This type of integration testing reflects the realities of the development process.

It describes the continuous testing of an application as new functionality is added.

It implies the various aspects of an application's functionality are independent enough to work separately before all the parts of the program are completed.

This type of testing is done by programmers or by specially designated testers.

Functional Testing

Functional testing is a black box testing that bases its test cases on the specifications of the software component under test, which is geared to validate the functional requirements of an application.

Functional testing can amount to a trace of the requirement to confirm its implementation in code, or it can be an actual scenario-driven performance evaluation.

System Testing

System testing is a type of specialized black box type testing that focuses on the overall requirement specifications. This is the process of testing an integrated hardware and software system to verify that the system meets its specified requirements. This testing process is conducted by the testing teams in both development and target environment. It is very similar to functional testing because it is attempting to validate whether the system performs as specified.

The obvious difference is that the tests are being done on both software and hardware.

End-to-End Testing

End-to-end testing is similar to system testing, because it inhabits the "macro" end of the test scale. It involves testing of a complete application environment in a situation that mimics real-world use, such as interacting with a database, using network communications, or interacting with other hardware, applications, or systems if appropriate. This testing process is performed by QA teams.

Sanity Testing

Sanity testing determines whether a new software version is performing well enough to accept it for a major testing effort. Sanity testing is a very important part of a good development practice. As such, it is an integral part of certain development approaches such as Boehm's spiral. For example, if the new software is crashing every 5 minutes, putting the system on its knees or trashing databases, it may not be in a "sane" enough condition to warrant further testing until it has been "tweaked" a bit more. This testing process is performed by the testing teams.

Regression Testing

Regression testing seeks to uncover software errors after bringing changes to the program, and it is one of the most common types of tests. It is also one of the most costly testing methods, because it is retesting after fixes or modifications have been made to the software or its environment. Because of the cost implications and the fact that it takes place after a problem has been identified, it can be difficult to determine how much retesting is going to be required. This testing process is performed by the testing teams. Automated testing tools can be useful for this type of testing.

Acceptance Testing

Acceptance testing, which is sometimes called factory acceptance testing (or FAT), is the final testing of the product against the specifications of the end user or customer. It is the formal testing conducted to determine whether or not a system satisfies its acceptance criteria and to enable the customer to determine whether or not to accept the system. It is usually based on "hands-on" use of the product by the end users/customers over some limited period of time.

Normally, there are heavy-duty financial implications to this type of testing so there may be rigorous audits of all deliverables by the customer. This testing process is usually performed by customer representatives or UAT team.

Load Testing

Load testing puts demand on a system or device and measures its response. It involves testing an application under heavy loads such as testing a website under a range of loads to determine at what point the system's response time degrades or fails. Load testing is frequently performed on an ad hoc basis during the normal developmental process. It is particularly useful because it can quickly and economically identify performance problems without hand checking. It is usually conducted by the performance engineers.

Stress Testing

Stress testing evaluates a system or component at or beyond the limits of its specified requirements. This is a term that is often used interchangeably with "load" and "performance" testing by professionals. It serves the same purpose as load testing in the sense that it is looking to predict failure thresholds. Stress tests normally test system functioning under specific conditions such as unusually heavy loads, heavy repetition of certain actions, input of large numerical values, and large complex queries to a database system.

It differs from load testing in the sense that any potential area of failure under stress is targeted (not just load). This testing process is usually conducted by the performance engineer.

Performance Testing

Performance testing is conducted to evaluate the compliance of a system or component with specified performance requirements. This term is also often used interchangeably with "stress" and "load" testing. However, it differs from the other two in that it normally references criteria that are established in advance or benchmarks that are created in the testing process, for instance, if what is being examined is performance degradation over time. Ideally, "performance" testing criteria for every artifact are defined "upfront" in the requirements documentation or in the software quality assurance (SQA) or test plan. Like the other two testings, performance testings are always supported by software and testing scenarios. This testing process is usually conducted by the performance engineer.

Usability Testing

Usability testing is one of the more common general testing approaches. It verifies the ease with which a user can learn to operate, prepare inputs for, and interpret outputs of a system or component. Usability testing could be understood as testing for "user friendliness" or user comfortability. This testing process is usually performed by the end users. User interviews, surveys, video recording of user sessions, and other techniques can be used. *Programmers and testers are usually not appropriate as usability testers.*

Install/Uninstall Testing

Install/uninstall testing is a type of quality assurance work that focuses on what customers will need to do to install and set up the new software successfully. It may involve full, partial, or upgrades install/uninstall processes. It is typically done by a software testing engineer in conjunction with the configuration manager.

Recovery Testing

Recovery testing evaluates how well a system recovers from crashes, hardware failures, or other catastrophic problems. This testing process is performed by the testing teams.

Security Testing

Security testing determines that an information system protects data and maintains functionality as intended, and how well the system protects against unauthorized internal or external access or willful damage. It may require sophisticated testing techniques. Security testing can be performed by testing teams or by specialized security testing companies.

Comparison Testing

Comparison testing is a comparison of the software's weaknesses and strengths to competing products. This testing technique compares the product with previous versions or other similar products. It can be performed by testers, developers, product managers, or product owners.

Alpha Testing

Alpha testing is a type of testing of a software product or system conducted at the developer's site. It is typically done by end users or others and definitely not by programmers or testers. It takes place when an application is nearing completion. Some minor design changes can be made as a result of such testing, so it is not as widely circulated.

Beta Testing

Beta testing is the final testing before releasing the application for commercial purpose. This is by far the most common method of final testing a new product in the real world. Beta testing takes place when development and testing are essentially completed and final bugs and problems need to be found before final release. It is typically done by end users or others and not by programmers or testers.

Automated Testing

Automated testing is the testing technique that uses automation testing tools to control the environmental setup, the execution of tests, and reporting of the results. This testing process is performed by a computer and is used inside the testing teams. This requires a formalized "manual testing process" that currently exists. The tester must first establish an effective testing process.

The real use and purpose of automated test tools is to automate regression testing. This means that a tester must have or must develop a database of detailed test cases that are repeatable and these tests should be run every time there is a change to the application to ensure that the change does not produce unintended consequences.

Agile Testing

Agile is basically a SDLC methodology. Agile testing is the software testing practice that follows the principles of the agile manifesto, emphasizing testing from the perspective of customers who will utilize the system. This type of testing is usually performed by QA teams. There is an independent discussion about agile testing under SDLC.

Suggested Readings

1. CHAOS Manifesto 2013.
2. Dr. Paul Dorsey. Top 10 Reasons Why Systems Projects Fail. 2014. Available at: http://www.hks.harvard.edu/centers/mrcbg.
3. The dismantled National Program for IT in the NHS.
4. U.K. House of Commons. 2013. Available at: http://www.publications.parliament.uk/pa/cm201314/cmselect/cmpubacc/294/294.pdf.
5. Why do IT projects fail: Shuhab-u-Tariq. Available at: http://www.shuhab.com/Downloads/WhyDoITProjectsFail.pdf.

4

TESTING: PLAN AND DESIGN

Introduction

This chapter introduces the test plan, strategy, and stages. Part 1 introduces definition and real-time practical plan of how a plan should be designed. Part 2 introduces the step-by-step process of test design, requirement analysis, preparing test data, scheduling test, test estimation, etc. Part 3 discusses the test design process and the factors involved in the test designing. Part 4 introduces the test case design process, where it also introduces the sample test case.

Part 1: Plan and Strategy

Test Plan

A software project test plan is a document that describes the objectives, scope, approach, and focus of a software testing effort.

The test document helps people outside the test group understand the "why" and "how" of product validation in the plan.

Contents of a Test Plan

The following are some of the items that might be included in a test plan, depending on a particular project. Different companies practice different formats of test plan. This document is prepared based on IEEE Standard 829 and the personal work experience.

Test Plan Identification

Some unique company generates numbers to identify its test plan, its level, and the level of software that it is related to. Preferably, the level of test plan will be the same as the related software level.

PROJECT IDENTIFICATION			
Organization	ABC	Date	
Project name		Project code	
Application name		Iteration	
Release number		Change type	
Methodology			
Execution life cycle			
Project manager			
Approver—1			
Approver—2			

Document Change Control Log

This log is updated each time this document is updated. The log identifies the version number, the date the revisions were completed, a brief description of the changes, and the author.

VERSION #	DATE	SECTIONS/ AGE REVISED	DESCRIPTION	REVISED BY NAME AND TITLE	REVIEWED BY NAME AND TITLE
1.0	07/01/2015		Initial draft		
1.1	07/15/2015	All	Testing scope		
1.2	07/30/2015	Section 3.1	Updated project ID		
1.3	08/15/2015	Section 4.2			

Purpose of the Document

State the purpose of the plan, which is the executive summary part of the plan.

The purpose of the "Test Plan" should describe the scope of the objective and approach of intended testing activities. It should identify what items (systems, subsystems, major functional areas, etc.) will be tested and what types of tests will be performed, as well as the roles and responsibilities.

The test plan is a comprehensive release level document that should cover all test activities planned for the test.*

---

* IEEE Standard for Software and System Test Documentation, IEEE Std 829™-2008 (Revision of IEEE Std 829-1998).

References

All documents, including the scope of the project, project stakeholder requirements, and test strategy documents, should be available to support the test plan.

Sample Reference Metrics

DOCUMENT NAME	PHYSICAL SOURCE/LOCATION
Scope statement	
Requirement specifications	
Test strategy	
Project plan	
High-level design document	
Detail design document	
Development and test process standards	
Defect management standard	
Defect management procedure	
Corporate standards and guidelines	
Methodology guidelines and examples	

Software Product Overview/Project Description

Test Objectives

Assumptions/Constraints List
Assumptions

ASSUMPTION NUMBER	RELATES TO	CONSTRAINTS DESCRIPTION	STATUS CODE	STATUS DATE	STATUS COMMENT

Constraints

CONSTRAINTS NUMBER	RELATES TO	CONSTRAINTS DESCRIPTION	STATUS CODE	STATUS DATE	STATUS COMMENT

Software Risk Issue and Mitigation

The critical areas are as follows:

1. Delivery of a third-party product
2. Release of a new version of the software
3. User challenges to understand a new tool, etc.
4. Extremely complex functions
5. Modifications to components with a past history of failure
6. Poorly documented modules or change requests

(There will be a detailed discussion about the overall risk analysis and risk management in Chapter 8.)

Another key area of risk is a misunderstanding of the original requirements. This can occur at the management, user, and developer levels. Be aware of vague or unclear requirements and requirements that cannot be tested. It is also very important that each item of the requirement is similarly understood by business team (user), developers, and testers. Make sure that all parties are in the same page during the requirement analysis meeting. It is highly recommended for a test team to carefully read through each item of the requirement and make a note and ask questions during the requirement analysis meeting if any item is not clear.

One good approach to define where the risks are is to have several brainstorming sessions.

Note concerns and worries about the project/application.*

Communication and Status Reporting

The test lead for each stage will report test status to the project stakeholders on a regular basis. The report is a point in time snapshot that captures the critical tasks of testing that should include but is not limited to the following:

- Overall status of the test stage
- Requirements test coverage
- Execution summary
- Execution status

---

* Ibid.

- Test issues requiring immediate attention
- Defect summary
- Next steps

Test Tools

The following tools will be employed for this project:
List the tools to be used in the specific test release.

	TOOL	TOOL VENDOR/IN-HOUSE
Requirement repository	DOORS (for example)	IBM
Test case repository	Quality center (for example)	HP
Defect management repository	Quality center (for example)	HP

Test Scope

The progression testing of the application should focus on the release requirements that can be traced directly to use cases (or business functions) and business rules.

The test plan document should be modified in conjunction with changes to the requirements document. It should be clear and specific if only new requirements or enhancements would be tested or if any older requirement will be tested.

The regression test format should specifically mention the number of rounds of regression tests that are planned till the release. The plan should also mention the scope of the coverage.

Part 2: Test Approach and Stages

Requirements Analysis

The requirements should be documented, actionable, measurable, testable, traceable, related to identified business needs or opportunities, and defined to a level of detail sufficient for system design.

The test teams involved in the requirements review process should validate whether the stakeholder requirements are clear, succinct, testable, and capture the needs of the business accurately prior to moving beyond analysis. The test teams should note and log their findings captured during the review(s) based on the defect management standard.

Solution Specifications

Developers should implement the design specifications through source code by leveraging the solution specifications. They will also write unit test cases and conduct unit testing during the construction phase.

Testing Levels

(This is an example, but the role could be different, and the role should be detailed as shown in the example test plan.)

The testing for the project consists of unit, system/integration (combined), and acceptance test levels. It is hoped that there will be at least one full time independent test person for system/integration testing. However, with the budget constraints and time line established, most testing will be done by the test manager with the participation of development teams.

Unit Testing

Unit testing will be done by the developer and will be approved by the development team leader. Proof of unit testing (test case list, sample output, data printouts, and defect information) must be provided by the programmer to the team leader before unit testing will be accepted and passed on to the test person. All unit test information will also be provided to the test person.

System/Integration Testing

System/integration testing will be performed by the test manager/ test lead and development team leader with the assistance from the individual developers as required.

(If there is any specific test tool available for this project, it should be mentioned in this part.)

System Test

System test should start with a thorough analysis of the application to be tested utilizing all available information, including the scope, stakeholder requirements, design documents or solution specifications, approved change controls, and direct contact with business and business analysts.

The test scenarios should represent the positive and negative conditions that will be applied during testing. For each requirement, the system test team should define at least one test scenario. Each scenario should be transformed into a detailed test case by the inclusion of step-by-step directions to evaluate the test conditions against the expected results for each step. The system test team should create requirements coverage by linking each targeted test with one or more requirements. Tests may be grouped to meet the various testing goals, which may include testing as a specific function.

System Test Execution

Test execution should begin once the software is given to the system test team for testing, and all subsequent changes to the software must come under change control. The system test team must be aware of all changes that are moved into the test environment.

A "shake out" test may take place to validate that the application is ready for further testing for each deployment.

Defect Management

In handling definition of any defect or policy, the team should be referred to "Defect Management Standard" documents. In other words, there should be a "Defect Management Standard" in place. The goal for testing for all defects should be in a terminal state (closed, canceled, or deterred) prior to the production implementation.

Acceptance Testing

Acceptance testing will be performed by the actual end users with the assistance of the test manager and development team leader.

The acceptance test will be done in parallel with the existing manual ZIP/FAX process for a period of 1 month after completion of the system/integration test process.

Test Data Preparation

The system test team should work with the development and business analyst to ensure the full coverage of the expected test attributes.

Test Environments

System test should be conducted in the test environment.
User test should be conducted in the acceptance environment.

Sample Entry/Exit Criteria

The following criteria could be followed for each iteration of system test.

Entry Criteria

- Development test/unit test has been completed
- Development team documented build notes with all known issues and defects
- Test data have been defined, obtained, populated, or prepared and are ready for use as per the test data/preparation section
- System test plan is complete and approvals received
- Test scripts for the relevant code build have been completed, reviewed, accepted, and are ready for use
- Test environments have been configured as per the test environment section earlier
- Build is complete and deployed to the test environment
- Test environment shake out is successful and no show stopper incidents are found

Exit Criteria

- 100% execution of all test scripts
- The pass rate shall be 90% or higher (pass rate % depends on company's policy)

- Zero (0) open critical defects (depends on company policy)
- Zero (0) open high defects (depends on company policy)
- All medium and low defects are documented and communicated to user test team(s)
- Business and technology sign-off (acceptance of test results) received

Test Schedule

It is very important to maintain a test schedule. A high-level test schedule can be prepared by the project manager to keep the whole project on time. However, the test team can also create their own internal test schedule, especially it is needed when the team size is big, in that circumstances, the test team needs to distribute the tasks among team members and maintain the schedule.

Scheduling system testing is a portion of the overall scheduling of a software development project. It is a part of overall software project plan, and it could be managed by the project manager, or the test team can manage this portion by their internal team as long as the test team meets the project plan deadline.

It is very important to outline a schedule and the milestones for the test project. The system test group is constrained to distribute its testing effort to accommodate the marketing requirement to release the product within the approved time frame. The team must complete the system testing phase on time without much delay in product delivery and without compromising the quality of a product.

Example

A high-level test schedule for this test project is shown in Table 4.1 using the MS Project Gantt chart. This sample project plan is not necessarily applicable. It is just a sample example. The test team can keep their own schedule in MS Project or in MS Excel.

Defect Reporting and Tracking

Details of defect reporting should be specified in the test plan. Details of defect management will be discussed in Chapter 7.

Table 4.1   The Test Schedule and Timeline of the Project in Microsoft Project Format

ID	Task Name	Duration	Start	Finish	Predecessors	Resource Names
1	**Initiating**	**7 days?**	**Mon 7/20/15**	**Mon 7/27/15**		**Abu**
2	Develop project charter	6 days?	Mon 7/20/15	Sat 7/25/15		Onevada
3	Meet with stakeholders	1 day?	Mon 7/27/15	Mon 7/27/15	2	Norma
4	**Planning**	**85 days**	**Thu 6/11/15**	**Tue 10/6/15**		**Alisa**
5	Create detailed WBS and schedule	10 days?	Sat 7/25/15	Thu 8/6/15		Jack
6	Estimate project costs	5 days?	Mon 8/10/15	Fri 8/14/15		Johny
7	Create project team	3 days?	Mon 8/17/15	Wed 8/19/15	6	Norma
8	Sign project team to contracts	1 day?	Thu 8/20/15	Thu 8/20/15	7	Alamgir
9	Create communication plan	3 days?	Mon 8/17/15	Wed 8/19/15		Willey
10	Organize a comprehensive project plan	5 days?	Thu 8/20/15	Wed 8/26/15	9	
11	**Executing**	**131 days**	**Mon 8/31/15**	**Mon 2/29/16**		
12	Award and manage contract for conversion	5 days?	Mon 8/31/15	Fri 9/4/15		Norma
13	Install new software on servers	29 days?	Mon 9/7/15	Thu 10/15/15	12	Alamgir
14	Install new hardware and software on client machines	65 days?	Fri 10/16/15	Thu 1/14/16	13	Jack
15	Test new billing systems	20 days?	Fri 1/15/16	Thu 2/11/16	14	Johny
16	Train users on new system	25 days?	Fri 2/12/16	Thu 3/17/16	15	Norma
17	**Controlling**	**153 days**	**Mon 8/24/15**	**Wed 3/23/16**		**Abu**
18	Document suggested changes	5 days?	Mon 8/24/15	Fri 8/28/15		Willey
19	Review with change control board	5 days?	Mon 8/31/15	Fri 9/4/15	18	Jack
20	Document suggested changes	5 days?	Mon 1/11/16	Fri 1/15/16		Kartik
21	Review with change control board	5 days?	Mon 1/18/16	Fri 1/22/16	20	Rakesh
22	Document suggested changes	5 days?	Tue 6/2/15	Mon 6/8/15		Kartik
23	Review with change control board	5 days?	Fri 3/4/16	Thu 3/10/16		Norma
24	Checkpoint for quality, risk, and cost	6 days?	Tue 3/1/16	Tue 3/8/16		Rakesh
25	**Closing**	**0 days**	**Wed 3/30/16**	**Wed 3/30/16**		**Abu**
26	Sign-off	6 days?	Tue 3/1/16	Tue 3/8/16		Abu
27	Update lessons learned	5 days?	Thu 3/24/16	Wed 3/30/16		Abu

Project: group project av1
Date: Thu 10/1/15

Legend:

Task	Inactive Task	Manual Summary
Split	Inactive Milestone	Start-only
Milestone	Inactive Summary	Finish-only
Summary	Manual Task	External Tasks
Project Summary	Duration-only	External Milestone
External Tasks	Manual Summary Rollup	Progress
External Milestone		Deadline

Roles and Responsibilities

ROLE	PROJECT POINT OF CONTACT	RESPONSIBILITY
Project manager		Management and oversight
Technology and development manager/team		Development and error remediation
		Technology and development manager
QA test Manager/lead Testers		• Test script development and execution (system test) • Defect management • Test reporting
Business sponsor		Test script development and test execution (user test and production deployment test) Defect prioritization
Technology sponsor		Test script development and test Execution (user test and production deployment test)
User test		Test script development and test Execution (user test and production deployment test) • Defect prioritization • Test reporting (user test)
Architect		• Business lead • Architect

Appendix

Reference Documents

Note that some of the documents embedded here may become outdated since they can be updated after the submission of this test strategy. The latest versions of documents are always available via the "Repository Links" in the right-hand column.

DOCUMENT NAME	DOCUMENT LOCATION	REPOSITORY LINK
Scope statement		
Stakeholder's requirements		
Project risk log		
Defect management standard		
Defect management procedure		

Testing Estimation

In testing, cost and time together are called test effort, and the whole estimation is called level of effort (LOE).

Measuring test estimation or LOE is basically being completed by test manager or test lead. However, correct LOE is very important because project time, scope, resource, and cost are involved with correct LOE.

Test estimation has two major components:

- The number of test cases created by one person in 1 day
- The number of test cases executed by one person in 1 day

Usually LOE is completed in the planning stage to estimate the cost of the test and the time to complete the test.

In most cases, the estimation of the system test effort is combined with the estimation of entire software project. However, it is useful to separate the test effort estimate from the estimate of the entire project so that enough time is allocated to plan for the system testing from the beginning and conduct it as soon as the entry criteria are satisfied. There are a few key factors in estimating test effort, which are as follows:

1. A number of test cases need to be designed
2. How much effort is required to create each detailed test case
3. How much effort is required to execute each test case
4. How much effort is needed for requirement analysis and for result analysis

Following is a sample LOE that may give some idea about the structure of test estimation (Table 4.2).

Lessons Learned

Project Description

PROJECT OVERVIEW	
Project name/release number	
Client/project Mgr. name	
Project type	
Testing team	
Project start and end dates	
Lessons learned review date	

Table 4.2 The Test Schedule and Timeline of the Project in Microsoft Project Format

	TASK	SUBTASK	DURATION (HOURS)	DEPENDENCY	PLANNING LOE: 322
REQUIREMENT ANALYSIS	Conduct test kickoff		2	Stakeholder requirements signoff	Execution LOE: 616
	Draft test scope		8	Conduct test kickoff	
	Define test strategy		44		
		Draft test strategy	16	Draft test scope	
		Review test strategy	8	Draft test strategy	
		Document test strategy review	1	Review test strategy	
		Update test strategy based on review	2	Review test strategy	
	Revise testing tasks/LOE (as needed)		16	Define test strategy	
DESIGN AND DEVELOPMENT	Develop system test scenarios		48	Requirements checkpoint	
	Define test plan		52		
		Draft test plan	24	Develop system test scenarios and develop user test scenarios	
		Review test plan	16	Draft test plan	
		Document test plan review	4	Review test plan	
		Update test plan based on review	8	Review test plan	
	Revise testing tasks/LOE (as needed)		32	Define test plan	

(Continued)

Table 4.2   (Continued) The Test Schedule and Timeline of the Project in Microsoft Project Format

	TASK	SUBTASK	DURATION (HOURS)	DEPENDENCY	PLANNING LOE: 322
IN CONSTRUCTION	Develop system test cases		160	Requirements/design PQO checkpoint OR test plan signoff	
	Draft test case specification (initial)		16	Develop system test cases	
	Define requirements traceability		104		
		Trace system test cases	16	- Business tracing requirements to scope - Development tracing solution Specifications to requirements - Develop system test cases	
		Trace user test cases	16	- Business tracing requirements to scope - Development tracing solution specifications to requirements - Develop user test cases	
		Draft RTM	40	- Trace system test cases - Trace user test cases	
		Review RTM	16	Draft RTM	
		Document RTM review	8	Review RTM	
		Update RTM based on review	8	Review RTM	

(Continued)

Table 4.2 (Continued) The Test Schedule and Timeline of the Project in Microsoft Project Format

	TASK	SUBTASK	DURATION (HOURS)	DEPENDENCY	PLANNING LOE:	322
IN SYSTEM TEST	Progression testing, defect remediation, and test incident reporting		240	Migration to test environment		
	Regression testing, defect remediation, and test incident reporting		256	Progression testing, defect remediation, and test incident reporting		
	Define test reports		120			
		Draft system test results summary	16	Regression testing, defect remediation, and test incident reporting		
		Draft test incident report	8	Regression testing, defect remediation, and test incident reporting		
		Draft test case specification (final)	16	Regression testing, defect remediation, and test incident reporting		
		Review system test results summary	16	Draft system test results summary		
		Document system test results summary review	32	Review system test results summary		
		Update system test results summary based on review	32	Review system test results summary		

938

Assumptions:

Any performance-related scope items will be focused on functionality alone. Manual performance measurement will not be tested in system testing.

These LOE are high level and subject to change upon the actual requirement.

What Went Well

WHAT WENT WELL	BENEFITS TO THE PROJECT

What Could Have Gone Better

WHAT COULD HAVE GONE BETTER	IMPACT TO PROJECT	RECOMMENDED IMPROVEMENT	COMMENT

NEW Opportunities

LOE Accuracy

Top Three Recommended Improvements

1. Recommended improvement #1.

....

2. Recommended improvement #2.

....

3. Recommended improvement #3.

....

Part 3: Test Design Factors

Software Requirement

Software requirement is basically a field within software engineering that deals with establishing the needs of stakeholders that are to be solved by the software. The IEEE Standard 610, Glossary of Software Engineering Technology, defines a software requirement as

1. A condition or capability needed by a user to solve a problem or achieve an objective.
2. A condition or capability that must be met or possessed by a system or system component to satisfy a contract, standard, specification, or other formally imposed document.
3. A documented representation of a condition or capability as in 1 or 2.

The activities related to working with software requirements can broadly be broken up into elicitation, analysis, specification, and management.*

Requirement Identification

Requirements are a description of the needs or desires of users that a system is supposed to implement.

Requirement Identifier Requirements must be expressed in such a form that the users and other stakeholders can easily review and confirm their accuracy. Some use User Story, specifically in the agile methodology, Microsoft Testing Tool Team Foundation Server has an item named User Story, another Testing Software Rally also uses the term User Story. IBM tool DOORS has its item as requirement, some companies use MS Word document for requirement. Therefore, the "form" of a requirement is crucial to the communication between users (and their surrogates) and the representatives of a software development organization.

Requirements also should be discussed and analyzed thoroughly to ensure that the requirements are communicated unambiguously to the developers and testers so that there are no surprises when the system is delivered. It is very important that the business stakeholders, developers, and testers are exactly on the same page in understanding the requirements. The interpretation of the requirements must come from the business team or users.

---

* "Guide to the Software Engineering Body of Knowledge" IEEE Computer Society, Retrieved 11 January, 2013.

It is undesirable for the teams to interpret the requirements in their own ways. There are severe consequences for teams interpreting requirements in their own ways. First, the development team and the system test team may have conflicting viewpoints about the product or even about any defect that may arise.*

Software Requirement Specification

A software requirements specification (SRS) is a description of a software system to be developed, laying out functional, and nonfunctional requirements.

SRS establishes the basis for an agreement between customers and contractors or suppliers (in market-driven projects, these roles may be played by the marketing and development divisions) on what the software product is to do as well as what it is not expected to do. SRS permits a rigorous assessment of requirements before design can begin and reduces later redesign. It should also provide a realistic basis for estimating product costs, risks, and schedules.†

The SRS document enlists enough and necessary requirements that are required for the project development.

An example organization of an SRS is as follows:‡

- Overview/goal/purpose
- Assumptions
- Constraints
- Dependencies
- Definitions
- System overview
- References
- Description
  - Product perspective
    - System interfaces requirement
    - User interfaces requirement

---

* Kshirasagar Naik. *Software Testing and Quality Assurance Theory and Practice*, Wiley, A John Wiley & Sons, Inc., Publication.
† Kshirasagar Naik. *Software Testing and Quality Assurance, Theory and Practice*, Wiley, A John Wiley & Sons, Inc., Publication, 1958, 2008, p. 322.
‡ Wikipedia, SRS.

- – Hardware interfaces
- – Software interfaces
- – Communication interfaces
- – Memory constraints
- – Operations
- – Site adaptation requirements
- Product functions
- User characteristics
- Constraints, assumptions, and dependencies
- Stakeholder requirements
  - External interface requirements
  - Functional requirements
  - Performance requirements
  - Design constraints
    - – Standards compliance
  - Logical database requirement
  - Software system attributes
    - – Reliability
    - – Availability
    - – Security
    - – Maintainability
    - – Portability
  - Other requirements

Requirements Evaluation Matrix*

Project Name

Amendment History—Document Status (e.g., draft, final, and release #):

CR# (OPTIONAL)	DOCUMENT VERSION #	APPROVAL DATE	MODIFIED BY	SECTION, PAGE(S), AND TEXT REVISED

---

* Partial document of Masters in Computer Information Systems Class project by the author.

SOLUTION CRITERIA AND WEIGHTING FACTORS

Rq#	sc# wf	sc# wf	sc# wf	sc# wf	sc# wf	sc# wf	sc# wf	sc# wf	sc# wf	sc# wf	sc# wf	sc# wf	Value

Business Value of Requirements

Value of requirements determined by the estimated support for weighted solution criteria

Rows: Requirement or requirement set

Columns: Solution criteria numbers and weighting factors

Cells: Requirements estimated support for solution criteria

Scales/Measures

Affect -2 Significant deterrence from criteria

-1 Slight deterrence from criteria

0 No effect on criteria

1 Slight contribution to criteria

2 Significant contribution to criteria

Significant Requirement Conflicts and Enablers

HIGH-VALUE RQ#	CONFLICTING RQ#S	ENABLING RQ#S	EXPLANATION

Estimated Costs and Risks to Satisfy Requirements

	USING CURRENT COMPONENTS			USING AVAILABLE COMPONENTS			NEW
RQ#	COMPONENTS	SUPPORT	COSTS/ RISKS	COMPONENTS	SUPPORT	COSTS/ RISKS	COSTS/ RISKS

(Continued)

	USING CURRENT COMPONENTS			USING AVAILABLE COMPONENTS			NEW
RQ#	COMPONENTS	SUPPORT	COSTS/ RISKS	COMPONENTS	SUPPORT	COSTS/ RISKS	COSTS/ RISKS

Scales/Measures

Support 0 = no support for requirements, 1 = fully satisfies requirement

Costs project hours to modify; to acquire, to extend, and to integrate or to develop

Risks L = low risk; M = medium risk; H = high risk

Requirements Cost/Benefit and Prioritization Summary

	COSTS		BENEFITS		CHAPTER 251
REQUIREMENTS	ESTIMATED COSTS/ RISKS	CONFLICT ADJUSTMENT	CONTRIBUTION VALUE	ENABLER ADJUSTMENT	PRIORITY

| REQUIREMENTS | COSTS | | BENEFITS | | CHAPTER 251 |
	ESTIMATED COSTS/ RISKS	CONFLICT ADJUSTMENT	CONTRIBUTION VALUE	ENABLER ADJUSTMENT	PRIORITY

Notes and Assumptions

Part 4: Test Case Specification and Design

Test Case Specification

This phase involves creation, verification, and rework of test cases and test scripts. Test data are identified/created and are reviewed and then reworked as well.

- Create test cases, automation scripts (if applicable)
- Review and baseline test cases and scripts
- Create test data (if test environment is available)

Deliverables

- Test cases/scripts
- Test data

Test Environment Setup

Test environment decides the software and hardware conditions under which a work product is tested. The team needs to understand the required architecture, environmental setup, and prepare hardware and software requirement list for the test environment. Setup test environment and test data.

Deliverables

- Environment ready with test data setup
- Smoke test results

Sample Test Case*

Individual Plan and Test Case

Document name:
Publication date: mm/dd/yyyy
Prepared by: ....
Submitted to: ABC Software, Inc.

Introduction

ABC Software, Inc. created new software for nonprofit organizations. The name of the software is Raisers Help. Mr. ABCD is appointed as tester for V&V test. It is a fundraising software that runs in PCs, and it is used mainly by nonprofit organizations. It is used to enter donor information, gift management, creating queries, reports writings, and alumni relations.

Scope

The Raisers Help software has five modules: constituent management, gift management, query, report, and alumni management. Different users would have access to use different modules depending on their clearance level. When an icon is double clicked, the respective module is one of the first things to get loaded and viewed on the monitor. The first screen that is seen by the user is the login screen. This login screen consists of the username and the password fields. Below these fields, there are two command buttons: "OK" and "Cancel." The test plan is going to describe how the Raisers Help login screen will be tested to ensure that only valid users can log on. The test will also verify that the user has permission to use the specific module. It will also test the functionalities of the command buttons on the login screen. The testing plan deals with users accessing the network environment.

---

* All provided data and information are for example only, not necessarily usable.

Objective

The objective is to verify that only valid users can log on to the Raisers Help software and that the command buttons provided on the login screen are consistent with the tasks that they are supposed to perform.

Responsibility

The developer of the Raisers Help login screen is ABC Software, Inc. The testing is to be conducted by Mr. A. The results are to be reported to the development team leader and the developer.

Sample Test Cases

Testing Condition 1.1—Login with Correct User ID and Password

Reason for the test	To ascertain that • The Raisers Help login screen appears accurately • The user can log in successfully with the proper username and password
Testing environment	The testing environment setting is • Windows 8, with 8 GB RAM and 400 GB Hard Drive Space • Windows 7
Test procedures	Once the icon has been double clicked, the tester: • Left clicked on the username field and enters in the correct username "mahfuz" • Left clicked on the password field and enters in the correct password "abc123" • Left clicked on the "OK" command button
Results expected	The expected results include that • Upon completing the above steps, the user should be able to successfully log in to Raisers Help
Test results	The test results include that • The user mahfuz was able to successfully log in
Test pass/fail	Pass
Tester signature	ABCD

Testing Condition 1.2—Wrong User ID

Reason for the test	To ascertain that • The Raisers Help login screen appears accurately • The user cannot login successfully if the username is incorrect
Testing environment	The testing environment setting is • Windows 8, with 15 GB RAM and 400 GB hard drive space • Windows 7

Test procedures	Once an icon has been double clicked, the tester: • Left clicked on the username field and enters in the incorrect (or spelled wrong) username "mahfooz" • Left clicked on the password field and enters in the correct password "abc123" • Left clicked on the "OK" command button
Results expected	The expected results include that • Upon completing the above steps, the user should not be able to log in to The Raisers Help
Test results	The test results include that • An error message appeared on the screen indicating that the username and/or password is incorrect
Test pass/fail	Pass
Tester signature	ABCD

Testing Condition 1.3—Wrong Password

Reason for the test	To ascertain that • The Raisers Help login screen appears accurately • The user cannot log in successfully if the password is incorrect
Testing environment	The testing environment setting is • Windows XP, with 5 GB RAM and 400 GB hard drive space • Windows 7
Test procedures	Once the icon has been double clicked, the tester: • Left clicked on the username field and enters in the correct username "student" • Left clicked on the password field and enters in the incorrect password "123abc" • Left clicked on the "OK" command button
Results expected	The expected results include that • Upon completing the above steps, the user should not be able to log in to Raisers Help
Test results	The test results include that • An error message appeared on the screen indicating that the username and/or password is incorrect
Test pass/fail	Pass
Tester signature	ABCD

Testing Condition 1.4—Username Blank

Reason for the test	To ascertain that • The Raisers Help login screen appears accurately • The user cannot log in successfully if the username field is blank and the password is correct

Testing environment	The testing environment setting is
	• Windows XP, with 5 GB RAM and 400 GB hard drive space
	• Windows 7
Test procedures	Once the icon has been double clicked, the tester:
	• Left clicked on the username field and left the field blank
	• Left clicked on the password field and enters in the correct password "abc123"
	• Left clicked on the "OK" command button
Results expected	The expected results include that
	• Upon completing the above steps, the user should not be able to log in to Raisers Help
Test results	The test results include that
	• An error message appeared on the screen indicating that the username and/or password is incorrect
Test pass/fail	Pass
Tester signature	ABCD

Testing Condition 1.5—Password Blank

Reason for the test	To ascertain that
	• The Raisers Help login screen appears accurately
	• The user cannot log in successfully if the username is correct and the password is left blank
Testing environment	The testing environment setting is
	• Windows XP, with 5 GB RAM and 400 GB hard drive space
	• Windows 7
Test procedures	Once the icon has been pressed, the tester:
	• Left clicked on the username field and entered the correct username "mahfuz"
	• Left clicked on the password field and left the field blank
	• Left clicked on the "OK" command button
Results expected	The expected results include that
	• Upon completing the above steps, the user should not be able to log in to Raisers Help
Test results	The test results include that
	• An error message appeared on the screen indicating that the username and/or password is incorrect
Test pass/fail	Pass
Tester signature	AbuSayed Mahfuz

Testing Condition 1.6—Username and Password Blank

Reason for the test	To ascertain that
	• The Raisers Help login screen appears accurately
	• The user cannot log in successfully if the both the username field and the password field is left blank

Testing environment	The testing environment setting is • Windows XP, with 5 GB RAM and 400 GB hard drive space • Windows 7
Test procedures	Once the icon has been double clicked, the tester: • Left clicked on the username field and left the field blank • Left clicked on the password field and left the field blank • Left clicked on the "OK" command button
Results expected	The expected results include that • Upon completing the above steps, the user should not be able to log in to Raisers Help
Test results	The test results include that • An error message appeared on the screen indicating that the username and/or password is incorrect
Test pass/fail	Pass
Tester signature	ABCD

Testing Condition 1.7—Cancel Button Clicked

Reason for the test	To ensure that • The Raisers Help login screen appears accurately • User is not able to log in when the cancel button is pressed even after entering the correct username and password
Testing environment	The testing environment setting is • Windows XP, with 5 GB RAM and 400 GB hard drive space • Windows 7
Test procedures	Once the icon has been double clicked, the tester: • Left clicked on the username field and enters in the correct username "mahfuz" • Left clicked on the password field and enters in the correct password "abc123" • Left clicked on the "Cancel" command button
Results expected	The expected results include that • Upon completing the above steps, the user should not be able to log in to Raisers Help
Test results	The test results include that • The module has disappeared • The user was not able to successfully log in to Raisers Help
Test pass/fail	Pass
Tester signature	AbuSayed Mahfuz

Testing Condition 1.8—Invalid User

Reason for the test	To ensure that • The Raisers Help login screen appears accurately • The user cannot log in successfully if the user does not have permission to this specific module

Testing environment	The testing environment setting is
	• Windows XP, with 5 GB RAM and 400 GB hard drive space
	• Windows 7
Test procedures	Once an icon has been double clicked, the tester:
	• Left clicked on the username field and enters in the incorrect username "mahfuz"
	• Left clicked on the password field and enters in the correct password "abc123"
	• Left clicked on the "OK" command button
Results expected	The expected results include that
	• Upon completing the above steps, the user should not be able to log in to The Raisers Help
Test results	The test results include that
	• An error message appeared on the screen indicating that the user does not have permission to access this module
Test pass/fail	Pass
Tester signature	AbuSayed Mahfuz

Summary

Since the login screen for Raisers Help is only in the executable format, there was no code to review. After doing a series of tests on the login screen, the features that were tested were successfully approved by the tester. When the username and password were missing or incorrect, or the user does not have permission to that specific module, the system would not grant access. Also, when testing the command buttons, each command button served its purpose. The "OK" button would proceed to the next screen if the criteria for logging into the system were correct. If the criteria for logging in were incorrect, then the correct error message would be displayed alerting the tester that access was denied. The "Cancel" button would negate the task at hand and the module disappears.

5

TEST: EXECUTION AND REPORTING

Introduction

This chapter introduces basically what a tester or test lead needs to do before starting and during the test execution, and how to report after completing the test execution.

This chapter is divided into three major parts. Part 1 discusses the starting of a test execution, Part 2 discusses the reporting of test results, and Part 3 discusses the analysis of test results.

Part 1: Starting Test Execution

Getting Ready to Start Test Execution

Getting ready for test execution basically starts when you plan for a test or prepare test strategy that is the fundamental part of preparation. Test strategy and plan were discussed in Chapter 3; however, we will discuss necessary points that are related to the test execution. It is important to follow the test strategy, which was submitted and approved by the team. Sometimes, small companies do not go through formal test plan or test strategy documentation.

It is very important to have a proper strategy and plan prepared and agreed upon before the system test team starts the execution of system testing.

Not having a system test execution plan and strategy may create misunderstanding when the test execution starts, or something could be missed or repeated at the end.

There are a few questions that need to be addressed before the test execution starts (Table 5.1). For example,

- Is the test plan in place and approved?
- What software is to be tested and what are the critical areas?

Table 5.1   Overall Test Execution % and Defect Report at a Glance

PLANNING PHASE	
METRICS DATA ELEMENT	VALUE
Planned progression coverage	100%
Prerelease overall regression capability	90%
Prerelease overall regression automation	70%
Planned regression coverage	100%
Planned regression coverage—automated	40%
Expected initial pass rate	90%
EXECUTION PHASE	
METRICS DATA ELEMENT	VALUE
Actual progression coverage	100%
Progression coverage—automated	50%
Actual regression coverage	80%
Postrelease overall regression capability	
Postrelease overall regression automation	
Actual initial pass rate	80%
Final pass rate	100%
System test defects—critical/high	5
System test defects—medium/low	12
System test defects—deferred	2
PREPROD PHASE	
METRICS DATA ELEMENT	VALUE
UAT defects—critical/high	2
UAT defects—medium/low	3
UAT defects—deferred	1
System test leakage—critical/high	0
System test leakage—medium/low	1

- How many times are the test cases executed and when?
- How many rounds of regression testing are planned for?
- How should defects be resolved?
- In what order are the test cases executed?

Requirement Coverage

It is essential that the tests in the test plan meet the original requirements. In other words, design and development must be according to the expectation of the stakeholders requirements, and the developer prepares solution specification for the requirement, and the testing team prepares test cases based on solution specification or requirement. It is better to design test cases based on solution specification. However, since requirement is the ultimate expectation of the stakeholders, it is called requirement coverage.

In some testing tool, the test plan module provides tools to connect between requirement and test plan.

Some testing tools provide options in requirements module to connect; in most cases, requirement ID and test IDs are the most important to connect between requirement and test cases. In the case that the testers do not use any testing tool for test management, they can simply track requirement ID and test ID in an MS Excel sheet or even on paper. We will provide a sample document for requirement coverage under requirement traceability matrices (RTM) or requirement traceability metrics.

Requirements Test Coverage Statement

System test should cover 100% of stakeholder requirements. However, exceptions should be listed in the report (Figure 5.1).

Scheduling Test Runs

You can set conditions and schedule the date and time for executing tests. You can also set the sequence to execute the tests.

Assigning Test Execution

Usually in larger projects when there are multiple testers and huge numbers of test cases, it is appropriate to assign test cases to best suit test engineers by considering their expertise and interest. However, it depends on the organization's practice and differs from project to project. Usually, under some circumstances, when a test is expected to be executed from a different perspective or for cross-training purpose, test cases could be tested by different testers in a different cycle. Also, it could be a matter of time.

	Requirement	Covered	Req-not-covered	Req-covered%
Main website	15	15	0	100%
Login page	10	9	1	90%
Buttons	12	11	1	92%
Review page	5	5	0	
Total	42	40	2	

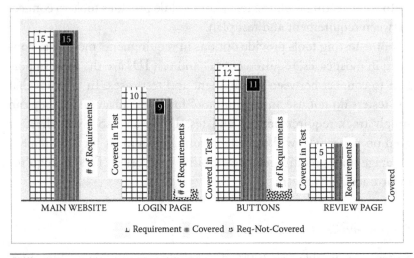

Figure 5.1   The requirement summary coverage, how many of them were required, and how many covered and %.

Before we start the test execution, we should make sure that everything is ready, that is why you need to set up prerequisite or entry exit criteria.

The first step is to set up the system test environment. Determine the operating system that will be used, the browser that will be used, and whether it should be tested in different browsers. In addition, we should make sure that all related software and hardware are ready. For example, if we need to test an application in Internet Explorer 11; in this circumstance, making ready the Internet Explorer 11 is not enough. If you have Windows 8, you also need to make sure that the software you are using to test is compatible with Windows 8.

You also need to think of the data level. For example, if you are using IE 11 and Windows, setting up Windows 8 and IE 11 is not enough; you will have to make sure all specific data are available in the database.

Sometimes, some companies do not follow the formal entry exit criteria. Many smaller companies do not even prepare the formal test plan. In that case, there must be rules and criteria.

Part 2: Test Result Reporting

Status Report

Status could be taken daily or weekly. In agile process, every day, there is a stand-up meeting for 10–15 minutes, where everyone gives a status report. Daily stand-up meeting usually happens in the morning at 9–10 AM. It is one of the practices of the team. Some team practices individual daily work status; what he or she did yesterday, what he or she plans for doing that day, while some team have a practice to report the user's story (Table 5.2).

Daily Stand-Up Update by Individual

In the agile methodology, requirement and works are managed through story, since agile methodology is basically breaking the product into small incremental builds. It breaks in to user's story, and the story is high-level user expectation—what the user wants. And during the iteration, the test execution team looks at the status of the story, who owns the story at this point, and what is the status of that story or how many percentages are completed. The team discusses the status of the story in everyday stand-up meetings.

Table 5.2 Daily Stand-Up Report

SAMPLE STATUS REPORT			
DATE	WHAT WAS ACCOMPLISHED YESTERDAY	WHAT ARE THE PLANS FOR TODAY	ANY QUESTIONS?
11/27/2015	Completed test case specification	1. Working of the system test case development	
11/28/2015	Peer review	1. Peer review	
11/29/2015	Test case review	Peer review	
11/30/2015	Test cases review	Test case mapping in QC	
12/03/2015	Completed peer review		
12/04/2015	Test case execution	Test case execution	

Weekly Status Report Template

Some team may provide a weekly status report, which may help to track major project issues, achievements, pending tasks, and milestones. It may also help the team to prepare future tasks (Table 5.3 and Figure 5.2).

Table 5.3　The Weekly Status Report

Project ID:

Project name:

Release #:

Status report prepared by:

Project manager:

Date:

Current status:

1. Issues:
2. Issues holding the QA team from delivering on schedule:
3. (You can mark these issues in red color. These issues may require management help in resolving)
4. Issue description: possible solution: issue resolution date:
5. Issues that management should be aware of:
6. (These are the issues that do not hold the QA team from delivering on time but management should be aware of them. Mark these issues in yellow color. To report these, you can use the same template as above)
7. Project achievements:
8. Next week's priorities:
9. Pending deliverables:
10. (Reason: if necessary why they are pending)
11. New tasks:
12. Defect status:
13. Open defects:
14. Closed defects:
15. Test cases:
16. # of total test cases

Kanban Storyboard			
Defined	In Dev.	In Test	Accepted
US 110-Abu	US230-Kishor		
Login Page	Member Log		
US 120-Norma	US222 Saleh		
Security	Configuration		
US 130-Merian	US250-Rahma		
User Verification	Expense		
US 124-Oneyada	US290		
Bank Information	Profile		

Figure 5.2　Kanban Board Display Status of Different Requirement Stories and who is Doing What

Test Result Summary Report

PROJECT IDENTIFICATION		
Organization	ABC	Date
Project name		Project code
Application name		Iteration
Release number		Change type
Methodology		
Execution life cycle		
Project manager		
Approver—1		
Approver—2		

Document Change Control Log   This log is updated each time this document is updated. The log identifies the version number, the date the revisions were completed, a brief description of the changes, and the author.

VERSION #	DATE TEST RESULT PREPARED	SECTIONS/PAGE REVISED	DESCRIPTION	REVISED BY NAME AND TITLE

Purpose of the Document   The test results summary report is a management report providing key metrics and status of the overall testing effort in the testing phase of a project execution life cycle.

References: (Sample Reference Metrics)

DOCUMENT NAME	PHYSICAL SOURCE/LOCATION
Scope statement	
Requirements specifications	
Test strategy	
Project plan	
High-level design document	
Detail design document	
Development and test process standards	
Defect management standard	
Defect management procedure	
Corporate standards and guidelines	
Methodology guidelines and examples	

Progression Test Case Execution Status

(Sample)

SCOPE ITEM/ FUNCTIONAL AREA	TOTAL # OF TEST CASES	# OF EXECUTED TEST CASES	% OF EXECUTED TEST CASES	# OF PASS TEST CASE (FINAL)	# OF INITIAL FAILED TEST CASES	# OF DEFECTS DETECTED	# OF CLOSED DEFECTS	# OF DEFERRED DEFECTS
User interface	20	20	100%	20	3	1	1	0
Session timeout	4	4	100%	4	0	0		0
Reauthentication users	6	6	100%	6	1	1	1	0
Main page	20	20	100%	20	2	2	2	0
Application log out flow	5	5	100%	5	0	0	0	0
Total	55	55	100%	55	6	4	4	0

Regression Test Case Execution Status

SCOPE ITEM/ FUNCTIONAL AREA	TOTAL # OF TEST CASES	# OF EXECUTED TEST CASES	% OF EXECUTED TEST CASES	# OF PASS TEST CASE (FINAL)	# OF INITIAL FAILED TEST CASES	# OF DEFECTS DETECTED	# OF CLOSED DEFECTS	# OF DEFERRED DEFECTS
User interface								
Session timeout								
Reauthentication users								
Main page								
Application log out flow								
Total								

Part 3: View and Analyze Test Results

After you run tests, determine whether the actual results match the expected test results. It depends on which tools you use; many tools have their own analyzer, a tester can analyze the result himself or herself by using MS Excel. Some test analysis samples and report samples are provided in this chapter.

Defect: As a Part of Test Result

Chapter 6 of this book discusses defects in detail; however, defects are the major part of test execution. Test execution and defect management are almost a parallel job. The whole project team needs to be fully prepared to address defect from the first day of the test execution. A defect can happen the first day and first hour of the test execution starting day. If the team is not prepared to address the defect, one simple defect can stop the progress of the project.

It is recommended to set up a defect discussion meeting at the end of each day or every other day if necessary.

If a defect has been detected, the tester should create a new defect and link it to the test set, test instance, test run, or run step, or link an already-existing defect.

Requirement Test Case—Defect Traceability Metrics

REQ. ID	TEST CASE ID	DEFECT ID	DESCRIPTION	STATUS	SEVERITY	ROOT CAUSE

Defect Details   Defect is mostly sequential. Status of the defect should be based on defect life cycle, which is mentioned in detail in Chapter 7.

DEFECT ID	STATUS	SEVERITY	DESCRIPTION	ROOT CAUSE

Deferred Defects   If any defect is deferred, it must be mentioned with details of the defect and reason for deferring.

DEFECT ID	HEADLINE	REASON FOR DEFERRING

Defects by Root Cause

Defect count by root cause for all valid defects should be mentioned (Figure 5.3).

Canceled Defects

The canceled defects should have defect ID, headline or name of the canceled defect, and an explanation or a reason for cancellation of the defect (Table 5.4).

Defect Summary

Our proposed project has four functional areas: login page, about the company page, buttons, and contact us page. The login page has three open defects and five closed defects. The about page has two open and two closed defects, and button page has four closed defects. There is no other defect (Figure 5.4).

Issue Log

If there are any issues related to test or overall project they need to be logged on.

Defect by root cause							
	Code	Requirement	Design	Data	Environment	Test	Total
Main website	4	0	2	0	0	0	6
Login page	2	0	1	0	0	0	3
Buttons	2	0	1	0	0	0	3
Review page	1	0	0	0	0	0	1
Total	9	0	4	0	0	0	13

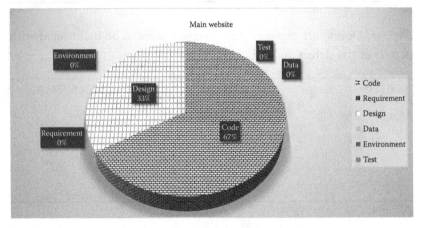

Figure 5.3   The defect root cause and its %.

Table 5.4   Defect That Has Been Canceled and the Reason Why Defect Was Canceled

DEFECT ID	HEADLINE	REASON FOR CANCELATION

Exit Criteria

- 100% of all integration test cases have been executed with at least 85% passed and artifacts documented.
- All priority 1, 2, and 3 defects have been resolved and successfully retested.
- 100% of all regression test cases have been executed/passed, and artifacts are documented.
- All priority 1, 2, and 3 defects found in regression tests have been resolved and successfully retested.

Defect status summary

Functional area	New	Open	Closed	Canceled	Deferred	Total
Login page	0	3	5	0	0	8
About page	0	2	2	0	0	4
Buttons	0	0	4	0	0	4
Contact us page	0	0	0	0	0	0
Total						16

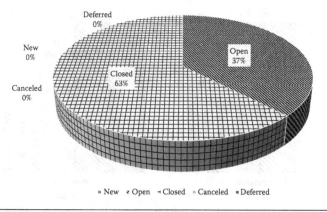

Figure 5.4   The latest defect status summary.

- All system test deliverables completed and checked into subversion in advance of production readiness review.
- Requirements that are covered by each test case of the test suite along with the status of the test case.

Requirement Traceability Matrices (RTM)

SCOPE ITEM ID OR DESCRIPTION	REQUIREMENT ID	REQUIREMENT DESCRIPTION	SOLUTION SPECIFICATION ID	SYSTEM TEST CASE ID	TEST CASE NAME

System Test Coverage Metrics (Sample)

It is very helpful if a visual report can be provided. A visual report gives a good idea about the whole project in a glance. The following are some sample graph reports provided (Figures 5.5–5.7).

Test Execution Quality Metrics

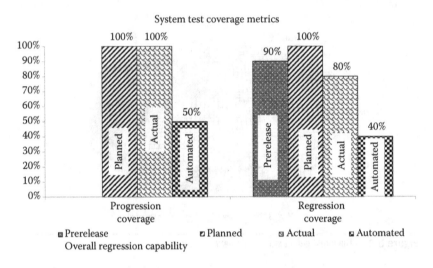

Figure 5.5   The metrics of planned and actual status of system test coverage.

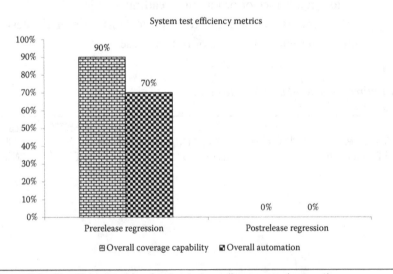

Figure 5.6   The efficiency metrics of system test overall coverage and automation.

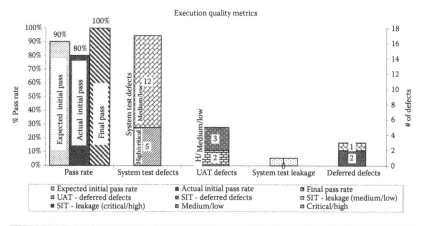

Figure 5.7   The execution quality metrics.

Defect Tracking Overview

Track defects until application developers and testers determine that the defects are resolved. Defect records inform members of the development team and quality assurance team of new defects discovered by other members.

Defect Linkage

When a test case fails, it does not necessarily mean a defect. There could be multiple reasons for a test case failure. Similarly, when a defect is found, it does not necessarily mean that it happened due to a test case failure. However, it is recommended and the best idea to have all defects linked to failure test cases.

When a defect is found, which is not connected to a test case, it is better to create a new test to link that defect. Even though it is possible to find a defect without test cases, it is better to link with test case.

A defect could be linked to a test case and to the requirements, test sets or test instances, and other defects.

During a manual test run, if you add a defect, some testing tools automatically create a link between the test run and the defect.

Figure 8.7

SECTION III
CHALLENGES

6

INCIDENT MANAGEMENT

Introduction

This chapter introduces types of incidents and how to manage an incident. Part 1 defines the incident, accident and failure, roots and sources of any incident that may occur. Part 1 also discusses initial documentation and classification of any incident.

Part 2 discusses why investigation is needed and investigates and analyzes the process of an incident. Part 3 discusses the overall incident, and handling and preventing the future incident. Part 4 discusses the documentation of an issue. Part 5 discusses reporting and responding to security incidents.

Overview on Incident Management

Incident management plays a major role in software quality, reliability, and overall business. Several methods of incident management can be considered. However, the incident management life cycle process as recommended by NASA* seems to be meaningful.

NASA recommended "incident management life cycle" displays as (1) preparation, (2) identification, (3) containment, (4) eradication, (5) recovery, and (6) follow-up and documentation, analysis, and communication. NASA *Info Security Handbook* recommends documentation, analysis, and communication as part of incident management throughout the life cycle (Figure 6.1).

Information technology infrastructure library provides the activities of an incident management process, which includes the following

- Incident recognition and reporting
- Classification and initial support

---

* *Information Security Handbook*, Incident Response and Management: NASA Information Security Incident Management Office: OCIO/Deputy CIO for Information Technology Security, pp. 2, 12–17.

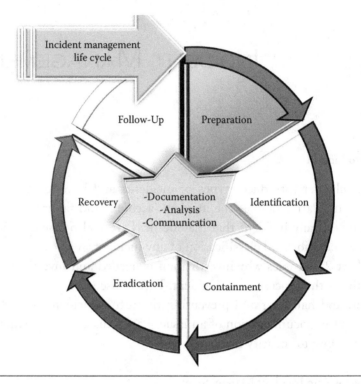

Figure 6.1   Incident management life cycle.

- Investigation and diagnosis
- Resolution and recovery
- Incident closure
- Incident ownership, monitoring, tracking, and communication

According to the *Incident Handling Guide*, prepared by National Institute of Standards and Technology, U.S. Department of Commerce, the incident response process has several phases. The initial phase involves establishing and training an incident response team (IRT) and acquiring the necessary tools and resources.

Why Incident Management Is Important

An incident can cause a defect or security problem so it becomes a risk, which consequentially becomes a software quality issue and reliability issue. That is why any incident should be given full attention and should be taken seriously and need to be documented and reported (Figure 6.2).

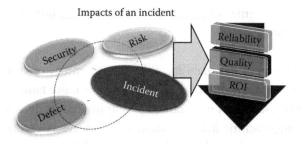

Impacts of an incident

Figure 6.2   Impact of an incident. An incident can cause a severe defect and vulnerable risk, which can ultimately cause reliability or quality issues.

Part 1: Identification

Definition

Incident   An incident is any unplanned or unintended event or sequence of events that does not result in death, injury, illness, or damage to property (including data and intellectual property) but has the potential to do so.

   IEEE 610 defined incident as a part of software test and defined it as "Any event occurring during the execution of a software test that requires investigation."*

Information Security Incident

According to NASA, *Information Security Handbook*, the definition of "An Information Security incident is an adverse event or situation associated with electronic and non-electronic information that poses a threat to the integrity, availability, or confidentiality of that system."†

Accident   An accident is any unplanned or unintended event or sequence of events that results in death, injury, illness, or damage to property (including data and intellectual property).

---

* IEEE Std 610.12-1990 (Revision and redesignation of IEEE Std7SZ.1983) *IEEE Standard Glossary of Software Engineering Terminology*, p. 68.
† NASA, *Information Security Handbook*, Incident Response and Management: NASA Information Security Incident Management Office: OCIO/Deputy CIO for Information Technology Security.

Defect   A Six Sigma defect is defined as anything outside of customer specifications.

Failure   Failure is the inability of a system, entity, or component to perform its required function owing to one or more fault conditions.

Compromise—An unwarranted and uninvited incursion, infringement, or encroachment of a system that defeats safety and security mechanisms in order to harm the system or data.

According to the definition given in IEEE 610, the failure is "The inability of a system or component to perform its required functions within specified performance requirements."*

Even though an incident may not be necessarily a failure or defect by default, however, an incident may cause serious harm and an incident could be just a symptom or a serious issue.

Incident Identification

Hence, the first thing that needs to be done is to recognize the incident and report it immediately. When an incident happens, the team should search the functionality of the incident and try to match the incident with another incident that occurred earlier and was saved in the known error database (KEDB). This is a database where known errors (and possible solutions) are stored. An incident with the same symptoms could also be already opened before, and a workaround may exist. Incident matching procedures help to prevent doing the same thing several times. KEDB and problem matching should contain all relevant information.

Identifying Ways   The incident management team should focus on incidents that use common attack routes. Different types of incidents merit different response strategies. Several ways of attack are there. Following are some of the possible ways of attack:

- External/removable media.
- Web: An attack executed from a website or a web-based application.

---

* IEEE Std 610.12-1990 (Revision and redesignation of IEEE Std7SZ.1983) *IEEE Standard Glossary of Software Engineering Terminology*, p. 32.

- E-mail: An attack executed via an e-mail message or attachment, for example, exploit code disguised as an attached document or a link to a malicious website in the body of an e-mail message.
- Impersonation: An attack involving replacement of something benign with something malicious, such as structured query language (SQL) injection attacks.
- Improper usage: Any incident resulting from violation of an organization's acceptable usage.
- Loss or theft of equipment: The loss or theft of a computing device or media used by the organization, such as a laptop, a smartphone, or an authentication token.*

Identifying the Attacking Hosts

Identifying an attacking host can be a time-consuming and a futile process that can prevent a team from achieving its primary goal; however, it is important. When an attack occurs, find out the attackers, and the host ID team may

- Validate attacking host IP address
- Research the attacking host in search engines
- Check with incident database to match the attacking host

Incident Initial Documentation

An IRT that suspects that an incident has occurred should immediately start recording all facts regarding the incident. This is the first thing that needs to be done before even reporting.

---

* *Computer Security Incident Handling Guide*, National Institute of Standards and Technology, U.S. Department of Commerce, Special Publication 800-61 Revision 2, p. 21.

The IRT should maintain records about the status of incidents, along with other pertinent information. The issue tracking system should contain information on the following:

- The current status of the incident (new, in progress, under investigation, resolved, etc.)
- A brief statement of the incident
- Signs related to the incident
- Other incidents related to this incident
- Actions taken by all incident handlers on this incident
- Impact assessments related to the incident
- Contact information for other involved parties (e.g., system owners and system administrators)
- A list of evidence gathered during the incident investigation
- Comments from incident handlers
- Next steps to be taken (e.g., rebuild the host and upgrade an application)

The IRT should precaution incident data and restrict access to it, only authorized personnel should have access to the incident database. Incident communications (e.g., e-mails) and documents should be encrypted or otherwise protected so that only authorized personnel can read them.*

Incident Classification

When an incident happens, either small or big, even if it seems simple, it should be documented and reported immediately. And the incident management or response team should respond to it accordingly. The response team needs to have a plan on how to respond.

There are a few things that could be included in the incident response plan.

The incident should be reported immediately as soon as the incident was discovered, and the incident should be reported by the person who discovered it.

IRT needs to have detailed information about the person who reported the incident and all possible people of interest.

The incident team member should contact the incident response manager immediately. In the case there is no specific incident manager

---

* *Information Security Handbook*, Incident Response and Management: NASA Information Security Incident Management Office: OCIO/Deputy CIO for Information Technology Security.

assigned, however, there should be a procedure about where and how to report any incident. The incident should be reported through all possible means, such as e-mail and phone messages, in addition, other appropriate personnel and designated managers should also be informed. The staff member could possibly note the following information:

1. What is the nature of the incident?
2. The severity of the possible impact?
3. Is the incident inside the trusted network?
4. Is the incident existent or alleged?
5. Is the incident still in progress?
6. Is the incident business critical?
7. What are the details of the system/s being targeted, their operating system, IP address, and location?
8. Is IP address or any information about the attacker available?
9. What data or property is endangered and how critical is it?
10. What is the impact on the business should the attack succeed? Minimal, serious, or critical?
11. What system or systems are targeted, where are they located physically and on the network?
12. Can the incident be recovered sooner?
13. Will the response alert the attacker and will that impact the investigation?

Type of Incident   What type of incident is this? Example: virus, worm, intrusion, abuse, damage.

The incident should be categorized as

- Is it a threat to public safety or life?
- Is it a threat to sensitive data?
- Is it a threat to computer systems?
- Is it a disruption of services?

Initial Assessment   Team members should make an assessment on the incident and create a procedure based on possible assessment.

- Worm
- Virus
- System failure

- Active intrusion—is critical data at risk?
- Inactive intrusion
- System abuse
- Property theft
- Website denial of service
- Database or file denial of service
- Spyware

An incident must be reported before the situation can be corrected and minimization of damage.

- Reporting the results of an investigation and lessons learned can reduce the chance of reoccurrence.
- Perception management. Customers and employees gain the impression that the organization is being open and on top of the situation.
- A company may be required to report to shareholders, customers, public, or regulators.
- Pursuit of legal action requires incident reporting.

Part 2: Investigation and Analysis

Reasons to Investigate

Investigation is extremely important and necessary to determine what, how, why something happened or did not happen and why it was allowed to happen.

To ascertain the extent of the consequences and the corresponding need for recovery mechanisms and remedial measures. To gather the information necessary to file an accurate report of the accident/incident and to evaluate legal issues.

Investigation Process

When an incident happens, it must be recorded, reported, and investigated. A minor incident or near incident also requires a thorough investigation and may disclose significant potential for a serious incident if the conditions are left uncorrected.

In the investigation process, the investigator should

- Analyze cause, extent, and consequences of the failure/compromise
- Initiate recovery mechanisms
- Report accident/incident
- Deploy remedial measures
- Evaluate legal issues

Incident Root Cause   There are two major components that contribute to the cause of an incident. They are the "element" and the "root cause."

- The "element" is the condition or act that directly caused the incident.
- The "root cause" is the system failure that allowed the work element to become deficient or to fail.

A thorough investigation will reveal the root cause of the incident. The purpose of an incident investigation is to determine the work element and root causes of incident and to assist in providing the company with a solution to prevent recurrence.

Companies should have an incident investigation process to ensure that

- All incidents (including near misses) are investigated.
- An investigation identifies the root cause.
- Corrective actions are tracked until they are completed.
- Trends are reviewed, gaps are identified, and improvement plans are developed to prevent future occurrence.*

Collecting Evidence Evidence is very important and critical. Sometimes, it is very critical and complex to collect evidence. There are some basic rules that may help the process.

---

* Incident Investigation Process and Exercise, a training research paper prepared by Rochester Institute of Technology.

Instant Picture or Screenshot   Some web-related evidence may not be found later on; it could be even removed, and hence, the best thing is to take an instant picture or screenshot.

Interviewing Involved Individual   In this case, the involved individual may feel apprehensive about being interviewed. In this circumstance, put the individual at ease—make sure they know that the primary purpose of the interview is to prevent a recurrence of the incident and that it can only be done with their help. Avoid finger pointing and laying blame.

Treat people with tact and respect. Make them aware that they need to be thorough and truthful in their account of the incident and that you are not there to get anyone into trouble, only to find out what happened and why, so that it will not happen again.

Ask any necessary questions to determine what happened, what was done, and how it was done. Try to avoid asking why questions that may make people defensive.[*]

Six Steps for Successful Incident Investigation   According to the article, "Six steps for successful incident investigation"[†] (Figure 6.3), these six steps are as follows:

> Step 1—Immediate action
> Step 2—Plan the investigation
> Step 3—Data collection
> Step 4—Data analysis
> Step 5—Corrective actions
> Step 6—Reporting

Incident Analysis

Goal of the analysis is to figure out what happened, how it happened, why it happened, and what were the consequences.

An accurate indicator does not necessarily mean that a security incident has occurred. Some indicators, such as a server crash

---

[*] Ibid.

[†] *Six Steps for Successful Incident Investigation* by Risktec, an organization dedicated for Risk Management and Assessment for Business, http://www.risktec.co.uk/knowledge-bank/technical-articles/six-steps-for-successful-incident-investigation—.aspx.

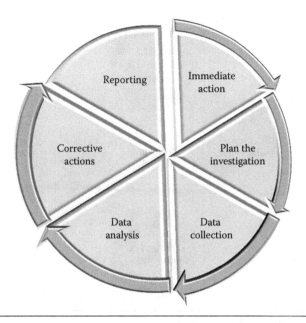

Figure 6.3 Investigation steps.

or modification of critical files, could happen for several reasons other than a security incident, including human error. To determine whether a particular event is actually a security incident needs to be analyzed. It may be necessary to cooperate with other technical and information security personnel to make a decision.

The IRT should work quickly to analyze and validate each incident. When the team believes that an incident has occurred, the team should rapidly perform an initial analysis to determine the incident's scope, such as which networks, systems, or applications are affected; who or what originated the incident; and how the incident is occurring (e.g., what tools or attack methods are being used, what vulnerabilities are being exploited) (Figure 6.4).*

Some Examples of Analyzing an Incident

Barrier Analysis Determine which defensive layers failed or were missing.

- Aids in determining the cause for the incident.

---

* *The Handbook for Computer Security Incident Response Teams (CSIRTs)* by Carnegie Mellon Software Engineering Institute, p. 79 and 119.

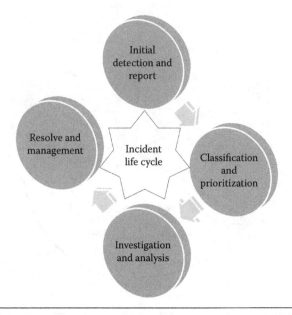

Figure 6.4   Different aspects of incident life cycle.

- People with first-hand knowledge of system can provide valuable insight.
- Need to be careful interviewing so that witness does not feel threatened or fearful of being disciplined.

Damage Mode Effect Analysis   Event and causal factors

- Describe the sequence of events that led to an incident.
- The primary event of incident.
- The immediate cause and the reasons that contributed.
- This is easy for stakeholders to understand

Scenario Analysis

- All system entities, modes, and environments are examined.
  - Attempts to speculate all possible, logical, credible scenarios that could have caused or contributed to the incident.
  - Do not examine evidence but develop theories.
  - Useful for situations where there is little history.

- Try to draw a diagram of linked, sequentially timed events, and their causal relationships to demonstrate how an incident occurred.
- Describe direct converging and underlying events.
- More detail than an event and causal factor chart, events are associated with actors and time.

Time/Loss Analysis for Emergency Response Evaluation

- Analyzes the following information:
    - Effect of human intervention following an incident
    - Controllability of an incident
    - Effectiveness of mitigating threat control measures over time
- Performed in the operations phase of the software development life cycle (SDLC)

Analyzing Warning Time

- Investigates the effect of the difference between available and actual response times
    - Propagation time—time between initiating event to incident
    - Detection time—time from occurrence to earliest indication
    - Response time A—time for automatic corrective action
    - Response time B—time for human-initiated corrective action (Figure 6.5)
- Performed in the operations phase of the SDLC

Part 3: Response and Recovery

Incident Response

The team must take an action in response to the incident and document what was done. Response team should also document the following

1. How the incident was discovered
2. The category of the incident

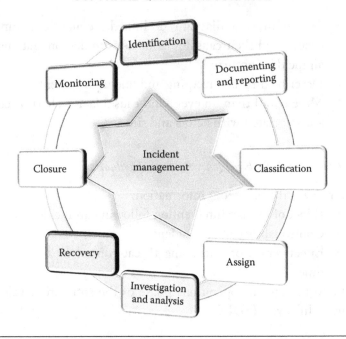

Figure 6.5   Other aspects of incident management.

3. How the incident occurred, whether through e-mail, firewall, and so on
4. Where the attack came from, such as IP addresses and other related information about the attacker
5. What the response plan was
6. What was done in response
7. Whether the response was effective

IRT should review system logs, looking for gaps in logs, reviewing intrusion detection logs, and interviewing witnesses and the incident victim to determine how the incident was caused. Only authorized personnel should be performing interviews or examining evidence, and the authorized personnel may vary by situation and the organization.

1. IRT should recommend changes to prevent the occurrence from happening again or infecting other systems.
2. Upon management approval, the changes will be implemented.

3. IRT should restore the affected system(s) to the uninfected state. IRT may
   a. Reinstall the affected system(s) from scratch and restore data from backups if necessary. Preserve evidence before doing this
   b. Make users change passwords if passwords may have been sniffed
   c. Be sure that the system has been hardened by turning off or uninstalling unused services
   d. Be sure that the system is fully patched
   e. Be sure real-time virus protection and intrusion detection is running
   f. Be sure the system is logging the correct events and to the proper level
4. Evidence preservation—make copies of logs, e-mail, and other communication. Keep lists of witnesses. Keep evidence as long as necessary to complete prosecution and beyond in case of an appeal.
5. Notify proper external agencies if necessary, including the police and other appropriate agencies if prosecution of the intruder is possible.
6. Assess damage and cost—assess the damage to the organization and estimate both the damage cost and the cost of the containment efforts.
7. Review response and update policies—plan and take preventative steps so the intrusion cannot happen again.
   a. Consider whether an additional policy could have prevented the intrusion.
   b. Consider whether a procedure or policy was not followed that allowed the intrusion, and then consider what could be changed to ensure that the procedure or policy is followed in the future.
   c. Was the incident response appropriate? How could it be improved?
   d. Was every appropriate party informed in a timely manner?
   e. Were the incident–response procedures detailed and did they cover the entire situation? How can they be improved?

f. Have changes been made to prevent a reinfection? Have all systems been patched, systems locked down, passwords changed, antivirus updated, e-mail policies set, and so on?

g. Have changes been made to prevent a new and similar infection?

h. Should any security policies be updated?

i. What lessons have been learned from this experience?[*]

Initiate Recovery Mechanisms

Review Preliminary Investigation Results

- Determine what can and cannot be recovered (systems, computer hardware, computer software, applications, and data)
- Ascertain when each system, entity, and component can and should be restored
  - Technical considerations
  - Operational priorities
  - Safety and security priorities
- Determine how each system, entity, and component should be restored
  - Level of service
  - Actions and commands necessary for recovery
  - Verifying effectiveness of recovery efforts
- Notify customers, end users, and other stakeholders
  - Problem experienced
  - Emergency precautions
  - Estimated recovery time[†]

---

[*] "Incident Response Plan Example" an online document prepared by California Department of Technology Incident Response Plan Example. www.cio.ca.gov/.../incident_respon.

[†] Prepared based on notes taken from Professor Dan Shoemaker's class at University of Detroit Mercy and some information from a "Incident Investigation" document by Blue Cross Blue Shield Michigan.

Preventing Incidents

Prevention of incidents is very important. If prevention is not assured, more large-scale incidents may occur, overwhelming the IRT. This can lead to slow and incomplete responses, which translate to more extensive damage, longer periods of service, and unavailability of data.

The following items provide a brief recommendation for securing networks, systems, and applications:

- Risk assessments: Periodic risk assessments of systems and applications should determine what risks are posed by combinations of threats and vulnerabilities.*
- Host security: All hosts should be properly patched, and hosts should be configured to follow the principle of least privilege granting users only the privileges necessary for performing their authorized tasks.
- Network security: The network perimeter should be configured to deny all activities that are not expressly permitted. This includes securing all connection points, such as virtual private networks (VPNs) and dedicated connections to other organizations.
- Malware prevention: Software to detect and stop malware should be deployed throughout the organization.
- User awareness and training: Users should be made aware of policies and procedures regarding appropriate use of networks, systems, and applications.

Incident Notification

Each update occurring in an IRT needs to notify the appropriate individuals so that all who need to be involved will play their roles.

Who should be reported and notified about an incident. This policy may vary among organizations, but parties who are typically notified include the following:

- CIO
- Head of information security

---

* Guidelines on risk assessment are available in NIST SP 800-30, *Guide for Conducting Risk Assessments*, at http://csrc.nist.gov/publications/PubsSPs.html#800-30-Rev1.

- Local information security officer
- Other IRTs within the organization
- External IRTs (if appropriate)
- System owner
- Human resources (for cases involving employees)
- Public affairs
- Legal department (if applicable)
- Law enforcement (if applicable)*

Evidence Collection and Documentation

It is important to clearly document how all evidences, including compromised systems, have been preserved. Evidence should be collected according to procedures that meet all applicable laws and regulations.

In addition, evidence should be accounted for at all times; whenever evidence is transferred from person to person, chain of custody forms should detail the transfer and include each party's signature. A detailed log should be kept for all evidences, including the following:

- Identifying information (e.g., the location, serial number, model number, hostname, media access control (MAC) addresses, and IP addresses of a computer)
- Name, title, and phone number of each individual who collected or handled the evidence during the investigation
- Time and date (including time zone) of each occurrence of evidence handling locations where the evidence was stored[†]

---

* *Computer Security Incident Handling Guide*, National Institute of Standards and Technology, US Department of Commerce, Special Publication 800-61 Revision 2, p. 34.
† Ibid, p. 36.

Part 4: Issues

Issues List

Project Name: _____
Project #: _____
Issue ID: _____   **Creation Date:**   **Completion Date:**

                                              (MM/DD/YY)   **(MM/DD/YY)**

Requester: _____
Brief Description: _____
Detailed Description: _____
Person Responsible to Solve: _____
Status: _____
(OPEN/RESOLVED)
Brief Status Description: _____
Impact to Plan
  (Budget/schedule/other): _____
When detected: Subproject: _____   **Phase:** _____
Root cause: _____
**Process Improvement to Prevent future
occurrences:** _____
Notes: _____

Project Issues List Instructions

Purpose:
The purpose of this form is to document all issues related to a project. Documenting project issues is necessary to properly address the issues and resolve them properly. This form will also provide documentation that can help to improve the management of future projects.

Project Name:
Project name, preferably the same name for the project that is in the organization's effort tracking system.

Project ID:
The unique project number # that has been created for this project in the organization's effort tracking system.

Issue ID:
Unique ID for this issue.

Creation Date:
Date that the entry is recognized as an issue to be documented and addressed by the project team.

Completion Date:
Date that the issue is considered complete.

Requester:
Name of person or group who generated the request for this issue to be addressed.

Brief Description:
A short name by which the issue will be referred to in subsequent documentation, including status reports.

Detailed Description:
A narrative describing all pertinent points of the issue. It should be complete so that a third party could read and understand the nature and complexity of the issue.

Person Responsible to Solve:
Team member responsible for organizing the resources to resolve the issue.

Status:
Current status of the issue.

Brief Status Description:
Narrative describing the circumstances surrounding the current issue. Required: Yes.

Impact to Plan:
Describe the changes that must be made to the plan, such as added cost and lengthened schedule.

When Detected:
Use these fields to identify during what subproject/phase of the project the issue arose.

Root Cause:
When the item is completed, rejected, or accepted, take time to analyze and document why this item occurred.

Prevent Future Occurrences:
Prevent similar issues in the future.

Notes: _____

_____

Project Issues Log

Project Name:
Project #:

ISSUE ID	CREATION DATE (MM/DD/YY)	BRIEF DESCRIPTION	REQUESTOR	PERSON RESP.	STATUS (OPEN/ RESOLVED)	COMPLETION DATE (MM/DD/YY)

Part 5: Security Incidents

Security Incidents Reporting

Prevention is better than cure, this concept applies to security incidents as well. It is the best strategy to enact all plans and actions to prevent a security incident in advance. Team needs to ensure that the incident's impact is minimized.

Before an Incident Happens the Team Should

1. Establish security policy and procedure.
2. Assess the vulnerabilities and risk analysis periodically/routinely.
3. Check all computer systems and network devices regularly.
4. IT staff and end users need to have security training.
5. Monitor and check network traffic and system performance.
6. Check all logs and logging mechanisms regularly.
7. Check the backup.
8. Establish computer security IRT to handle security incidents.*

After an Incident Happens

1. Remain calm "Do not panic!"
2. Report to incident management team immediately.

---

* "Responding to IT Security Incidents," an online article published by Microsoft TechNet, https://technet.microsoft.com/en-us/library/cc700825.aspx.

3. Document all necessary information. Keep copies of any altered files before restoring your system!!
4. Make backups.

This is necessary in handling and reporting incidents.

Responding to a Security Incident

The IRT should serve as the focal point for IT incidents, while information systems security officers should serve as security contacts.

The IRT should identify computer security incidents, characterize the nature and severity of incidents, and provide immediate diagnostic and corrective actions when appropriate.

Tips for Responding to Security Incidents

Steps to Take during the Incident

- Evaluate the situation
- Disconnect or shut down if appropriate
- Analyze and respond
- Make proper notifications
- Document the incident

Responding to Security Violations

When an incident occurs that is proven to be a security violation some actions need to be taken immediately.

Improper use of the financial data or systems may constitute the violation of international, federal, state, and local civil and criminal laws including other state and federal criminal laws regarding computer crime.

An individual's computer use and privileges may be suspended until an investigation is completed. Such suspected violations should be reported to the appropriate supervisors, possibly to a security officer, and data security where applicable. Security violations may result in revocation of access and disciplinary action.

If an incident is suspected where the financial system's internal security has been compromised, the administration should have authority to suspend all users from gaining access to the financial data and systems.

Security Office Actions   Security officer should contact the user's supervisor and inform them that access to the financial data and systems will be suspended upon further investigation of the violation. It may also be necessary to contact the data security and/or enterprise Internet services and have the user ID temporarily revoked.

7

DEFECT MANAGEMENT

Introduction

This chapter, as the name implies, deals with the conceptual aspects of defect management. There are three parts in this chapter. Part 1 discusses the basic concepts of a defect and why a defect happens. Part 2 introduces the practical methodologies of how to manage the defects. In this section, some sample documents and templates are provided to manage the defect properly. Part 3 discusses and analyzes the root causes of defects and provides recommendations of how to prevent defects in the future.

Part 1: Definition and Analysis

Definitions

Defect A defect in simple terms is a variance from expectation. Another definition is that a defect is a condition in a process/product which does not meet a documented requirement. In other words, a defect is an error in a process or product's behavior that causes it to malfunction or to produce incorrect or unexpected results.

The root cause of a defect may originate from different sources such as code, requirements, design, environment, build/compilation, test case, and data.

Defect in Hardware In IEEE 610, defect or fault is defined as "A defect in a hardware device or component; for example, a short circuit or broken wire."

Defect in Software   "An incorrect step, process, or data definition in a computer program."*

This definition is used primarily by the fault tolerance discipline. In common usage, the terms "error" and "bug" are used to express this meaning.

Definition of an Error

In IEEE 610, the error is defined as

- "The difference between a computed, observed, or measured value or condition and the true, specified, or theoretically correct value or condition."
  - For example, a difference of 30 m between a computed result and the correct result.
- "An incorrect step, process, or data definition."
  - For example, an incorrect instruction in a computer program.
- "An incorrect result."
  - For example, a computed result of 12 when the correct result is 10.
- "A human action that produces an incorrect result."
  - For example, an incorrect action on the part of a programmer or operator.†

Defect Repository   Defect repository is the defect management tool/repository used to track defects and all defects associated with the application under test. There are many tools available. However, many companies typically use HP Quality Center or IBM Clear Quest for defect repository.

What Causes Defects in Software

Certainly, it is very important and necessary to understand why an error happens. Honestly speaking, that is the point. When the cause

---

* IEEE Std 610.12-1990 (Revision and redesignation of IEEE Std7SZ.1983) *IEEE Standard Glossary of Software Engineering Terminology*, p. 32.
† Ibid., p. 31.

could be identified, almost half of the problem is resolved. In this arena, it is called defect root cause. In this chapter, we have dedicated one important part on root cause analysis (RCA), and we will try to evaluate them.

When the software code has been built, it is executed and then any defects may cause the system to fail to do what it should do (or do something it should not), causing a failure. Interestingly and alarmingly, sometimes a defect may not be obvious even though it exists; in programming language, it is called a logic error.

In computer programming, a logic error is a bug in a program that causes it to operate incorrectly, but not to terminate abnormally (or crash). A logic error produces unintended or undesired output or other behavior, although it may not immediately be recognized as such.

Logic errors may occur in both compiled and interpreted languages. Unlike a program with a syntax error, a program with a logic error is a valid program in the language, even though it does not behave as intended. The only clue to the existence of logic errors is the production of wrong solutions.

This example function in C is to calculate the average of two numbers that contains a logic error. It is missing brackets in the calculation so it compiles and runs but does not give the right answer due to operator precedence (division is evaluated before addition).

```
int average (int a, int b)
{
    return a + b / 2;    /* should be (a + b) / 2*/
}
```

In simple math,

$(2 + 5) \times 2$ and $2 + 5 \times 2$ is not the same.

In $(2 + 5) \times 2$ the result is 14; on the other hand, $2 + 5 \times 2 = 12$ because here you have to do the multiplication first then the addition. There is a rule called PEMDAS which represents as

P = Parenthesis
E = Exponents
M = Multiplication
D = Division
A = Addition
S = Subtraction

In these circumstances, if the developer writes the wrong code such as forgetting to put (2 + 5) in parenthesis, then the result will be wrong even though for the tester it may look like the correct result.

Detecting a Defect Early

It is indeed better to find the defect as early as possible. In software development, if there is a mistake in requirement and you found it in production that could lead to a big mess.

To fix this defect, no matter how much it may cost, you may not find all people you need—developer, tester, designer—everyone may not be available then, and it is not a simple thing. For example, it is easier to build a new building than repair an old building. It could be a total disaster.

What Is the Cost of Defects Not Detected Early?

In addition, considering the impact of failures arising from defects, which we have not found, we need to consider the impact once we find those defects. The cost of finding and fixing defects rises considerably across the life cycle; think of the old English proverb "a stitch in time saves nine." This means that if you mend a tear in your sleeve now while it is small, it is easy to mend; but if you leave it, it will get worse and need more stitches to mend it.

When a defect exists in the requirement specification and is not detected until acceptance testing or until production, then it will be much more expensive to fix (Figure 7.1).

It is quite often the case that defects detected at a very late stage are not corrected because the cost of doing so is too expensive. Also, if the software is delivered and meets an agreed specification, if the specification was wrong, then the software will not be accepted. The project team may have delivered exactly what they were asked to deliver, but it is not what the users wanted. In some cases, where the defect is too serious, the system may have to be completely reinstalled.

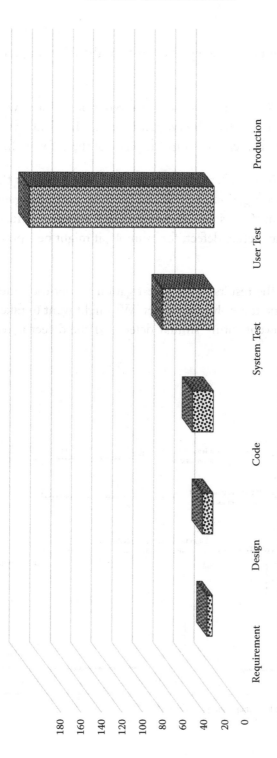

Figure 7.1 The cost of a defect is much higher in production than in requirement.

Defect Life Cycle Steps

The IEEE 1044 defect life cycle consists of the following four steps (Figure 7.2):

Step 1: Recognition or Identification Recognition occurs when we observe an anomaly, that observation being an incident, which is a potential defect. This can occur in any phase of the software life cycle.

Step 2: Investigation After recognition, the investigation of the incident occurs. Investigation can reveal related issues. Investigation can propose solutions. One solution is to conclude that the incident does not arise from an actual defect; for example, it might be a problem in the test data.

Step 3: Action The results of the investigation trigger the action step. We might decide to resolve the defect. We might want to take action indicated to prevent future similar defects. If the defect is resolved,

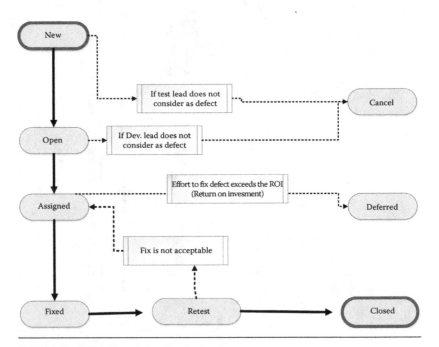

Figure 7.2 Defect life cycle from new to closed.

regression testing and confirmation testing must occur. Any tests that were blocked by the defect can now progress.

Step 4: Disposition   With action concluded, the incident moves to the disposition step. Here, we are principally interested in capturing further information and moving the incident into a terminal state.

Objectives of Testing

Reduce the Risk of Failure   Most of the complex software systems contain faults, which cause the system to fail from time to time. This concept of "failing from time to time" gives rise to the notion of *failure rate*. As faults are discovered and fixed while performing more and more tests, the failure rate of a system generally decreases. Thus, a higher level objective of performing tests is to bring down the risk of failing to an acceptable level.

Reduce the Cost of Testing   The different types of costs associated with a test process include the cost of designing, maintaining, and executing test cases; the cost of analyzing the result of executing each test case; the cost of documenting the test cases; and the cost of actually executing the system and documenting it.

Therefore, the fewer test cases designed, then the cost of testing is reduced. However, producing a small number of arbitrary test cases is not a good way of saving money. The highest level objective of performing tests is to produce low-risk software with fewer test cases. This idea leads us to the concept of *effectiveness of test cases*. Therefore, the test engineers must judiciously select fewer, more effective test cases.

Analyze Root Causes

According to Capability Maturity Model Integration (CMMI), the objective of defect RCA is to determine causes of defects.

Root causes of defects and other problems are systematically determined.

Address Causes of Defects   Root causes of defects and other problems are systematically addressed to prevent their future occurrence.

Institutionalize a Defined Process   A root cause is a source of a defect; if it is removed, the defect is decreased or removed.

Determine which defects and other problems will be analyzed further.

When determining which defects to analyze further, consider the impact of the defects, the frequency of occurrence, the similarity between defects, the cost of analysis, the time and resources needed, safety considerations, and so on.

Perform causal analysis of selected defects and other problems and propose actions to address them.

The purpose of RCA is to develop solutions to the identified problems by analyzing the relevant data and producing action proposals for implementation.

Conduct causal analysis with the people who are responsible for performing the task.

Causal analysis is performed with those people who have an understanding of the selected defect or problem under study, typically in meetings.

An action proposal usually documents the following:

Originator of the action proposal
Description of the problem
Description of the defect cause
Defect cause category
Phase when the problem was introduced
Phase when the defect was identified
Description of the action proposal
Action proposal category

Projects operating according to a well-defined process will systematically analyze the operation where problems still occur and implement process changes to eliminate root causes of selected problems.

Implement the Action Proposals

Implement the selected action proposals that were developed in causal analysis.

Action proposals describe the tasks necessary to remove the root causes of the analyzed defects or problems and avoid their recurrence.

Only changes that prove to be of value should be considered for broad implementation.

Part 2: Process and Methodology

Defect Management Process

There are several high-level steps to be taken in a typical defect management process. The following items are highly recommended, which are also supported by IEEE standards.

Identifying

The first thing that needs to be done is to identify the defect: what is it and how did this happen? The first person who identifies the defect should submit it as defect to his or her lead and the team lead should evaluate, verify, and identify it as a defect, and then it remains an open defect.

Categorizing

When a defect is reported and verified by the test team, it remains as open, then it should be assigned to someone, usually to a related developer. Once the defect is categorized, the defect moves on in the process to the next step that is prioritization.

Prioritizing

Prioritization is typically based on a combination of the severity of impact on the user, relative effort to fix, along with a comparison against other open defects. The priority should be determined with representation from the management, the customer, and the project team.

Assigning

Once a defect has been prioritized, it is then assigned to a developer or other technician to fix.

Resolving

The developer fixes (resolves) the defect and follows the organization's process to move the fix to the environment where the defect was originally identified.

Verifying

Depending on the environment where the defect was found and the fix was applied, the software testing team or customer typically verifies that the fix has actually resolved the defect.

Closing

Once a defect has been resolved and verified, the defect is marked as closed.

Management Reporting

Management reports are provided to appropriate individuals at regular intervals as defined reporting requirements. In addition, on-demand reports are provided on an as-needed basis.

Roles and Responsibilities in Software Development Life Cycle

Business Owner

The business owner requests funding, sets business requirements, and works with the technology owner to make strategic decisions.

Stakeholders

Stakeholders include anyone who will be impacted by a project, including security, risk, compliance, and governance organizations.

Stakeholders should actively work with the analysts, testers, and developers to ensure that the defects have been logged and addressed in a timely manner, participate in defect review meetings, and provide input into the final defect disposition.

Analyst

The analyst's role is responsible for reviewing any defects that impact business and system operations. The analyst should participate or represent someone in defect review meetings to ensure that proper severity and priority have been assigned to the defects. The analyst should work with the testing and development team to confirm that the defects have been properly fixed and retested.

Developer

A developer is responsible for researching and remediating any assigned defects that have been opened by the testers or any other stakeholders. Developers should work with the testers and analysts to provide additional defect information, research the defect, and provide a fix to prevent the defect from recurring. Developers must participate in defect review meetings and provide updates to the defect fixes that are pending disposition as well as discuss any temporary workarounds that apply until a permanent fix is identified and implemented.

Tester

A tester is a project team member performing testing activities such as system testing or user testing. Testers are responsible for testing the application, registering and tracking all testing defects, and documenting any issues that will need to be escalated or reviewed with the management. Testers should work with the business and development team to determine priorities, severities, and remediation dates. Testers must participate in defect review meetings to ensure that all defects are tracked and are appropriate.

Conflict Resolution and Escalations during Defect

If there is any dispute or disagreement regarding any defect or about the interpretation of any terminology, and if the dispute cannot be resolved within the business unit, the business owner shall attempt to resolve the dispute.

Defect Management Methodology

> Identifier:
> Effective Date: mm/dd/yyyy
> Version: 0.00

Document Change Control

VERSION CHANGE DATE	VERSION #	WHAT KIND OF CHANGE/ REVISION	WHERE CHANGED HAPPENED (SECTION/PAGE)	REVISED BY NAME AND TITLE	APPROVED BY NAME AND TITLE

Documentation

PROCEDURE NAME	DEFECT MANAGEMENT PROCEDURE	COMMENT
Version number:	1.00	
Procedure identifier:		
Superseded procedure(s):	N/A	
Date approved:		
Effective date:		
Procedure author(s):		
Procedure owner:		
Procedure approver:		
Procedure repository:		
Supporting documentation:	Defect management standard	
	Software development life cycle (SDLC) Standard	
	End user computing (EUC) standard	
	Security vulnerability remediation standard	
	Infrastructure hardware change (IHC) procedure	
	Incident management standard	
	Incident management procedure	
	Technology incident management standard	
	Technology incident management procedure	

Statement of Purpose

The primary goal of this procedure is to provide clear definitions and a list of values for all software defect attributes. This procedure will ensure that all defect repositories will use a consistent defect reporting and management process.

Risks

It is important that the company or team exhibit suitable and effective controls managing defects, ensuring their timely resolution based on their severity, and update their resolution progress to the stakeholders as it is critical for the company's finance and other key business processes.

Defect Steps

STEP #	STATUS	DESCRIPTION	PRIMARY PERFORMER	OUTPUT/ EVIDENCE	INPUT
1. SUBMITTING THE DEFECT					
1	New	The submitter identifies and records in a defect repository.	Test team Business team	Defect record is "submitted" in the defect repository.	
2. RESOLVING THE DEFECT (PENDING)					
2	Open pending resolution	Acknowledge the submitted defect. The defect is assigned to the development team.	Development team/ business team	Defect record is moved to a "pending resolution" state in the defect repository.	
3. RESOLVING THE DEFECT (RESOLVED)					
3	Fix and resolved	Resolve the acknowledged defect. The defect is sent to the submitter for re-test.	Development team	Defect record is moved to "resolved" state in the defect repository.	

(Continued)

STEP #	STATUS	DESCRIPTION	PRIMARY PERFORMER	OUTPUT/ EVIDENCE	INPUT
4. REOPENING THE DEFECT					
4	Reopen pending resolution	The submitter retests the resolved defect and the defect still exists. Reopen the resolved defect. The defect is reassigned to the development team for further analysis or resolution.	Test team Business team	Defect record is moved to a "pending resolution" state in the defect repository.	
5. CLOSING THE DEFECT					
5	Closed	The submitter retests the resolved defect and the defect does not exist. Close the resolved defect.	Test team Business team.	Defect record is moved to "closed" state in the defect repository.	
6. DEFERRING THE DEFECT					
6	Deferred	Business team determined to defer the acknowledged defect.	Business team	Defect record is moved to "deferred" state in the defect repository.	
7. CANCELING THE DEFECT					
7	Cancelled	Business or development team cancels the acknowledged or deferred defect. Submitter concurs.	Test team Business team	Defect record is moved to "cancelled" state in the defect repository.	

Defect States

The mandatory states of a defect are
  Submitted/New
  Open
  Resolved
  Closed
  Canceled
  Deferred

ATTRIBUTES	DESCRIPTION	TYPE	OPTIONAL (O) REQUIRED (R) CONDITIONALLY REQUIRED (CR)	BUSINESS RULES
Defect ID	Defect name of ID	System list	R	
Project ID	Project name or ID	System list	R	Name or ID of the project. Most recent project name or ID must be used if a defect is found in production.
Application	System in which defect was identified	List	R	Unique application identifier. Should match to the CMDB and asset ID databases.
Functional area	Module/ subsystem/ component in which defect was identified	System list	R	List of functional areas, modules, or components. The defect is associated with an application.
Headline	One line summary of the defect	Text	R	
Description	Detailed description of problem that includes steps to reproduce the defect, actual results, and expected results	Text	R	
SDLC phase found	Phase where the defect was detected	List	R	Analysis (optional), design (optional), construction, system test, user test, implementation and postimplementation.
Found in environment	Environment in which defect was found	List	CR	Development, test, acceptance, production, integration and contingency. Not required if root cause is requirement or design.
Found in release number	Release number in which the defect is found	System list	R	

(Continued)

ATTRIBUTES	DESCRIPTION	TYPE	OPTIONAL (O) REQUIRED (R) CONDITIONALLY REQUIRED (CR)	BUSINESS RULES
Closed in release number	Release number for which the defect is closed	System list	CR	Conditionally required if the state is closed
Remedy incident ID	Problem ticket number for defects found in production	Text	CR	Conditionally required if the SDLC phase found is implementation or postimplementation
Test case ID	Associated test case ID	Text	CR	Not required if root cause is requirement or design
Functionality type	Lists the type of functionality that introduced the defect	List	R	New functionality, existing functionality
Severity	Impacts to application functionalities, business processes, or interfaces causing minor to critical disruption to application usage	List	R	Severity of the defect must be set in consensus with stakeholders to one of the following: Critical High Medium Low

Defect Attributes

When a defect is discovered, the following minimum set of defect information must be reported in the defect repository.

ATTRIBUTES	DESCRIPTION	TYPE	OPTIONAL (O) REQUIRED (R) CONDITIONALLY REQUIRED (CR)	BUSINESS RULES
Priority	Prioritizing defect based on how fast the defect should be fixed	List	R	Priorities will be set by the submitter of the defect to one of the following: Critical High Medium Low

(*Continued*)

ATTRIBUTES	DESCRIPTION	TYPE	OPTIONAL (O) REQUIRED (R) CONDITIONALLY REQUIRED (CR)	BUSINESS RULES
Root cause	Analysis of what caused the defect	List	R	
Root cause reason	Provide the reason for the root cause of the issue.	List	CR	Required if root cause is: Requirements Incomplete/missing Unclear Inconsistent Incorrect Not traceable Not testable
Resolution notes	Details regarding the resolution of defect	Text	CR	Conditionally required if the state is not submitted
State	Provides a current state of the defect's current flow while going through defect resolution process	System action	R	This is the defect state at any point in time. The values in this field are auto populated
Deferral Business Impact	Business impact description if defect is deferred as well as work around if applicable	Text	CR	Required if the defect is deferred
Submitter	Name of person that created the defect	System generated	R	
State updated By	Name of person that last changed the state of the defect	System list or system generated	CR	Name of the person that last change the state. Required if the state of the defect is deferred, closed, or canceled.
Update date	Date on which defect state	System	R	Defect repository will maintain the audit trail for the defect
Workaround	Lists the work around for deferred defects	Text	CR	Required if the state of the defect is deferred
System test	Identifies whether the defect was leaked from system test	List	CR	Required if the SDLC phase found is user test of higher
				Yes No

Defect Priorities

The defect priorities and definition may differ from one testing stage to another; sometimes in some projects, it may also differ from person to person. The basic definitions are provided below. The expected resolution timeframe for the defects depends on their priority.

Security defects have a prescribed timeframe for remediation that are spelled out in the security, vulnerability, and remediation standard.

PRIORITY DESCRIPTION	PRIORITY DEFINITIONS FOR DEFECTS IN NONPRODUCTION	PRIORITY DEFINITIONS FOR PRODUCTION DEFECTS
Critical	Immediate attention—critical may also mean that it might be blocking some other activities. The critical defect should be resolved immediately.	Immediate attention—must receive highest development priority and should be resolved immediately.
High	Should be reported immediately to the development team. A response or action plan must be provided within 2 working days since the defect causes more than one of the functional areas to be untestable.	Should be reported immediately to the development team. A response or action plan must be provided within 2 working days.
Medium	A response or action plan should be reported within 5 working days.	A response or action plan should be reported within 5 working days. This defect should be resolved in the next release.
Low	Fix dates are subject to negotiation. An action plan before the next release.	Fix dates are subject to negotiation. An action plan before the next release.

Defect Severities

The defect severity definition may also differ from one testing stage to another and also may differ among stakeholders as human perception may be different.

SEVERITY DESCRIPTION	SEVERITY DEFINITIONS FOR SYSTEM, USER, AND PRODUCTION	SEVERITY DEFINITIONS FOR REQUIREMENT DEFECTS
Critical	Critically severe defect causes severe business disruption, financial or reputational impact, and no workaround exists. The customer is unable to use the product, resulting in a critical impact to their operation. This defect must be resolved before exiting current phase or releasing to production.	The reason for the requirement defect could be considered such as Incomplete/missing Inconsistent Incorrect

(Continued)

SEVERITY DESCRIPTION	SEVERITY DEFINITIONS FOR SYSTEM, USER, AND PRODUCTION	SEVERITY DEFINITIONS FOR REQUIREMENT DEFECTS
High	Significant business disruption but a workaround exists. The customer is able to use the product but is severely restricted. This defect should be resolved before exiting current phase or releasing to production.	Content has a major inaccuracy or is missing important detail. The reason for the requirement defect could be considered such as Incomplete/missing Incorrect Unclear Inconsistent Not traceable Not testable
Medium	Minor business disruption but has a workaround, minor usability issues. This defect should be resolved before exiting current phase or releasing to production.	Content is correct but has a moderate flaw that needs amendment; for instance, because it is unclear, imprecise, or not concise. The reason for the requirement defect could be considered such as Unclear Not traceable Not testable
Low	The defect may be cosmetic in nature or a usability annoyance, such as warning messages, misspelled words, etc.	Formatting or organizational observation or a grammatical or spelling error not affecting the meaning. The reason for the requirement defect is usually unclear

Part 3: Root Cause Analysis

Definition

A root cause is an originating cause of either a condition or a causal chain that leads to an outcome or result.

In software development, we can see how defects may arise and are caused by any field.

Root cause of a defect identifies the process or source that introduced the defect.

Root Cause Fields

Standard acceptable values for the root cause field are listed in the following sections:

Requirements This field is required if the root cause of the defect is requirements and should list the actual issue of the stakeholder requirement document that introduced the defect.

Defect Cause in Requirement The possible cause of defect in requirement could be

Incomplete/Missing Necessary functionality is omitted from the requirements set. The defect should specify what needs to be documented to address the gap.

  Unclear: A requirement is not simple, specific, clear, and unambiguous.

Inconsistent A requirement is in conflict with one or more other requirements or other requirements make it redundant.

Incorrect A requirement does not reflect the needs of one or more project stakeholders.

Not Traceable A requirement cannot be traced to project scope, that is, it cannot be established as being within the approved scope of the project.

Not Testable A requirement does not specify observable functionality and so cannot be validated by testing.

Implementation Dependent A requirement does not describe desired system functionality independent of the technology and design that will be used to achieve it.

Design This root cause should be selected if the solution specifications or detailed design are missing, inconsistent with requirements, or otherwise incorrect.

Code This root cause should be selected if the application failed to produce expected result or the functionality is missing, not consistent with stakeholder requirements, solution specifications, standards, or otherwise incorrect.

Environment This root cause should be selected if the application failed to produce expected results due to incorrect environment, infrastructure, or application configuration set up. Examples of environment issues are errors in software compilation/build, incorrect application configuration settings, application processes not initialized, application password is expired, third-party packages are missing, dependent systems are not available, and so on.

Test This root cause should be selected if a defect was reported incorrectly because of inconsistent test case results with stakeholder requirements or solution specifications, premature test case execution, or the test case was not executed in the appropriate environment.

Data This root cause should be selected if the product failed to produce expected results due to the improper setup of test data in the pertinent databases or input files.

Analysis RCA is an effective technique to investigate the origin for defect occurrence. This analysis helps to prevent reoccurrences of defect in future.

The Most Common Root Cause Classifications

Despite the existence of various rationales, RCA techniques enable to classify the most common root causes and percentage of their contributions toward various defect patterns. They are communication (25%–30%), education (20%–25%), oversight (30%–40%), transcription (20%–25%), and miscellaneous (5%–10%). From the defect distribution and defect pattern analysis, it is evident that trivial defects contribute more toward defect injection (Table 7.1).

TABLE 7.1   A Sample Report of Defects in Different Stages and Severity Level Report, and % of Pass and Fail

PLANNING PHASE	
METRICS DATA ELEMENT	VALUE
Planned progression coverage	100%
Prerelease overall regression capability	90%
Prerelease overall regression automation	70%
Planned regression coverage	100%
Planned regression coverage—automated	40%
Expected initial pass rate	90%
EXECUTION PHASE	
METRICS DATA ELEMENT	VALUE
Actual progression coverage	100%
Progression coverage—automated	50%
Actual regression coverage	80%
Postrelease overall regression capability	
Postrelease overall regression automation	
Actual initial pass rate	80%
Final pass rate	100%
System test defects—critical/high	5
System test defects—medium/low	12
System test defects—deferred	2
PRE-PROD PHASE	
METRICS DATA ELEMENT	VALUE
UAT defects—critical/high	2
UAT defects—medium/low	3
UAT defects—deferred	1
System test leakage—critical/high	0
System test leakage—medium/low	1

In Table 7.1, in the planning phase:

Progression coverage was planned to cover 100% and actually 100% was covered.

Prerelease overall progression was planned to automate 70%, but the actual progression automation was covered 50%.

Regression coverage was planned to cover 60%, but actually team was able to cover 80%.

Initial pass rate was expected (as usually some tests fail) to reach 90% (line 9); however, the actual initial pass rate was 80% (line 19), which is less than expected. This also means more test cases failed than expected, but the good news is that the final pass rate is 100%, which means the development team was able to resolve and fix the defects.

There are 11 defects found by the system test team, where the severity level of 3 of them were critical/high (line 21) and 8 of them were medium/low (line 22); on the other hand, UAT or the user acceptance test team, found 5 defects in total, 4 which were already found by the test team, 1 defect that was found by UAT but the system test failed to find it defined and system test leakage.

So altogether, there were 12 defects; among these, 9 defects were resolved and closed, and 3 could not be resolved at this time. The team including stakeholders decided to work around for now and possibly resolve it in future release. These 3 unresolved defects are called deferred (Figures 7.3 and 7.4).

DEFECT ID	STATE	SDLC PHASE FOUR	ROOT CAUSE	DEFECT PHASE AGE
1001	Closed	System Test	Requirement	3
1002	Closed	Design	Code	−1
1003	Closed	System Test	Design	2
1004	Closed	System Test	Requirement	3
1005	Closed	System Test	Code	1
1006	Deferred	System Test	Code	1
1007	Deferred	User Test	Code	2
1008	Closed	Design	Code	−1
1009	Closed	Design	Requirement	1
1010	Closed	System Test	Code	1
1011	Closed	User Test	Design	3
1012	Deferred	User Test	Code	4

Defect Prevention

Awareness of defect injecting methods and processes enables defect prevention (DP). It is the most significant activity in software development. It identifies defects along with their root causes and prevents their recurrences in the future.

Benefits of Defect Prevention Prevention is better than a cure; it applies to defects as well. It is indeed better to prevent a defect

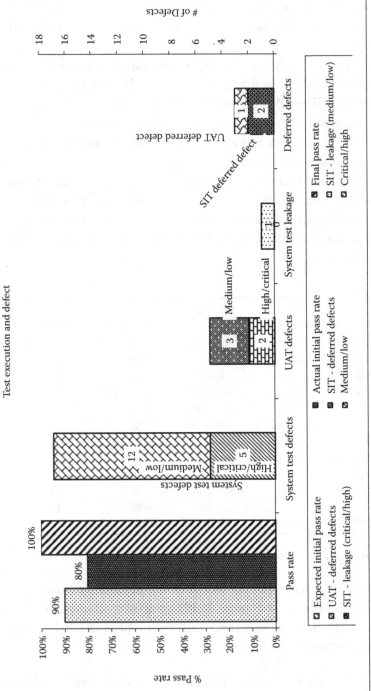

Figure 7.3 A sample report % of pass and defects.

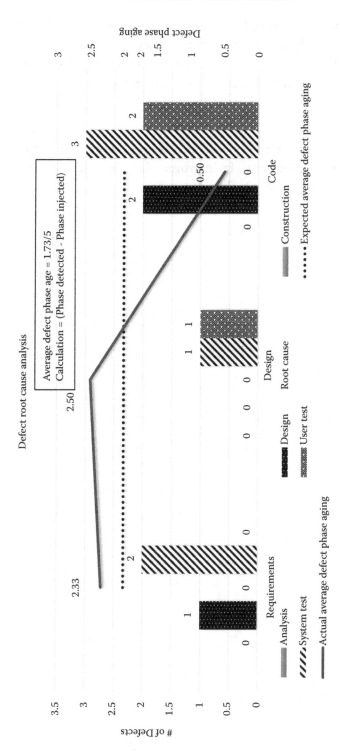

Figure 7.4 Defect root cause analysis, average phase age.

before it reaches its severity level. Validation, verification, inspection, and review helps to prevent defects or severe risk issues.

Therefore, it is imperative to introduce defect prevention at every level of SDLC to prevent defects at the earliest occurrence.

Defect Prediction

Defect prediction is a technique of identifying the quality of the software before deployment. It improves the performance. The main objective is Software Quality Assurance.

8

RISK, VULNERABILITY, AND THREAT MANAGEMENT

Introduction

This chapter, as the name implies, deals with the conceptual aspects of risk, vulnerability, and threat management. There are three parts and two appendices in this chapter. Part 1 discusses about identifying potential risks, Part 2 discusses how to analyze and assess the level of risk. It also discusses the effective method to identify risks; risk response strategy; mitigation and contingency plan; and vulnerability, risk, and threat analysis. Part 3 provides a comparative analysis between OCTAVE methods of risk management and other methodologies. The two appendices discuss sample documents of vulnerability and risk assessment and risk factors assumptions.

Part 1: Risk Management

Risk is the possibility of losing something valuable, sometimes in the exchange of gaining something else, like the famous saying of "no pain no gain." However, since software development itself is a process of developing or building a great production, the risk in the software development life cycle (SDLC) is a possible threat and vulnerability. From that perspective, in this chapter, we discuss the threat and vulnerabilities in relation to the risk management. Risk in software may cause a problem that may decrease product quality or the success of a project.

Risk management is part of a project. Risk has a possibility of happening anytime and could have either a positive or negative impact to a project. A risk may have multiple causes and multiple impacts.

The most remarkable aspect of risk is that it is an uncertain event, which may have an impact on the project cost, schedule, or performance. All projects contain some elements of risk.

Risk management is an ongoing process that should continue through the life cycle of a project. It should include a risk management plan, processes, identification, analysis, monitoring, and control.

The identification of risk or at least brainstorming should be started before the project is initiated, and potential risk should be documented. When a risk is identified, it is first assessed to ascertain the probability of occurring, the degree of impact to the schedule, scope, cost, and quality, and then prioritized.

As part of documenting a risk, two other important items need to be addressed.

The first is mitigation steps that can be taken to lessen the probability of the event occurring. The second is a contingency plan, or a series of activities that should take place either prior to or when the event occurs. Mitigation actions frequently have a cost. Sometimes, the cost of mitigating the risk can exceed the cost of assuming the risk and incurring the consequences. It is important to evaluate the probability and impact of each risk against the mitigation strategy cost before deciding to implement a contingency plan. Contingency plans implemented prior to the risk occurring are preemptive actions intended to reduce the impact or remove the risk in its entirety. Contingency plans implemented after a risk occurs can usually only lessen the impact.

Identifying and documenting events that pose a risk to the outcome of a project is just the first step. It is equally important to monitor all risks on a scheduled basis by a risk management team and report in the project status report.

Types of Risks

In software quality perspective, there are two main types of risks that could be identified.

1. Risk related to the product quality
2. Risk related to process and planning

These two types could be said in other words as product and process risk. The fundamental concepts of software quality perspective is

1. If the right product is produced. This item relates to the customer's expectation and demand. For example, the customer wanted to have a three level house with four bedrooms, and a

nice backyard. This item verifies the product as if there is any risk in the house, in rooms, or levels.

2. If the product is produced in a right method. This item relates to the plan, process, and methodology; sometimes due to process risk, you may not know the project's progress, weakness, and strength; nothing can be verified or trusted. Process risk may impact overall success of the project; sometimes may not be customers' immediate dissatisfaction; however, it may cause serious dissatisfaction in future.*

Impact of Risk

Figure 8.1 shows that risk can be anytime in a project, and risk management should be a continuous process in a project.

One of the remarkable aspects in risk management is the difference between incident management, defect management, and risk management, where the risk is hidden, whereas incident and defect are visible. Also, the severity of the risk may not be easy to assess; another remarkable aspect of risk management is that risk can be assumed during the whole project even after production.

Dealing with Risk

The fundamental point of risk management is dealing with the risk. Risk is normal expectation; the main question is how to manage such risk.

Figure 8.1   Risk in any part of SDLC can be harmful for software quality.

---

* Rex Black, Jamie L. Mitchell, and Rocky Nook. *Advanced Software Testing.* Vol. 3, 2011, p. 75.

Risk management includes three primary activities:

1. Risk identification, figuring out what the different project and quality risks are for the project.
2. Risk analysis, assessing the level of risk—typically based on likelihood and impact—for each identified risk item.
3. Risk response, mitigation consists of mitigation, contingency, transference, review, and monitoring (Figure 8.2).

Different people obviously can have different definitions, identifications, and management aspects of risk.

Risk Management Life Cycle

Risk Identification   The categorization and risk breakdown structure method helps to identify where risk may come from, and which area may have weaknesses and need more attention (Figure 8.3).

Ten Effective Methods to Identify Risks

There are 10 known effective methods that help in identifying risks:

Brainstorming   Brainstorming is a technique that is best accomplished when the approach is unclear. Team members think to identify possible risks. It is always important for the team members and

Figure 8.2   The risk management life cycle.

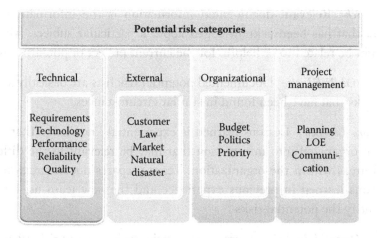

Figure 8.3 Potential risk categories from technical, external, and project planning.

stakeholders to have sufficient information about the project. In risk management, knowing the project, issues, and possible risks require knowledge about the system and the process.

Participation of all group members is important to have a structured and successful brainstorming. Brainstorming can also be used during planning to generate a list of migration strategies, possible causes for the risk, or other areas of impact. Each brainstorming session for risk identification should be documented.

Survey Survey is a method to get the perception of people who may not be directly involved in the process. The team prepares a list of questions about the potential risk. The organizer or question preparer needs to keep in mind that there might be a lot of people who may not like to complete the survey. Also those who complete the survey may not have accurate knowledge about the risk.

Interview Interviewing experienced people is another effective way to identify risk areas. Interviewing process could be taken individually or in a group. Group interviews may help to identify the starting point of risk identification.

Practical Experience and Understanding Practical experience and understanding are very important and could be effective. The team needs to ensure the knowledge is relevant and applicable to identify the risk.

Research Relevant documented information is the information or data that has been acknowledged about a particular subject, which might be related to or helpful for the current project or potential risk.

Potential Risk Lists Documented potential risk lists are basically a list of risks that have been found in similar circumstances.

Lessons Learned Lessons learned is experiential knowledge that has been organized into information that may be relevant to the different areas within the organization. Team prepares documentation of lessons learned in previous experience and the new team uses it to identify the potential risks.

Risk-Oriented Analysis There are two major techniques of risk oriented analysis: (1) Fault-based analysis and (2) event-based analysis. These are top-down analysis approaches that attempt to determine what events, conditions, or faults could lead to a specific top-level risk event.

Design Template A set of context diagrams and flow charts for various aspects of the development process. These templates are the groundwork of the project and conventional guidance to accomplish a top-down assessment of activities.*

Risk Assessment

In Part 1 of this chapter, we discussed about identifying the risk. Let us assume risk is identified, what next?

After identifying a risk, now you have to assess and measure it, what is the level of risk? How much is it going to cost? Is it recoverable, what kind of effect will be on return on investment (ROI).

In information technology (IT) environment, the third step is to perform the risk identification and assessment—a methodology for determining the likelihood of an event that could hinder the organization from attaining its business goals and objectives in an effective, efficient, and controlled manner.

It is extremely important for organizations to determine the substances of their risk portfolio periodically and perform activities to manage risks to an acceptable level. Auditors also need to identify the

---

* *Risk Identification Methods—12 Types*, Published by ClearRisk Manager, https://manager.clearrisk.com/Resources/RiskTool/Risk_Identification_Methods_-_12_Types

effectiveness and usefulness of risk assessment results. Auditors also need to understand.

What Is Risk Assessment? A risk assessment typically involves an overview of all project areas to identify the key risks that could impact project delivery and determine how well they are being tracked and mitigated. This type of review is also quite common if management believes that the project is not progressing well, costs are exceeding the budget, or the project has already experienced delays.

Risk Assessment Process In terms of risk identification and assessment and the *Global Technology Audit Guide* series, developing the IT audit plan suggests that risk management processes should have the following five key objectives:*

1. Risks arising from business strategies and activities need to be identified and prioritized.
2. Management and the board need to determine the level of risk acceptable to the organization, including the acceptance of risks designed to accomplish the organization's strategic plans.
3. Risk mitigation activities need to be designed and implemented to reduce or otherwise manage risk at levels that are acceptable to management and the board.
4. Ongoing monitoring activities need to be conducted to reassess risk periodically and the effectiveness of controls to manage risk.
5. The board and management need to receive periodic risk management process reports. The organization's corporate governance processes also should provide periodic communication of risks, risk strategies, and controls to stakeholders (Table 8.1).

Identify and understand IT strategy.
Detail IT infrastructure, operation, and application.

- Ranking Risk
- Measuring risk and its impact
- Leading IT Governance Frameworks

Insights on governance, risk, and compliance, February 2013

---

* Kirk Rehage. Developing the IT Audit Plan. Chevron Corporation Steve Hunt, Crowe Chizek and Company LLC, p. 12.

Table 8.1   A Sample Technology Risk Assessment and Mitigation Plan Document

Deliverable name	Technology risk assessment and mitigation (TRAM)
Phase	Should be in the planning phase
Confirmation	The e-mail should be sent to the TRAM team as evidence of Tram team position, list of all TRAM reports should be sent to PQO
Required?	Yes/no
Purpose	The purpose should be to find the technology risks that team members may not be aware of, Tram Team should be subject matter experts.
Deliverable link	Important links should be added
Major points	Major technology risk assessment and mitigation plan keypoints should be noted
Additional information	Any comment, note, procedural remark, related materials

Risk Assessment Involves Identified Risks   In the risk assessment, the following technical factors should be considered:

- Disorganized and poor management
- Time, resources, and budget constraints
- Unclear, unprofessional requirements, design
- Too many changes in requirement and code
- Complexity in code
- Employee lack of knowledge and training
- Intra team and inter team conflict
- MSP uncertainty
- Onsite and offshore resources
- Challenges with ongoing changes in technologies versus established technologies
- The lack of quality in the tools and technology
- High defect rates

Technology Risk Assessment and Mitigation (TRAM) (Sample)
See Table 8.1

Business Risk

- Potential damage to representation
- Loss of customers and business
- Potential financial losses or liability
- Civil or criminal legal sanctions
- Loss of licenses and permits*

---

* Ibid, pp. 82–83.

According to an article Risk Management Plan by the U.S. Department of Health & Human Services, The Risk Register contains five ratings for impact (Table 8.2);

Catastrophic (A) It may cause the following:

- Regulatory/compliance, violations/issues
- Inability to validate data
- Withdrawal of product manufacturer
- Tainted product
- Production delays
- Technical miscommunications
- Security/confidentiality breeches

Critical (B)

- A noncompliance finding resulting in process or operational degradation
- A security finding requiring immediate corrective action prior to continued operation
- Reoccurring violation of any safety regulation resulting in serious injury
- Production errors containing regulatory violations that pose direct consequence to the operation

Moderate (C)

- Security finding requiring a corrective action plan
- Production element errors that may pose indirect consequences to the operation

Minor (D)

- No regulatory action anticipated
- No compliance impact anticipated
- No evident security threat affected
- Minor errors in completed company policy and procedures
- Production errors containing quality system and/or opportunities for improvement

Table 8.2   Risk Assessment Matrix

	Determining the Level of Risk
Critical	Act immediately to mitigate the risk. Either eliminate, substitute, or implement engineering control measures.
High	Act immediately to mitigate the risk. Either eliminate, substitute, or implement engineering control measures. If these controls are not immediately accessible, set a timeframe for their implementation and establish interim risk reduction strategies for the period of the set timeframe.
Medium	Take reasonable steps to mitigate the risk. Until eliminate, substitution or engineering control can be implemented, institute administrative or personal protective equipment controls.
Low	Take reasonable steps to mitigate and monitor the risk. Institute permanent controls in the long term. Permanent controls may be administrative in nature if the hazard has low frequency, rare lilelihood and insignficant consequence.

How to Prioritize the Risk Rating

Once the level of risk has been determined, the following table may be of use in determining when to act to institute the control measures.

Hierarchy of Control—Controls identified may be a mixture of the hierarchy in order to provide minimum operator exposure.

(*Continued*)

Risk Assessment Matrix
Negligible (E)

- No regulatory/compliance violation
- No security/confidentiality element affected
- On time production
- Validated experiments "Clean" product
- Properly executed communications*

RISK ASSESSMENT SUMMARY

TOPIC:				DATE:			ISSUE NO. REVIEW DATE:
IDENTIFY HAZARDS AND SUBSEQUENT RISKS	ANALYZE RISKS EVALUATE RISKS			IDENTIFY AND EVALUATE EXISTING RISK CONTROLS			FURTHER RISK TREATMENTS
Hazards/ Issues/Risks	Conse- quence	Likeli- hood	Risk level	What we are doing now to manage this risk	Effectiveness of our strategies	New risk level	Further action needed Opportunities for improvement

Risk Response

Risk response is the most important part of risk management; in other words, basically risk management is risk response. How do you respond to a risk that is the core point and your response will bring the outcome? For each identified risk, a response must be recognized. It is the responsibility of the project team to select a risk response for each risk. The project team will need the best possible assessment of the risk and description of the response options in order to select the right response for each risk.

The possible response options are as follows:

Avoid If there is safe possibility to avoid the risk that is the first action to be think of. Avoidance could be done by changing scope, objective, or strategy.

Transfer Shift the impact of a risk to where it could be less impact on the project. It does not eliminate it; it simply shifts the impact

---

* *Risk Management Plan*, by U.S. Department of Health & Human Services, http://www.phe.gov/about/amcg/toolkit/Documents/risk-management.pdf

temporarily, or transferring risk to a third party such as insurance company, especially when risk is out of control.

Reduce   Reducing the impact of a risk could be the best solution if possible. Take steps to reduce the probability and/or impact of a risk. Taking early action, close monitoring, more testing, etc.

Accept   Simply accept that this is a risk. It is what it is. Sometimes accepting the risk could be the best solution; it may cost more money, and schedule could be delayed (Figure 8.4).

Risk Mitigation   What is risk mitigation? According to the definition given by BusinessDictionary.com risk mitigation is "A systematic reduction in the extent of exposure to a risk and/or the likelihood of its occurrence. Also called risk reduction."*

According to the article, "Risk Management Plan" by the U.S. Department of Health & Human Services,[†] risk mitigation involves two steps:

1. Identifying the various activities or steps to reduce the probability and/or impact of an adverse risk.

Figure 8.4   Risk response strategy.

---

* BusiessDictionary.com, http://www.businessdictionary.com/definition/risk-mitigation.html

† *Risk Management Plan*, by U.S. Department of Health & Human Services, http://www.phe.gov/about/amcg/toolkit/Documents/risk-management.pdf

2. Creation of a contingency plan to deal with the risk should it occur.

Mitigation activities should be documented in the risk register and reviewed on a regular basis. They should include the following:

- Identification of potential failure points for each risk mitigation solution.
- For each failure point, document the event that would raise a "flag" indicating that the event or factor has occurred or reached a critical condition.
- For each failure point, provide alternatives for correcting the failure.

Risk Contingency Plan

Contingency planning is the act of preparing a plan or a series of activities. Having a contingency plan helps the project team to think in advance (Tables 8.3 and 8.4).

- Identify the contingency plan tasks (or steps) that can be performed to implement the mitigation strategy.
- Identify the necessary resources such as money, equipment, and labor.
- Develop a contingency plan schedule. Since the date, the plan that will be implemented is unknown, this schedule will be in the format of day 1, day 2, day 3, etc., rather than containing specific start and end dates.
- Define emergency notification and escalation procedures, if appropriate.
- Develop contingency plan training materials, if appropriate.
- Review and update contingency plans if necessary.
- Publish the plan(s) and distribute the plan(s) to management and those directly involved in executing the plan(s).[*]

---

[*] Ibid.

Technology Contingency Plan (TCP) (Sample)

Table 8.3   Technology Contingency Plan

DTM deliverable name	Technology contingency plan (TCP).
Phase	Current phase checkpoint.
Confirmation	Latest status, evidence, document location link, list of all valid TCP reports should be generated and sent to PQO.
Required?	Yes/no
Purpose	The plan should be based on the criticality of the application and potential business impact.
Deliverable link	Important links should be added.
Major points	
Additional information	Any comment, note, procedural remark, related materials.

Table 8.4   Application Risk Questionnaire Sample

DTM deliverable name	Application risk questionnaire (ARQ):
Phase	ARQ should be completed in the planning phase.
Evidence	Evidence should indicate the various governing areas and if a review is required by the corresponding body.
Required?	Yes/no
Purpose	The purpose of ARQ is to enable the various governing bodies to assess the changes and identify potential risks.
Deliverable link	Important links should be added.
Major points	
Additional information	Any comment, note, remark, related materials.

Application Risk Questionnaire (ARQ)
Project Risk Log

- Purpose
- Risk type
- Risk rating
- Risk response procedure (Table 8.5)

Part 2: Vulnerability, Risk, and Threat Analysis

Information security is not just a software challenge; it involves inter-action among hardware, software, and people. Business organizations and software companies install firewalls and virus scanners and e-mail encryption when they realize the importance to protect their IT base. However, the effectiveness of these measures is limited due to lack of vulnerability and risk analysis. Vulnerability and risk analysis is all about defining the problem.

Table 8.5 Project Risk Log Sample

Date ....

Risk ID ....

Risk type ....

Risk description ....

Probability of occurrence % ....

Probable severity ....

Risk scope ....

Levels of occurrence ....

Risk response style ....

Response strategy ....

Contingency plan ....

Assigned to ....

Update ....

Vulnerability and Risk

So what is the vulnerability and risk analysis and how does it work?

The first step of vulnerability and risk analysis is to define the boundaries of the system to be protected.

It is comprised of four activities:

1. Determine what is being protected and why
2. Identifying the system
3. Characterize system operations
4. Ascertain what one does and does not have control over

Step 1: Determine What Is Being Protected and Why

Before information security can be implemented, the systems and data being protected need to be identified. Not all systems or components need to be protected or need the same level of protection.

The first step is identifying what is being protected.

1. Systems that process or generate data
2. Systems that display data
3. Backup, archival, or online storage systems
4. Control systems that act on real-time data
5. Communications systems
6. Voice, video, image, or textual data
7. Hardcopy output
8. Input devices

Next step is to define why these items need to be protected. Need to identify specific reason and justification need to be explained? Goals need to be defined before they can be achieved. A clear, concise, unambiguous statement

- Ensures systems are not over or under protected.
- Focuses on what is to be accomplished not how.

Sample Statement

GOAL	JUSTIFICATION
1. Protect the privacy and integrity of customer records from accidental or malicious intentional unauthorized disclosure, manipulation, alteration, abuse, corruption, and theft	• Customer loyalty depends on sound business ethics • Local (or national) regulations require privacy protections • Liability lawsuits may result from a failure to protect customer records. • Fraud lawsuits may result from a failure to protect customer records
2. Protect personal identifying information: name, address, phone number, e-mail, account number, etc.	
3. Protect customer payment information and history	
4. Protect customer purchase history and preferences	
5. Protect customer online, voice, fax, and hardcopy transactions	

Step 2: Identify the System

What Is a System?

1. "System is defined as "a set of connected things or parts forming a complex whole, in particular."
2. "A set of things working together as parts of a mechanism or an interconnecting network."

The following are the types of system entities that InfoSec must consider, it is possible for an item to be from more than one entity:

- Logical: software name
- Physical: software executes and is stored on physical entities such as computers, hard drives, floppy drives, PROMs, PLCs, and ASICs.

- Animate: human users, system administrators, trainers, and maintenance staff are then animate entities within a system.
- Inanimate: all other system entities are inanimate; for example, system archives.
- Primary: Primary entities are those that contribute directly to accomplishing a system's function; for example, the CPU, operating system, applications software, and end users.
- Support: the electric power grid and the telecommunications backbone are examples of support entities. They are essential but contribute indirectly to the accomplishment of a system's function.
- Dynamic: system configurations and operational procedures are dynamic entities. Both tend to evolve or be modified frequently over the life of a system due to enhancements, maintenance, and changes in technology. A change in a dynamic entity should trigger the revalidation of protection strategies.
- Static: The entities that are static will vary from system to system. In one case, a maintenance schedule may be static; in another, the electromechanical components may be static.

Step 3: Characterize System Operations

A systems operations characterization takes two forms: operational mode or states and operational profiles. This information will serve as an input to the vulnerability and threat analysis.

Operational mode or state represents the state or mode an entity can exist. Examples common to most systems are normal operations such as start-up, shutdown or abnormal operations such as operator error, hardware failure, etc.

Capture the knowledge of how a system can be used, operational profiles should be developed for the maintenance staff, trainers, system administrators, super users, testers, and potential intruders.

Step 4: Ascertain What One Does and Does Not Have Control Over

Most system owners are surprised to learn how few entities they have total control over.

This discovery has a significant impact on the vulnerability and threat analyses, as well as the development of contingency plans.

Vulnerability and Threat Definitions

Vulnerability—a weakness in a system that can be exploited and violate the system's safety, security, reliability, availability, and integrity. They are inherent in the design, operation, or environment of a system.

Threats—the potential danger that a vulnerability may be exploited intentionally or accidentally.

Hazard—a source or situation with potential to harm.

Risk—a combination of the likelihood of a hazard occurring and the severity of the consequences should it occur.

Severity—represents the consequences of a potential hazard, the extent of harm, or damage that could be inflicted.

Four Levels of Threats

1. Catastrophic—fatalities or multiple severe injuries. Loss of one or more major systems.
2. Critical—single fatality or severe injury; loss of a major system.
3. Marginal—minor injury; severe system(s) damage.
4. Insignificant—possible single minor injury; system damage.

Likelihood—probability of threat occurring.

Frequent—likely to occur; the hazard will be experienced continually.

Probable—will occur several times; the hazard can be expected to occur.

Occasional—likely to occur several times over the life of the system.

Remote—likely to occur at some time during the life of the system.

Improbable—unlikely but possible to occur during the life of the system.

Incredible—extremely unlikely to occur during the life of the
system.

Risk is the composite of threat likelihood and the severity of
the consequences of a potential hazard should a vulnerability
be exploited. Risk is evaluated for every potential vulnerabil-
ity\threat pair. A system risk assessment must evaluate the
likelihood and severity of individual events AND combinations of events.

Four Steps of Threat Assessment

Step 1: Analysis Techniques Are Selected and Used
Once the system definition is used to identify goals that the techniques
need to support, the high-level potential failure points need to be used
to identify which represent potential attack points (Figure 8.5). They
could include

- Web server failure
- Local area network (LAN), workstation, or printer failure

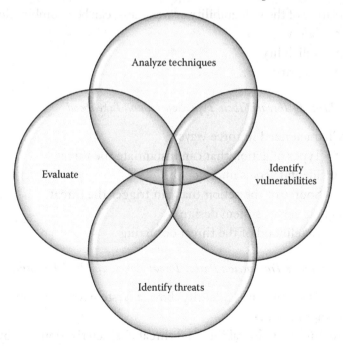

Figure 8.5 The four steps of risk assessment.

- Failure to links with other systems
- Failure of links to other organizations
- Telecom failure
- Power failure
- User actions
- Failure scenarios are devised for each potential failure point, using the system operational characterization and entity control analysis as input.
- IA analysis techniques are used to further decompose failure scenarios to identify and characterize vulnerabilities.

Step 2: Identify Vulnerabilities, Their Type, Source, and Severity
Vulnerabilities are classified as follows:

- Type of action that caused the vulnerability to manifest itself. Accidental action (or inaction) versus malicious action (or inaction).
- Method by which vulnerability is exploited. Direct versus indirect involvement of the perpetrator.
- Nature of the vulnerability or weakness, can be a combination:
  - Safety
  - Reliability
  - Security

Step 3: Identify Threats, Their Type, Source, and Likelihood

- Characterized in three ways:
  - Types of action that can instantiate the threat
- Accidental versus intentional
  - Source of the action that can trigger the threat
- People versus system design
  - Likelihood of the threat occurring

Step 4: Evaluate Transaction Paths, Threat Zones, and Risk Exposure

- Transaction paths identify how a system can be (or was) compromised.
- Reinforces vulnerability and threat characterizations are by
  - Uncovering new vulnerabilities and methods of exploitation.
  - Refines threat source and likelihood estimates.

- Examine different threat perspectives.
- Evaluate how different operational modes and states and time affect risk.
- Optimize the use of threat control measures by identifying common lower-level events within transaction paths.
- Transaction paths capture the most logical sequence of events that could cause an event to occur. They focus on what is logically possible, not whether it is feasible, economical, or probable.
- An individual path represents a unique route from the top to bottom event.
- Paths can be developed as part of the analysis or be used to reconstruct how an accident/incident occurred.
- First define the boundaries of the system.

Evaluate Transaction Paths

- The transaction paths "drill down" until they reach their lowest level.
- In the example, the Air Traffic Control system can be compromised in four ways.
- There are five ways to tamper with aircraft communications with radar.
- There are then seven ways to intercept/retransmit signal to/from radar.

Evaluate Threat Zones

Threat and analyses are generally performed from the perspective of the system owner. To be complete, vulnerability and threat analyses should be done from the perspectives of all groups who will be impacted by the system. Transaction paths bring this multiple perspective.

Threat zones represent a segment of the transaction path that is associated with a specific operational mode/state, operational profile at any point in time.

Goal is to find the weakest link in the chain that will most likely lead to failure.

Opportunity, motive, and intent for an attack must also be considered (Figure 8.6).

Figure 8.6   OCTAVE® (operationally critical threat, asset, and vulnerability evaluation) is a risk-based strategic.

Part 3: OCTAVE and Risk Management

What Is OCTAVE?

OCTAVE® (Operationally Critical Threat, Asset, and Vulnerability Evaluation) is a risk-based strategic assessment and planning technique for security. It is a single source comprehensive approach to risk management.

It is a suite of tools, techniques, and methods for risk-based information security strategic assessment and planning.

The OCTAVE approach was developed by the Software Engineering Institute (SEI) at Carnegie Mellon University in 2001 to address the information security compliance challenges faced by the U.S. Department of Defense (DoD). SEI is a U.S. federally funded research and development center sponsored by the DoD.

The OCTAVE approach is a framework that enables organizations to understand, assess, and address their information security risks from the organization's perspective. It is a process-driven methodology to identify, prioritize, and manage information security risks (Figure 8.7).

The OCTAVE methodology helps stakeholders to

- Develop qualitative risk evaluation criteria based on operational risk tolerances
- Identify assets that are critical to the mission of the organization
- Identify vulnerabilities and threats to the critical assets

Figure 8.7 Key aspects of operational risk, security practices, and technology of OCTAVE.

- Determine and evaluate potential consequences to the organization if threats are realized
- Initiate corrective actions to mitigate risks and create practice-based protection strategy*

OCTAVE plays a kind of management role concerned with the security of the organization and evaluates the key aspects such as operational risk, security practices, and technology.

The OCTAVE approach tries to address operational risks, which is driven by operational risk and security practices. Technology is examined only in relation to security practices, enabling an organization to refine the view of its current security practices. By using the OCTAVE approach, an organization makes information-protection decisions based on the risks to confidentiality, integrity, and availability of critical information-related assets. All aspects of risk (assets, threats, vulnerabilities, and organizational impact) are factored into decision making, enabling an organization to match a practice-based protection strategy to its security risks.†

---

* http://en.wikipedia.org/wiki/OCTAVE#cite_note-1
† Christopher Alberts, Audrey Dorofee, James Stevens, and Carol Woody. *Introduction to the OCTAVE® Approach*, August 2003, Carnegie Mallon, Software Engineering Institute, p. 3.

OCTAVE Phases

OCTAVE has three phases.*

OCTAVE is organized around these three basic aspects, basically enabling management leadership to construct a comprehensive model of the company's information security needs (Figure 8.8).

The phases are listed in the following sections.

Phase 1: Build Asset–Based Threat Profiles

This is an organizational evaluation. The analysis team determines what is most important to the company and what is being done to protect those properties. It also identifies threats to each critical asset, creating a threat profile for that asset. The two major functions of this phase are gathering information from across the organization and defining threat profiles for critical assets. In this phase, the team gathers detail information, strength and weaknesses, threat and vulnerabilities. Distinguish between operational area knowledge and security requirements.

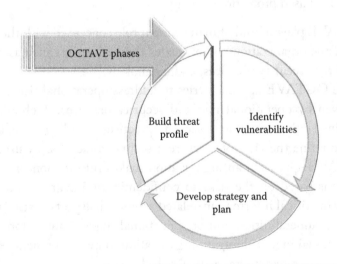

Figure 8.8   The three major phases of OCTAVE.

---

* http://en.wikipedia.org/wiki/OCTAVE#cite_note-2. Also see *Introduction to the OCTAVE® Approach*, by: Christopher Alberts, Audrey Dorofee, James Stevens, and Carol Woody, August 2003, Carnegie Mallon, Software Engineering Institute, p. 5.

Phase 2: Identify Infrastructure Vulnerabilities

This phase helps in the assessment of the information infrastructure. The team investigates network access paths, identifying classes of information technology components related to each critical asset, and determines the magnitude to which each class of component is resistant to network attacks.

During this phase, the analysis team evaluates the key components of systems supporting the critical assets for technological vulnerabilities.

Phase 3: Develop Security Strategy and Plans

Phase 3 is basically making a decision and action plan. The analysis team identifies risks to the organization's critical assets and decides what to do about them. The team creates a protection strategy for the organization and mitigation plans to address the risks to the critical assets based upon an analysis of the information gathered.

The primary purpose of this phase is to evaluate risks to critical assets and develop an organizational protection strategy and risk mitigation plans (Figure 8.9).*

OCTAVE Way of Risk Management

The OCTAVE approach to manage risks is administrated by the OCTAVE principles, which are essential requirements comprising

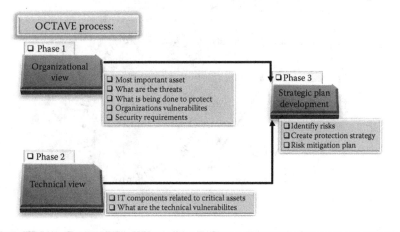

Figure 8.9   The OCTAVE process.

* The OCTAVE® Approach to Information Security Risk Assessment, Parthajit Panda.

principles, attributes, and outputs. Principles are the fundamental concepts driving the OCTAVE evaluation process. Attributes are derived from principles and are the tangible elements, and outputs are the required results that must be achieved.

OCTAVE is a comprehensive, systematic, context-driven and self-directed evaluation approach. Organizations that successfully apply this approach are consistently able to maintain a proactive security posture and are able to bring the organizational point of view to information security risk management activities.*

OCTAVE in Risk Management   An information security risk evaluation is part of an organization's activities for managing information security risks. OCTAVE is an evaluation activity, not a continuous process. Thus, it has a defined beginning and end. Figure 8.10 shows the relationship among these activities and where OCTAVE fits in.

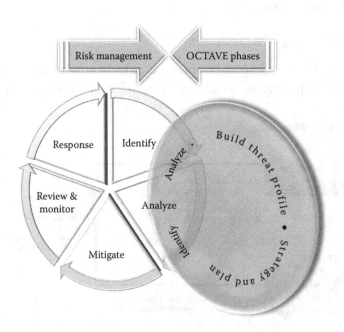

Figure 8.10   The common criteria of risk management process and OCTAVE phases.

---

* The OCTAVE® Approach to Information Security Risk Assessment, Parthajit Panda.

Appendix A—Sample

Vulnerability/Risk Assessment

For Pharmacy Handheld Technology (This document is based on a class project prepared by the author for Master in Information Systems at University of Detroit Mercy.)

Introduction   In today's health industry, technology is becoming a significant factor in the success of how information will be distributed and how it will be protected electronically at the physical level. Pharmacy Handheld Technology is one company that is planning for the future by making a strong effort to make information flow more secure by allowing physicians to electronically prescribe medical prescriptions using a personal digital assistant. In order for Pharmacy Handheld Technology to achieve the goal of information efficiency, it needs to face the variables that challenge the scope of information security.

Statement of Goals

GOAL	JUSTIFICATION
Protect the privacy and integrity of patient's records from accidental or malicious, intentional unauthorized disclosure, manipulation, alteration abuse, correction, and theft.	Patient's loyalty depends on sounds business/medical ethics
Protect personal identity information: Name, address, phone number, e-mail address, account number, and fax number.	The Health Insurance Portability and Accountability Act of 1996 (HIPAA) compliances
Protect patient's payment information and history	Liability lawsuit may result from a failure to protect customer's records
Protect patient's diagnoses and preferences of medication and preference history.	Patient's privacy
Protect patient online, voice, fax, and hardcopy transactions.	Fraud lawsuit may result from a failure to protect patient records

High-Level System Entity Control Analysis

SUBSYSTEM	COMPONENT	SUBCOMPONENT	CONTROL STATUS	EXPLANATION
1. People	1.1 Patients	–	None	Patients are not responsible for enforcing any operational processes
				(Continued)

SUBSYSTEM	COMPONENT	SUBCOMPONENT	CONTROL STATUS	EXPLANATION
	1.2 Doctors	–	Partial	Doctors are partially responsible for maintaining the system
	1.3 Pharmacy staff	–	Total	They are responsible for all operational processes.
	1.4 Insurance staff	-	Partial	Insurance company is partially responsible for maintaining the system.
2. Pharmacy Relational Database Management System (RDBMS)	2.1 Insurance group record	2.1.1 Health plan categories	Total	Authorized personnel at the pharmacy have complete access for the insurance group records.
		2.1.2 Insurance billing system	Partial	Insurance billing system is partially accessed through the pharmacy database.
	2.2 Listed doctor/ hospital database	2.2.1 Wireless communication system (E-Scripts)	Partial	Wireless has partial access due to the vulnerability of the wireless technology.
		2.2.2 In Network	Partial	Doctors/hospital in-network has partial access of the database.
		2.2.3 Out of network	None	No access for out-of-network doctors/hospitals.
	2.3 Listed pharmacy database	2.3.1 E-Refill system	Partial	The database has list of pharmacies (CVS, Walgreens, Rite Aid, etc.)
		2.3.2 In-Network pharmacy	Partial	The system facilitates in-network pharmacy

(Continued)

SUBSYSTEM	COMPONENT	SUBCOMPONENT	CONTROL STATUS	EXPLANATION
		2.3.3 Out-of-network pharmacy	None	No access of database given to out-of-network.
	2.4 Patient medical records	2.4.1 Patient medical data	Partial	Authorize DB personnel have partial access to patient records.
		2.4.2 Report generation system	Partial	System can generate various reports for the patient records.
		2.4.3 Past/current prescription records	Partial	System keeps relevant information about past and current
3. Health plan insurance companies	3.1 Billing system	3.1.1 Payment methods and procedures	Partial	Health Insurance companies keeps the billing record for the patient prescriptions.
	3.2 Prescription authorization system	3.2.1 Authorization notification via e-mail/fax	Total	Total access is given to the insurance companies for prescription authorization.
4. Physician network	4.1 Local LAN	–	Partial	LAN is connected to the pharmacy RDBMS through the VPN.
	4.2 Wireless Personal digital assistant (PDA)	–	Partial	Wireless PDA facilitates the communication for the electronic prescriptions.
5. Remote patient access	5.1 Web Access	5.x.1 Personal computer	None	Patient accesses his/her prescription using the Web.
	5.2 Phone Access	5.x.2 Touch Tone phone	None	Patient can use the touch telephone for electronic refills

Vulnerability and Threat Analysis

FAILURE POINTS	FAILURE SCENARIO	VULNERABILITY	TYPE OF ACTION	METHOD OF EXPLOITATION	TYPE OF WEAKNESS
Network Connectivity	Patients cannot connect to network due to Network/ System unavailability.	No control over Network Links	Accidental Inaction / Intentional	Direct / Indirect	Reliability, Security
Network Connectivity	Doctor cannot access network through his PAD /PC	No control over Network Links (wireless/ cables)	Accidental Inaction / Intentional	Direct / Indirect	Reliability, Security
Network Connectivity	Pharmacy staff cannot give medicines	Network not available	Accidental Inaction / Intentional	Direct / Indirect	Reliability, Security
Network Connectivity	Insurance Staff cannot check/ validate Patient Insurance	Network not available	Accidental Inaction / Intentional	Direct / Indirect	Reliability, Security
Software Glitches	Patients, Doctors, Pharmacy Staff and Insurance staff cannot access system due to software glitch	Partial control over software	Accidental Inaction / Intentional	Indirect	Reliability, Integrity
User action	User authorization not checked in order to speed up system response times, security compromised	End user and system administrator lack sufficient training, limited understanding of system security features and procedure	Accidental Inaction / Intentional	Indirect	Security
User action	Patient records/ history hard copy thrown open trash bins	careless disposal of hard copy print out	Accidental Inaction / Intentional	Indirect	Security

(Continued)

FAILURE POINTS	FAILURE SCENARIO	VULNERABILITY	TYPE OF ACTION	METHOD OF EXPLOITATION	TYPE OF WEAKNESS
User action	Pharmacy hub backup and archives generated sporadically or not at all; backups and archives not verified and unreliable	unsecured backup, archives	Accidental Inaction / Intentional	Indirect	Security
Web server	Conflicts between COTS application and Pharmacy HUB cause unpredictable behavior, unauthorized user can access COTS applications	COTS components installed with back doors	Accidental Inaction / Intentional	Direct	Security, Reliability

VULNERABILITY	SOURCE OF VULNERABILITY	HAZARD CONSEQUENCES	SEVERITY
No control over Network Links	Failure to get connected from patient system to Pharmacy hub	Patient cannot register him.	Critical
No control over Network Links (wireless/cables)	Doctor cannot access pharmacy hub, unable to get/give patient information. Unable to write prescription	Critical /sensitive data cannot be transmitted/ received, patient cannot get medicines	Catastrophic
Network not available	Pharmacy staff can not access prescription and unable to give medicines to patient	Patient cannot get his medicines	Catastrophic
Network not available	Insurance staff cannot validate patient insurance	Patient needs to pay at Doctors Clinic or Pharmacy	Critical
Partial control over software	Software manufacturer do not follow proper software standards	whole or partial system will not work	Critical
			(*Continued*)

VULNERABILITY	SOURCE OF VULNERABILITY	HAZARD CONSEQUENCES	SEVERITY
End user and system administrator lack sufficient training, limited understanding of system security features and procedure	Failure to develop operational profile and scenario	System security features are routinely disable/ or by pass	Critical
careless disposal of hard copy print out	Physical security issue not considered	Critical /sensitive data can be stolen, copied, and distributed	Critical
unsecured backup, archives	Inadequate operation procedures physical security not considered	Physical sensitive data can be intentionally altered, deleted, copied, or stolen	Critical
COTS components installed with back doors	Inadequate analysis of COTS	COTS components perform incorrectly, and may breach security	Critical

Physical Structure

Virtual Private Network as a Risk   Virtual Private Network (VPN) is a remote access technology designed to create highly secure point-to-point "tunnels" through the private Internet. VPN will provide an access service to the Pharmacy's HUB Network with potentially faster connection speeds than PPP when used with digital subscriber line (DSL), Cable-modem, and LAN connection technologies. VPN uses advanced encryption and tunneling to permit remote users to establish secure, end-to-end, private network connections over third-party networks, such as the public Internet via cable modem or DSL providers. VPNs are logically partitioned, private networks constructed over a shared or public infrastructure that utilizes a range of technologies to ensure traffic separation and privacy of data, either self-implemented or provided by a service provider.

Corporations are deploying two types of VPNs:

- Site-to-site VPNs—linking corporate headquarters to remote offices over a shared, prioritized network and extending services to outside users such as customers and business partners.

- Access VPNs—connecting telecommuters and mobile users to the corporate network over dial, DSL, ISDN, wireless, and cable technologies.

The Major Strengths of Utilizing Internet-Based VPN Services

- Lower hardware and maintenance costs
- Lower network costs (compared to private/leased-line service or remote dial-in service using long-distance facilities)
- Network security (if using tunneling, encryption, authentication, and authorization in the VPN)

By opting for VPN service, each location can avoid paying the often exorbitant costs associated with alternatives such as high-speed private-line services and (long-distance) dial-up remote access to the central Hub site. VPN service will also provide customers with more flexibility in terms of adding new sites to the network, a sometimes expensive proposition when it comes to fully meshed and high-speed private-line networks. VPN service has also become increasingly attractive as a means of communicating between locations spread across the globe.

Also, market place will dictate and expect that Internet-based VPN service offerings will be enhanced to become full suites of services bundled together, including such offerings as IP fax services, IP e-mail services (including e-mail-to-e-mail and e-mail-to-fax capabilities), IP telephony services, IP multicasting and video services, and much more.

Assumptions   Doctor will have a PDA, a wireless service that is going to be connected to LAN services.

1. While the doctor is out of range either out of country or somehow out of area, the patient will contact the nurse and the nurse will have access to the doctor at anytime and anywhere.
2. The system doctor will have content delivery network (CDN) system.
3. The connection will be dedicated between the pharmacy and the doctor Internet only. In other words, this

connection will not be available to any other site. This connection will be absolutely for doctor–patient–pharmacy triangle.

4. The connection between the pharmacy to the health plan/ or the pharmacy manager will be through UPN.
5. The vulnerability of system boundaries in Internet connection is by VPN.
6. Doctor is responsible for his LAN (VPN) system.
7. Doctor's LAN connected to Internet will be used only for patient and pharmacy purposes.
8. Doctor is connected to the database. So doctor can see the history and situation of the patient time-to-time VPN via hubs.
9. HIPAA will interact with VPN hub and VPN hub will interact with the pharmacy hub.
10. When the medicine is ready, the system will make an auto phone call or send an auto e-mail to the patient informing that the medicine is ready.
11. The assumption for the patient is that the patient is assumed to have at least some kind of Internet communication.
12. The system of doctor and pharmacy is assumed to be compatible with any latest system the patient uses.
13. Patient is responsible for vulnerabilities of his/her connection system.
14. The patient's computer must be at least 128 bit encryption-supported browser.

Appendix B

Risk Factors Assumptions

(This document is prepared based on authors, class project in Master's degree in Computer Information Systems at University of Detroit Mercy.)

Investment Size   Overall risk factors are high. The investment in the software process improvement (SPI) personnel is comparatively higher than whole company in terms of the whole budget and individual hourly rate. It could be assumed that it looks like company resources are dependent on SPI. Also, the difference in payment between SPI and non-SPI employees may increase the risk. Average hourly payment is unnecessarily too high.

And the average hourly rate paid to SPI staff versus the average staff hourly rate is also high. Due to the wrong source line of code (SLOC) and its effect on other software assets the investment may not be justified. The ideal rate for reusing design code is 75% where as DMC project has possibility to reuse code at 60%. The defect removal efficiency percentage is 20%.

Cost in excess of budget is 150% while the ideal rate is only 5%, which is 97% more than it is supposed to be. That means from operational and cost point of view, this project is a failure. According to Robin Sharp, *The Six Rules of Return on Investment—From a Programmer's Perspective: A Developers' Guide to ROI*:

ROI = (Profits/Invested Capital) * 100

From that point of view, this project would not be able to produce sufficient ROI.

Management Process Maturity Also from the development statistic point of view, this project is an obvious failure. The total cost exceeded the budget by 180%, while it was supposed to be 5%. Project modules are not designed or well planned. Budget commitments could not be met if large expenditures were made unnecessarily.

The module in each project element is not well planned even though investment is higher. Each project schedule is not well defined so there are a lot of inconsistencies. The project schedule is especially inconsistent regarding milestone and deadline commitments.

No form of configuration management is employed. Change management is undisciplined.

There is no organizational standard operating procedure for conducting the business. Specifications of requirements prior to acquisition are mandated; however, updates to these are not controlled.

There has been a tendency to deal with the usual set of contractors. As such, the selection process has gotten a "clubby" atmosphere.

Degree of Technical Risk   The technology base and/or project base primarily geared 42% toward experimental and only 12% toward established technologies.

Technically, the system's architecture and software base are more complex than routine. The disciplined management mechanisms for integrating new technology are more ad hoc than disciplined. Mechanism for integrating new technology and processes into the technology base is basically ad hoc, and mechanisms for control of change within the technology base are 10% disciplined and 40% ad hoc.

There is not enough involvement between DMC and contractors during the development process, which has led to some very expensive disappointments showing up at the acceptance tests.

The architecture and technology complex rates are high. The coherence in technology and architectural design is totally unplanned and ambiguous.

Return Factors

- The outcome benefits of SPI are mostly negative. The investment made in SPI to meet identifiable internal and or external customer needs is mostly unrelated.
- The problems reported by the internal and external customers are not with quality or timelines.
- Mostly, the cost benefit analysis was not performed before committing to each project.
- Technical needs or considerations, the primary driver, are mostly not commitment decisions. Project decisions are rarely reviewed and authorized by the manager above the technical level.
- The rate of organizations primarily obtaining its software from acquisition is 35%. The cost and benefit results are not reliable or technically sound at all.

Conclusion   If we estimate the percentage of investment in SPI versus the total organizational budget, we see the SPI budget is too high and nonprofitable. Hourly rates paid to the SPI staff versus the average overall hourly rate of pay are higher. Percentage of source code line effected by SPI project in comparison with overall SLOC is high.

This project should not be operated. The assessment of risk factors provides information that from the return on investment point of view cost for this project is unmanageable. The overall investment size is higher than the average. In contrast, the maturity of management process is lower than its average. The degree of technical risk is 30% higher.

Moreover, life cycle for management systems is not set. All systems are fully supported until they become too costly to maintain. When that happens they are dropped. There is no set plan or standard operation procedure (SOP) for this.

The administrative operational statistics are very disappointing. Project failure rate and cost rate were too high to recover. Only 20% of the design code could be reused, while the ideal rate of reusing the design code is 75%.

In operation, the good news is that all software utilized by the administration is acquired, but the biggest problem is that there is no organizationally SOP for conducting the business.

SECTION IV
SOFTWARE
QUALITY
EXPECTATION

9

INFORMATION SECURITY

Introduction

Part 1 discusses the basic definition and importance of information security. Part 2 discusses strategy, methodology, and security standards, which provides the strategy and methodology, such as ISO 15408, control objectives for information and (related) technology (COBIT), operationally critical threat, asset and vulnerability evaluation (OCTAVE). In Part 3, a sample security document is provided.

Part 1: Definition and Importance

1. What is information security?
2. From what threats does information need to be secured?
3. What kind of information needs to be secured?

What Is Information Security?

Information security, or **InfoSec,** is a procedure to help protect information from unauthorized access, use, disclosure, disruption, modification, perusal, inspection, recording, or destruction. It is a general term that can be used regardless of the form the data may take.*

According to a definition by Techopedia.com, "Information security (IS) is designed to protect the confidentiality, integrity, and availability of computer system data from those with malicious intentions, which may also include possession (or control), authenticity, and utility."†

---

* http://en.wikipedia.org/wiki/Information_security.
† http://www.techopedia.com/definition/10282/information-security-is.

The definition of IS given by Professor Dan Shoemaker,* also defined by ISO 17799,† is the preservation of the following as shown in Figure 9.1:

Confidentiality: ensuring that information is available only to those authorized

Integrity: ensuring the accuracy and completeness of information and processing methods

Availability: ensuring that the authorized users can access the information when required

Another definition given by Professor Shoemaker is "The process of protecting data from accidental or intentional misuse by persons inside or outside the organization. That Information can be electronic, on paper, film, or spoken. Regardless of the form it takes it should be adequately protected."

IS relates to the protection of valuable assets against loss, misuse, disclosure, or damage. The information must be protected against harm from threats, leading to different types of vulnerabilities such as loss, inaccessibility, alteration, or wrongful disclosure.

Threats include errors and omissions, fraud, accidents, and intentional damage. Protection includes safeguards such as physical security measures, background checks, user identifiers, passwords, smart

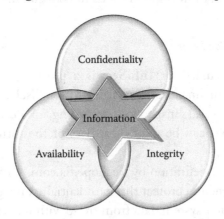

Figure 9.1   The definition of information security defined by ISO 17799.

---

* Professor Dan Shoemaker, at University of Detroit Mercy, Information Security Class lecture.
† ISO-17799.

cards, biometrics, and firewalls. These safeguards should address both threats and vulnerabilities in a balanced manner.

Security must be considered an integral part of the systems development life cycle process and explicitly addressed during each phase of the process. To be effective, the security must be dealt with in a proactive and timely manner.*

Difference between Privacy and Security

- Without security, there can be no privacy. In other words, security rules should be set first before privacy rules.
- Exception: HIPAA privacy rules published before security rules.
- Privacy is how data are used by one person who was given the information by another person.
- Security is about whether data are stolen or intercepted by an unknown party.

Key Points on Information Security

IS requires a balance. For a business to succeed, you need to let employees, customers, and business partners access data electronically, often through the Internet, which creates risks. Information security is about balancing those risks with the rewards of doing business electronically. Since risks and vulnerabilities are constantly changing, security is a never-ending process.

Computer viruses and worms can cause expensive downtime, lost sales, and damaged data and computers.

Severe financial losses can occur indirectly if customers and shareholders lose confidence in how the business is run.

From What Threats Does Information Need to Be Secured?

Cybercrime Cybercrime is basically computer-related crimes, which includes any illegal behavior committed by means of, or in relation to, a computer system or network, including such crimes as illegal

---

* IT Governance Institute. *Information Security Governance: Guidance for Boards of Directors and Executive Management*, p. 8.

possession and offering or distributing information by means of a computer system or network.[*]

The term "cybercrime" can include traditional computer crimes, as well as network crimes. As these crimes differ in many ways, there is no single criterion that could include all acts mentioned in the different regional and international legal approaches to address the issue.[†]

Types of Cybercrime   There are different types of computer crimes. Since our lives have become more dependent on computer systems every day, the type and nature of cybercrime is also becoming more complicated. However, there are some common types of cybercrime such as the following:

Hacking   Hacking or unlawful access to a computer system is one of the oldest computer-related crimes, which includes breaking the password of password-protected websites on a computer system.[‡]

Illegal Data Spying   When the computer system is connected to the network, criminals can possibly get access to the computer information via the network from anywhere in the world and where the network is connected.

Computer Virus   Cyber criminals can create a virus that basically deletes, suppresses, or alters computer data. The number of computer viruses has risen significantly.

And as I have mentioned, not only is the quantity of virus attacks increasing but also the techniques and functions of viruses have been changing and becoming more complicated.

In early years, computer-related viruses were circulated through storage devices such as floppy disks; however, nowadays, most viruses are spread via the Internet as attachments or even links either to e-mails or to files that users download.

---

[*] Marco Gercke. Understanding cybercrime: Phenomena, challenges and legal response, September 2012, ITU, p. 11.
[†] Ibid, p. 12.
[‡] Ibid, p. 17.

These new methods of virus circulation have vastly increased the rate of virus infection and the number of infected computer systems.

The computer worm SQL Slammer was estimated to have infected 90% of vulnerable computer systems within the first 10 minutes of its distribution. The financial damage caused by virus attacks in 2000 alone was estimated to be USD 17 billion. In 2003, it was still more than USD 12 billion.*

Scam Sometimes, you may receive a fake e-mail from a friend who might live next to you or is even sitting next to you. The e-mail explains that he was traveling to Spain, and at the airport, his wallet, passport, and everything was stolen and he needs help and wants you to send him some money. Well, obviously that is a fraud.

Mostly, scams were performed by a dishonest individual, group, or company in an attempt to obtain money or something else of value. Scams also happen in "con games", where an individual would misrepresent themself as someone with skill or authority, that is, a doctor, lawyer, investor; or in new forms of scams such as lottery scams, e-mail deceit, phishing, or requests for help.

Money Laundering A money launderer is one who wants to hide his real identity to avoid tracing and possesses a false identity.

In U.S. law, financial institutions are instructed to keep a record of reports for large currency transactions and also verify the individual's identity.

Phishing Phishing is an attempt to acquire the user's personal information such as user names, passwords, and/or credit card details by pretending to be a trustworthy entity in an electronic communication. In October 2013, e-mails purporting to be from American Express were sent to an unknown number of recipients.[†]

---

* Ibid, p. 20.
† Andrew Paul. "Phishing Emails: The Unacceptable Failures of American Express." E-mail Answers. Retrieved 9 October 2013.

Phishing Types   There are several types of phishing, and phishing is becoming more sophisticated as techology complexity increases. Following is a list of a few types of phishing.

Spear Phishing   Spear phishing is an e-mail fraud attempt that targets a specific organization, seeking unauthorized access to confidential data. Spear phishing attempts are not typically initiated by "random hackers" but are more likely to be conducted by perpetrators out for financial gain, trade secrets, or military information.

Clone Phishing   Clone phishing is a clone or copy of a legitimate, previously delivered e-mail containing an attachment or link and has had its content and recipient address taken and used to create an almost identical or cloned e-mail. The attachment or link within the e-mail is replaced with a malicious version and then sent from an e-mail address spoofed to appear to come from the original sender.

Whaling   The content of the whaling type of phishing usually is designed to target an upper manager and the person's role in the company. The content of a whaling attack e-mail is usually written as a legal subpoena, customer complaint, or executive issue. Whaling scam e-mails are designed to masquerade as a critical business e-mail, sent from a legitimate business authority, usually involving some kind of falsified company-wide concern. Whaling criminals also have fake official-looking FBI subpoena e-mails and claim that the manager needs to click a link and install a special software to view the subpoena.

Link Manipulation   Most methods of phishing use some form of technical fraud designed to make a link in an e-mail (and the spoofed website it leads to) appear to belong to the spoofed organization. Misspelled URLs or the use of subdomains are the common tricks used by phishers. In the following example URL, http://www.AmericanBank.example.com/, it appears as though the URL will take you to the example section of your bank website; actually, this URL points to the "your bank" (i.e., phishing) section of the example website. Another common trick is to make the displayed text for a link (the text between the <A> tags) suggest a reliable destination, when the link actually goes to the phisher's site.

Once a victim visits the phishing website, the deception is not over. Some phishing scams use JavaScript commands in order to alter the address bar. This is done either by placing a picture of a legitimate URL over the address bar or by closing the original bar and opening up a new one with the legitimate URL.

Not all phishing attacks require a fake website. Messages that claimed to be from a bank told users to dial a phone number regarding problems with their bank accounts. Once the phone number (owned by the phisher, and provided by a voice over IP service) was dialed, prompts told users to enter their account numbers and PINs. Vishing (voice phishing) sometimes uses fake caller-ID data to give the appearance that calls come from a trusted organization.

What Kind of Information Needs to Be Secured

Some Examples of Recent Phishing These are some examples of phishing e-mails seen on campus. Do NOT assume a suspect e-mail is safe, just because it is not listed here. There are many variants of each, and new ones are being sent out every day.

Your E-mail Account
April 30, 2015
ABC E-mail Account
Security info replacement
Someone started a process to replace all of the security info for your e-mail account.
If this was you, you can safely ignore this e-mail. Your security info will be replaced with 1232456 within 3 business days.
If this was not you, someone else might be trying to take over your e-mail account. Click here to fill in details and verify your current information in our servers and we will help you protect this account.
Thanks,
Mr. A
For: ABC E-mail Team
Phone: 650-723-2300
E-mail: alert@abc.com

"Subject: update" (to CS students, at least)

From: Help Desk <online2793774@telkomsa.net>

Date: June 20, 2014 at 7:57:55 AM PDT

To: info@xyzcompany.com

Subject: update

It had been detected that your xyz company e-mail account. Mail delivery system had been affected with virus. Your e-mail account had been sending virus included with your mail to recipient's account and as such a threat to our database. You will need to update the settings on your zyz.com e-mail account by clicking on this link: http://forms.logiforms.com/formdata/user_forms/66949_9366478/321793

From

CS. zyz

ITS Helpdesk

Your Apple ID was used to sign in to iCloud on an iPhone 4

February 8, 2014

Dear customer,

Your Apple ID was used to sign in to iCloud on an iPhone 4.

Time: February 06, 2014

Operating System: iOS 6.0.1

If you recently signed in to this device, you can disregard this e-mail. If you have not recently signed in to an iPhone with your Apple ID and believe someone may have accessed your account, please click here to confirm your details and change your password.

Apple Support

My Apple ID | Support | Privacy Policy

Copyright © 2014 iTunes S.à r.l. 31-33, rue Sainte Zithe, L-2763 Luxembourg. All rights reserved.

Your e-mail access has been suspended for your security.

To regain your access click here.

Voice Message from Unknown Caller

This e-mail appeared to be a message from the voicemail system with a voice message attached as a file. The message appeared to come from Unity Messaging System.

Bank Phishing Example Phishing and spoofing e-mails look like official Bank of America e-mails and try to trick you into visiting a fake website and providing your personal account information. These e-mails may also ask you to call a phone number and provide account information. See an example of a fraudulent e-mail.

Ways to identify phishing and spoofing e-mails include the following:

1. **Links that appear to be bank links but are not**
   If you place your cursor over a link in a suspicious e-mail, your e-mail program most likely shows you the destination URL. Do not click the link, but look closely at the URL: A URL that is formatted bankname.xyzwebsite.com is taking you to a location on fakewebsite.com. "bankofamerica" is part of the URL but does not guarantee that the site is an official Bank of America site.

2. **Requests for personal information**
   Usually this kind of phishing e-mail will ask you for your personal information such as your Social Security number (SSN), ATM or PIN, in fact, no authentic bank should ask you for such sensitive personal information.

3. **Urgent appeals**
   This kind of phishing e-mail claims your account may be closed if you fail to confirm, verify, or authenticate your personal information via e-mail within a certain time.

   Offers that sound too good to be true.
   Obvious typos and other errors.

   These are often the mark of fraudulent e-mails and websites. Be on the lookout for typos or grammatical errors, awkward writing, and poor visual design.

Identity Theft

The definition of identity theft varies in different countries and different fields.

Generally speaking, the definition of identity theft falls into two major distinctive categories:

"Identity theft" is defined by the Oxford English Dictionary as comprising the dishonest acquisition of personal information in order to perpetrate fraud, typically by obtaining credit, loans, and so on, in someone else's name.*

Another definition was given by Ian Walden, when people's identities are unlawfully acquired by others.[†]

The most common and harmful type of financial loss offense in relation to identity theft is definitely fraud. According to a US Federal Trade Commission (FTC) Survey Report.[‡]

An identity theft may involve fraudulent uses in three major ways: (a) appropriation of victim's credit card, (b) acquisition of new credit and bank account in victim's name, and (c) accumulation of overdraft fees or applications for other loans with personal details.[§]

By having this information, a thief can even change the billing address for the account so that the unauthorized purchases or loans remain uncovered.[¶]

Information That Is Considered Identity

Social Security Numbers   SSN is very personal information for an individual. This is the unique ID for a person in the United States.

Date of Birth   Date of birth (DOB), in conjunction with other pieces of information, can be used in many ways to compromise a person's identity.

Current and Previous Addresses and Phone Numbers   Both can be used in cybercrime and identity theft to enable an offender to assume the identity of the victim or to obtain more information thereabout.

---

* Oxford English Dictionary, http://dictionary.oed.com. Accessed 1 August 2008.
† Ian Walden. *Computer Crime and Digital Investigations*, Oxford University Press, Oxford, 2007, p. 115.
‡ http://www.ftc.gov/os/2007/11/ SynovateFinalReportIDTheft2006.pdf.
§ https://www.ftc.gov/sites/default/files/documents/public_statements/prepared-statement-federal-trade-commission-protecting-consumer-privacy-and-combating-identity-theft/p065404idtheft.pdf.
¶ An Analysis and Comparison of Government Legislative Strategies for Preventing Identity Theft.

Current and Previous Employment Information
Financial Account Information This may include checking and saving accounts, credit cards, debit cards, and financial planning information. Such information is a rich source for an identity thief to commit financial cybercrimes.

Mother's Maiden Name
Other Personal Information It includes passwords, passcodes, and e-mail addresses as well as photos.

Password for Nonfinancial Accounts

Password for Financial Accounts.

Criminal Activities That Lead to Cybercrime

There are certain activities that may not have anything to do with cyber-crime or cybersecurity. However, these could cause or lead to cybercrime.

1. Information from stolen wallets, credit cards, and checkbooks
2. Information gathered through family members or friends
3. Garbage diving
4. Information unlawfully obtained from legal resources

Phishing attacks harness the technology of the Internet and software to create fraudulent e-mails to lead consumers to counterfeit websites designed to trick recipients into divulging financial data such as account usernames and passwords. In other words, phishing is an online activity that combines social engineering strategies and technical measures.

Spyware Spyware can be loosely defined as "deceptive" practices of the unauthorized installation of programs that monitor a consumer's activities without their consent. The installed spyware can then be used to send the user unwelcome pop-up advertisements, take control of the user's web browser, monitor the user's Internet surfing habits, record the user's keystrokes, and even steal personal confidential information stored in the computer.

---

* *Handbook on Identity-Related Crime*, United Nations, New York, 2011 © United Nations, April 2011. All rights reserved, p. 12.

Objective of Information Security

According to information security guidance, IT Governance Institute, "the goal of Information Security is the knowledge of understanding 'to protect'."

While the goal of information security is generally understood, it is considerably more difficult to state which assets need how much protection against what.

Organizations typically have little knowledge of what information exists within the enterprise. There is generally no process to purge useless, outdated, or potentially dangerous information, data or unused applications. It is extremely rare to find a comprehensive catalogue or index of information or a process to define what is important and what is not, or even who "owns" it.*

The objective of information security is to develop, implement, and to manage an information security program that achieves the following five basic outcomes identified in *information security governance:*

1. Strategic alignment of information security with business strategy to support organizational objectives
2. Effective risk management by executing appropriate measures to manage and mitigate risks and reduce potential impacts on information resources to an acceptable level
3. Value delivery by optimizing information security investments in support of organizational objectives
4. Resource management by utilizing information security knowledge and infrastructure efficiently and effectively
5. Performance measurement by measuring, monitoring, and reporting information security governance metrics to ensure the achievement of organizational objectives[†]

Why Is Security Important?

Technology and software are among the most widely used products in human history. Certainly, it is a great success; however, these have one of the highest failure rates of any product in human history.

---

* W. Krag Brotby (Senior Security Consultant). *Information Security Governance: Guidance for Information Security Managers*, IT Governance Institute, CISM, USA, p. 29.
[†] Ibid, p. 8.

In the United States, more than USD 250 billion is spent each year on IT application development of approximately 175,000 projects. The average cost of a development project for a large company is USD 2,322,000.

Within that, the United States will be the biggest spending country by a long shot, and—as a sign of the times—apps will be the single-biggest spending category of all.*

One example, given by Standish Group report, is the City of Denver that failed to produce reliable software to handle baggage at the new Denver airport costing the city $1.1 million per day.†

Over 100 million people in the United Sates use computers every day either for business or for fun and it is increasing every day. Over 200 million people use devices that contain embedded software such as smart phones, home appliances, and entertainment devices.

In the United States, about 15 million companies use computers and software for their business purposes.

Based on a report published in the United States, about 77,186 software companies and another 10,000 U.S. companies create devices with embedded software. A large number of embedded software and the device companies themselves have moved to China, Taiwan, Japan, India, and other countries.‡

There are risk areas that could have a significant impact on critical business operations. Because new technology provides the potential for drastically enhanced business performance, improved and demonstrated information security can add real value to the organization by contributing to interaction with trading partners, closer customer relationships, improved competitive advantage, and protected reputation. It can also enable new and easier ways to process electronic transactions and generate trust.

---

* See, http://techcrunch.com/2013/07/15/forrester-2-1-trillion-will-go-into-it-spend-in-2013-apps-and-the-u-s-lead-the-charge/.
† *The Standish Group Report CHAOS*, © The Standish Group 1995. Reprinted here for sole academic purposes.
‡ Capers Jone and Olivier Bonsignour. *The Economics of Software Quality*, Addison-Wesley, 2011, p. 34.

What Is the Benefit of Information Security?

Without security, software cannot be reliable and cannot be a quality product. You cannot depend on software if it is not secure. Unsecured information could be very harmful and dangerous. When software is secured, it has less risk, it is more reliable, and the quality of the product goes up, which brings better return on investment (ROI).

A secure and high quality product also

- Provides the potential for an increased profitability
- Builds up the brand and makes the product more profitable

Secured and higher quality leads to

- Increased production
- Lower warranty costs
- Lower marketing costs
- Fewer surprises
- Positive customer experiences that delight the consumer and lead to additional sales

Part 2: Methodology

The Strategy

A good "information security strategy" should address and mitigate risks while complying with the legal, contractual, and statutory requirements of the business; provide demonstrable support for the business objectives of the organization; and maximize value to the stakeholders.

Ultimately, the goal of information security is business process assurance, regardless of the business. While the business of a government agency may not result directly in profits, it is, nevertheless, in the business of providing cost-effective services to its constituency and must protect the assets for which it has custodial care. Whatever the business, its primary operational goal is to maximize the success of business processes and minimize impediments to those processes.

Security Standards

ISO 15408   ISO 15408, commonly known as common criteria, provides the framework for testing the effectiveness of most security systems. However, it is not intended to measure the effectiveness of an organization's security program.

Control objectives for information and (related) technology (COBIT). It is developed for IT auditors and made available through the Information Systems Audit and Control Association (ISACA).

ISO 17799/BS7799 ISO 17799 Information Technology—Code of Practice for Information Security Management began in the United Kingdom as BS 7799 in 1995 as a comprehensive set of controls comprising best practices in information security. It was revised in May 1999 and fast tracked as in international standard in December 2000. Its chief strength is its flexibility.

Written in an open framework, the standard is a compilation of "best practices" that can be applied by any organization regardless of its size or type of industry.

ISO 17799 is technically a standard, and it reads more like a set of recommendations. It outlines security measures that organizations should have but not specifically how to implement them. It simply sets the expectations.

Note: A comprehensive standard is provided at the end this chapter, which is prepared primarily based on ISO 17799 Standard.

COBIT COBIT provides a framework for assessing a program, developing a performance baseline, and measuring performance over time.

OCTAVE OCTAVE is by Carnegie Mellon's CERT Coordination Center (wwww.cert.org/octave). It provides measures based on accepted best practices for evaluating security programs.

ISO 15408 vs. ISO 17799 ISO 17799 consists of 10 security controls, which are used as the basis for the security risk assessment.* There are 10 areas covered by the standard as follows:

Security Policy Security policy control addresses management support, commitment, and direction in accomplishing information security goals, including the following:

Information Security Policy Document—A set of implementation independent, conceptual information security policy statements governing the security goals of the organization. This document, along with a hierarchy of standards, guidelines, and procedures, helps to implement and enforce the policy statements.

---

* References: Info Security Mgt ISO 17799.

Organizational Security   Organizational security control addresses the need for a management framework that creates, sustains, and manages the security infrastructure, including the following:

Management information security forum—provides a multidisciplinary committee chartered to discuss and disseminate information security issues throughout the organization

Information system security officer (ISSO)—acts as a central point of contact for information security issues, direction, and decisions

Information security responsibilities—individual information security responsibilities are unambiguously allocated and detailed within job descriptions

Authorization processes—ensures that security considerations are evaluated and approvals obtained for new and modified information processing systems

Specialist information—maintains relationships with independent specialists to allow access to expertise not available within the organization

Organizational cooperation—maintains relationships with both information-sharing partners and local law enforcement authorities

Independent review—mechanisms to allow independent review of security effectiveness

Third-party access—mechanisms to govern third-party interaction within the organization based on business requirements

Outsourcing—organizational outsourcing arrangements should have clear contractual security requirements

Asset Classification and Control   Asset classification and control addresses the ability of the security infrastructure to protect organizational assets, including the following:

Accountability and inventory—mechanisms to maintain an accurate inventory of assets, and establish ownership and stewardship of all assets

Classification—mechanisms to classify assets based on business impact

Labeling—labeling standards unambiguously brand assets to their classification

Handling—handling standards, including introduction, transfer, removal, and disposal of all assets that are based on asset classification

Personnel Security Personnel security control addresses an organization's ability to mitigate risk inherent in human interactions, including the following:

Personnel screening—policies within local legal and cultural frameworks ascertain the qualification and suitability of all personnel with access to organizational assets. This framework may be based on job descriptions and/or asset classification.

Security responsibilities—personnel should be clearly informed of their information security responsibilities, including codes of conduct and nondisclosure agreements.

Terms and conditions of employment—personnel should be clearly informed of their information security responsibilities as a condition of employment.

Training—a mandatory information security awareness training program is conducted for all employees, including new hires and established employees.

Recourse—a formal process to deal with violation of information security policies.

Physical and Environmental Security Physical and environmental security control addresses risk inherent to organizational premises, including the following:

Location—organizational premises should be analyzed for environmental hazards.

Physical security perimeter—the premises security perimeter should be clearly defined and physically sound. A given premises may have multiple zones based on classification level or other organizational requirements.

Access control—breaches in the physical security perimeter should have appropriate entry/exit controls commensurate with their classification level.

Equipment—equipment should be sited within the premises to ensure physical and environmental integrity and availability.

Asset transfer—mechanisms to track entry and exit of assets through the security perimeter.

General—policies and standards, such as utilization of shredding equipment, secure storage, and "clean desk" principles, should exist to govern operational security within the workspace.

Communications and Operations Management Communication and operations management control addresses an organization's ability to ensure correct and secure operation of its assets, including the following:

Operational procedures—comprehensive set of procedures in support of organizational standards and policies

Change control—process to manage change and configuration control, including change management of the information security management system

Incident management—mechanism to ensure timely and effective response to any security incidents

Segregation of duties—segregation and rotation of duties minimize the potential for collusion and uncontrolled exposure

Capacity planning—mechanism to monitor and project organizational capacity to ensure uninterrupted availability

System acceptance—methodology to evaluate system changes to ensure continued confidentiality, integrity, and availability

Malicious code—controls to mitigate risk from introduction of malicious code

Housekeeping—policies, standards, guidelines, and procedures to address routine housekeeping activities such as backup schedules and logging

Network management—controls to govern the secure operation of the networking infrastructure

Media handling—controls to govern secure handling and disposal of information storage media and documentation

Information exchange—controls to govern information exchange, including end-user agreements, user agreements, and information transport mechanisms

Access Control   Access control addresses an organization's ability to control access to assets based on business and security requirements, including the following:

Business requirements—policy controlling access to organizational assets based on business requirements and "need to know."

User management—mechanisms to
  * Register and deregister users
  * Control and review access and privileges
  * Manage passwords

User responsibilities—informing users of their access control responsibilities, including password stewardship and unattended equipment.

Network access control—policy on usage of network services, including mechanisms (when appropriate) to
  * Authenticate nodes
  * Authenticate external users
  * Define routing
  * Control network device security

System Development and Maintenance

System development and maintenance control addresses an organization's ability to ensure that appropriate information system security controls are both incorporated and maintained, including the following:

System security requirements—incorporates information security considerations in the specifications of any system development or procurement

Application security requirements—incorporates information security considerations in the specification of any application development or procurement

Cryptography—policies, standards, and procedures governing the usage and maintenance of cryptographic controls

System Integrity—mechanisms to control access to, and verify integrity of, operational software and data, including a process to track, evaluate, and incorporate asset upgrades and patches

Development security—integrates change control and technical reviews into development process

Business Continuity Management

Business continuity management control addresses an organization's ability to counteract interruptions to normal operations, including the following:

Business continuity planning—business continuity strategy based on a business impact analysis

Business continuity testing—testing and documentation of business continuity strategy

Business continuity maintenance—identifies ownership of business continuity strategy as well as ongoing reassessment and maintenance

Compliance

Compliance control addresses an organization's ability to remain in compliance with regulatory, statutory, contractual, and security requirements, including the following:

Legal requirements—awareness of
- Relevant legislation
- Intellectual property rights
- Safeguarding of organizational records
- Data privacy
- Prevention of misuse
- Regulation of cryptography
- Collection of evidence

Technical requirements—mechanism to verify execution of security policies and implementations

System audits—auditing controls to maximize effectiveness, minimize disruption, and protect audit tools

Precautionary Guidelines

People are encouraged to request and use password-protected credit cards, bank accounts, and phone accounts. They should avoid using easily available information such as their mother's maiden name, their birth date, the last four digits of their SSN, their phone number, or a series of consecutive numbers.

Refrain from Giving Out Personal Information

People must not give out their personal information on the phone, through e-mails, or over the Internet unless they have initiated the communication or are sure they know who they are dealing with. Identity thieves are cunning and pose as representatives of banks, Internet service providers (ISPs), and even government agencies to get people to reveal their SSN, mother's maiden name, account numbers, and other identifying information. Before consumers share any personal information, they must confirm that they are dealing with a legitimate organization.

Storing Financial Records

Computer users should be careful when storing their financial records, birth date, and bank account numbers on their computer and should ensure that virus protection software is updated regularly and patches for the operating system and other software programs should be installed to protect against intrusions and infections that can lead to the compromise of their computer files or passwords. Ideally, virus protection software should be set to automatically update each week.

Use Firewall Programs

People are recommended to use firewall programs, especially if they use a high-speed Internet connection such as cable, or DSL that leaves their computer connected to the Internet 24 hours a day. The firewall program will allow them to stop uninvited and unauthorized access to their computer.

Do Not Open Files Sent from an Unknown Source   It is advisable not to open files sent from an unknown source or stranger, click on hyperlinks, or download programs from untrustworthy sources. People should be careful about using file-sharing programs. Opening a file could expose their system to a computer virus or a program known as "spyware," which could capture their passwords or any other information as they type it.

Use a Secure Browser   Consumers and businesses are encouraged to use a secure browser and encryption software when entering into online transactions or sending their personal information to trusted sites.

Delete All Stored Personal Information

Before disposing of a computer, people must delete all stored personal information and format their hard drive. Nevertheless, deleting files or reformatting the hard drive may not be enough because the files could still be retrieved from the computer's hard drive. Thus, a "wipe" utility program could be used to overwrite the entire hard drive.

Do Not Disclose Passwords to Anyone   Passwords of any accounts should not be disclosed to anyone as accounts can be hijacked, and people can find unexpected charges on their bills and statements.

Beware of Phishing, Spoofing, and Spam Attempts

Finally, **beware of phishing, spoofing, and spam attempts** by being diligent, prudent, and skeptical about suspicious communications.

COBIT Security Baseline

COBIT security baseline, an information security survival kit, provides guidelines on information security, current risk, WHY IS INFORMATION SECURITY IMPORTANT? 39 STEPS TOWARD SECURITY.

It also provides Information Security Survival Kit guidelines for home users, professional users, managers, executives, senior executives and board of directors. However, due to space constraints, we are not participating in that discussion at this stage.

Business Model Information Security

ISACA advocates and has developed an information security business model to address the complexity of security. It is a business-orientated model that promotes a balance between protection and business.

BMIS was developed to address the complexity of security as well. It is a business-orientated model that promotes a balance between protection and business.*

---

* *The Business Model for Information Security*, A holistic and business-oriented approach to managing information security, and common language for information security and business management to talk about information protection, ISACA Also see, *The Business Model for Information Security*, 2010, ISACA.

The model developed by ISACA, as shown in Figure 9.2, has emphasizes on organization, people, technology and process; however, ISACA also recognizes that there are other factors involved in business model information security such as culture and human factors.

The key elements as ISACA advocates are

- Organization design and strategy
- People
- Process
- Technology

The other factors are

- Culture
- Architecture
- Governing
- Emergence
- Enabling and support
- Human factors

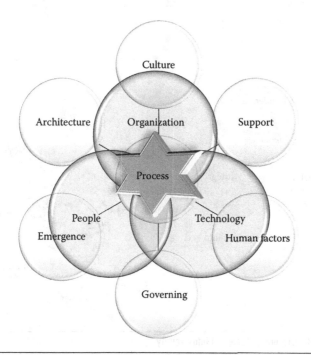

Figure 9.2   The business model for information security (BMIS) designed by ISACA.

BMIS can be viewed as a three-dimensional model best visualized as a pyramid. All aspects of the model interact with each other. If any one part of the model is changed, not addressed, or managed inappropriately, it will distort the balance of the model.

The Broader Scope of InfoSec

If we look at the broader scope of information security from different standards such as ISO 17799 and others, we see it's integrated to each other as shown in Figure 9.3.

Operational Procedure for Doctor

1. Doctor will use a login ID and password in order to access the pharmacy hub.
2. PDA cannot communicate with the system if the distance is more than 200 feet.
3. All logs of successful and unsuccessful logins are kept for 5 years.

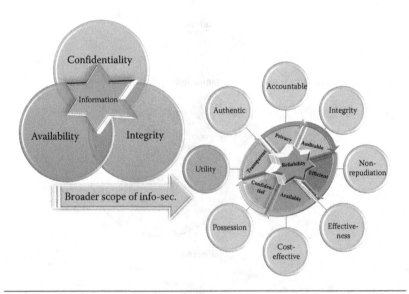

Figure 9.3   The broader scope of info-security.

4. After 20 minutes of inactivity, the doctor will automatically be logged out from the system.
5. Doctor can check patient's previous history at the pharmacy hub.
6. Doctor will write prescription on his/her PDA, which is then sent electronically to the pharmacy hub.
7. Once the prescription is sent to the pharmacy hub, the doctor can change the prescription, using his login and password, but a previous copy of the prescription will also be saved as backup.
8. In case of any error or trouble with connectivity or software, the doctor will call the technical help line at the pharmacy hub.
9. Uninterrupted power supply will be provided for power failure, which will give 60 minutes to complete the record and shut down system properly.

Operational Procedure for Pharmacy

1. Login ID and password will be assigned to the pharmacy staff in order to access the pharmacy hub.
2. After 20 minutes of inactivity, the pharmacy staff will be automatically logged out from the system.
3. Workstation will be provided to the pharmacy so that the staff can access the pharmacy hub.
4. Pharmacy staff can only view the patient's prescription and he/she does not have any privilege to modify it, but can add notes for the doctor.
5. Pharmacy staff can also view information from insurance XYZ about the patient's coverage on medicines.
6. Once pharmacy staff gave medicine to the patient, they will update the records, which they can change only if the patient returns the medicine.
7. All logs of successful and unsuccessful logins are kept for 5 years.
8. In case of any error or trouble with connectivity or software, the pharmacy staff will call the technical help line at the pharmacy hub.

9. Uninterrupted power supply will be provided, in case of power failure, the system will get power supply for 60 minutes to complete the record and shut down the system properly.

Common Information Security Criteria

If we observe most distinguished international standards on information security, we find some common information security criteria, especially among IEEE 9126, COBIT, and CMMI (Table 9.1)

TABLE 9.1   Common Information Security Criteria Among IEEE 9126, COBIT, and CMMI

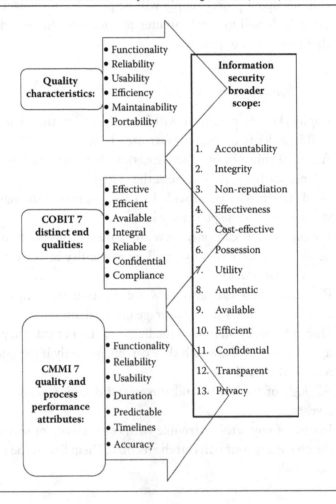

Operational Procedure for Patient

1. Login ID and password will be generated by the system for each patient, when the patient visits the doctor or registers online for the first time.
2. All logs of successful and unsuccessful logins are kept for 5 years.
3. After 20 minutes of inactivity, the patient will be automatically logged out from the system.
4. Patient can update his or her information any time through the Web.
5. Patient can view prescription and medicines but cannot modify it.
6. In case of any error or trouble with connectivity or software, the patient will call the technical help line at the pharmacy hub.

Operation Procedure for Pharmacy Hub

1. Login ID and password will be assigned to pharmacy hub operators.
2. All logs of successful and unsuccessful logins are kept for 5 years.
3. After 20 minutes of inactivity, the pharmacy hub operators will be automatically logged out from the system.
4. Backup of all systems will be done periodically.
5. Pharmacy hub operators do not have any type of access to the prescription.
6. Consultants are responsible for all the software- and networks-related problems at the pharmacy hub.
7. Backup of all systems and databases will be taken at separate location.
8. Uninterrupted power supply will be provided for power failures, which will provide power for 6 hours. If the power was not restored during this time, system will be switched to a secondary location.

Operational Change Control

All the changes at information processing facilities, such as doctor's office, pharmacy hub, and pharmacy should be controlled as these are the common causes of system and security failure. Whenever operational procedures are changed, an audit log will be maintained as it can impact on applications.

1. All the changes in operational procedure at the doctor's office, pharmacy hub, and pharmacy will be authorized by the management.
2. All the changes in the operational procedure at the doctor's office, pharmacy hub, and pharmacy will be recorded in an audit log.
3. Assessment of the potential impact of change should be done.
4. Change control forms must be filled electronically and sent to the pharmacy hub.
5. Pharmacy hub operators should send e-mail to all relevant persons.
6. In case of unsuccessful change, unsuccessful change form should be submitted electronically at the pharmacy hub, and pharmacy operators will send e-mail to all relevant persons.

Incident Management Procedure

Incident management procedure should be distributed to all persons to ensure quick, effective, and orderly response to security incidents.

1. All system failure and loss of service should be immediately reported to incident management team at the pharmacy hub.
2. By evaluating the type and threat of incident, the incident management team will report to management and if required to the government, that is, distributed denial of services by following *Cyber Threat Response and Guidelines*.
3. Incident management team will inform all relevant contractors or persons in order to put system back, recover data, or control security breach.
4. Incident management team will communicate with all relevant persons who were affected by the recovery from the incident.
5. Incident management team will analyze and identify the cause of problem and plan remedies to prevent further recurrence.

6. Incident management team will document all emergency action taken, in detail.
7. Incident management team will collect all evidence and secure for further problem analysis.

External Facilities Management

External contractors are always potential security exposures. To avoid this risk:

1. Any external contractor should not have any type of access to data stored at the pharmacy hub.
2. If any physical or software maintenance is required at the pharmacy hub by external contractors, only management-approved personnel will do that.
3. Business continuity plans are made with external contractors.
4. In case of any security breach, all the incidents should be reported to the security response team.

System Planning and Acceptance

To minimize the risk of system failure, adequate resources should be dedicated to the system so it is available redundantly.

Capacity Planning

To fulfill the requirement of power in terms of processing and storage better hardware should be used.

System Acceptance

The entire requirement, which is mentioned, should be tested before the system is accepted. Managers should ensure that the requirement and criteria for the acceptance of new system are clearly defined.

1. Server performance and storage capacity should be upgradeable.
2. Cluster architecture should be implemented.

3. All network administrators should be trained and provided with contingency and error recovery procedure.
4. Managers make sure that all personnel using server have adequate training.

Protection against Malicious Software

To protect the integrity of software and information, all the data should be protected from malicious software. All possible steps should be taken to prevent and detect the introduction of malicious software. User should be made aware of the dangers of unauthorized or malicious software, and manager should introduce special controls to detect or prevent its introduction.

Control against Malicious Software   Detection and prevention controls to protect against malicious software and appropriate user awareness procedures should be implemented.

1. All software that are used should be licensed.
2. No unauthorized software should run on network.
3. Any access to data from a "foreign" domain should be granted with permission of management only.
4. Symantec Antivirus Enterprise edition will be used.
5. All the data that was sent/stored to the server should be scanned with antivirus.
6. A manager makes sure that all antivirus definitions are up to date.
7. All update patches should be installed.
8. Any unauthorized access of files or any malicious activity should be formally investigated.

Housekeeping

To maintain the integrity and availability of information processing, files should be backed up regularly.

Information Backup

1. All the data should be backed up at midnight when there is minimum activity on network.

2. Cluster environment should also provide the backup servers in case of any hardware failure.
3. All backup tapes should be protected properly from any security breach or environmental damage.
4. Backup media should be regularly tested to ensure that they are reliable for emergency situations.

Operator Logs

Operational staff should maintain logs of all the following activities:

- System starting and finishing times
- System errors and corrective action taken
- Confirmation of the correct handling of data files and computer output
- Name and designation of the person making log entry

These logs should be subjected to regular, independent checks against the operation procedure.

Fault Logging

- All faults logs should be reviewed to ensure that faults have been satisfactorily resolved.
- All corrective measures should be reviewed to ensure that controls have not been compromised and that the action taken is fully authorized.

Network Management

To ensure the safeguarding of information in networks and the protection of the supporting infrastructure, network controls should be adopted.

Network Controls

- Operational responsibilities for networks should be separated from computer operations.
- Remote management should be authorized only by the manager.
- VPN network was used on public network to protect data.

Media Handling and Security

To prevent damage to assets and interruptions to business activities, media should be controlled and physically protected.

Management of Removable Computer Media

- All previously removed media from pharmacy hub should be erased.
- Authorization from management should be required for all media removed from the pharmacy hub.
- All media should be stored in safe, secure environment, in accordance with the manufacturer's specifications.

Disposal of Media Media that contain sensitive information about patients should be disposed of securely, that is, by incineration or shredding or emptied of stored data by another application within the organization.

The following items should be securely disposed:

- Paper documents containing any information about the patient
- Carbon papers
- Output reports
- One-time printer ribbons
- Magnetic tapes
- Removable disks
- Optical storage media
- Test data
- System documentation
- Patient history
- Disposal of sensitive information at pharmacy hub should be logged

Exchange of Information and Software To prevent loss, modification, or misuse of information exchanged between pharmacy hub and nodes, all the information should be controlled by electronic data interchange (EDI).

Security of Media in Transit　Information can be vulnerable to unauthorized access, misuse, or corruption during physical transport, and the following controls should be applied:

- List of reliable courier should be used.
- All the packages should be sufficient to protect the contents from physical damage.

Electronic Commerce Security　EDI is vulnerable to a number of threats, which may result from fraudulently activity, contracts dispute and disclosure, or modification of information.

ANSI X12, ISO 9735, and UN/EDIFACT standards should be followed for all electronic commerce-related activity.

Security of Electronic Mail　Electronic mail should be protected with digital certificates. The 168 bit digital certificate for e-mail was used from Verisign for secure e-mails, so that e-mails are not forged, and to be certain that messages sent cannot be intercepted and read by anyone other than the intended recipient.

Business Requirement for Access Control

Access Control Policy　The purpose of this document is to define and clarify policies, principles, standards, guidelines, and responsibilities related to security. These measures ensure that only authorized users have access to specific computer resources, networks, data, and applications.

User Access Management　All users are set up as "View Only" unless otherwise requested. All users are set up to use Adobe Acrobat Reader software to view and print prescriptions. All users gain access to pharmacy database by using the VPN using their ISP except the patients. The pharmacy database website will verify your password, prior to letting you gain access to the database.

User Registration　All users must go through an initial registration process to receive a user ID and password.

Privilege Management

Home patients: Out of scope for this project.

Pharmacies: The primary and the secondary pharmacists will have privileged access for the system. In order to receive the privileged access, each pharmacist must have 8 hours of special security and authorization training.

Health plan location: The supervisor for this department and one other person will have privileged access for the system. In order to receive the privileged access, each person must have 8 hours of special security and authorization training.

Doctor's office: The doctor and office manager will have privileged access for the system. In order to receive the privileged access, each doctor and office manager must have 8 hours of special security and authorization training.

Pharmacy hub: The pharmacy hub's employees are responsible for the management of each privileged access for the stakeholders. Their responsibility is to monitor and supervise all other access to the system.

User Password Management

Home Patients: Out of scope for this project.

Pharmacies: All the passwords will be stored in the central server at the pharmacy hub. Every password will be encrypted for security purposes, storage, and use.

Health plan location: All the passwords will be stored in the central server at the pharmacy hub. Every password will be encrypted for security purposes, storage, and use.

Doctor's office: All the passwords will be stored in the central server at the pharmacy hub. Every password will be encrypted for security purposes, storage, and use.

Pharmacy hub: All the passwords will be stored in the central server here and will be backed up daily. Every password will be encrypted for security purposes, storage, and use.

Review of User Access Rights

Home patients: Out of scope for this project.

Pharmacies: Every 6 months, a formal review will be conducted regarding users' access rights and privileges. At this time, if any changes or modifications are required they will be conducted via formal process.

Health plan location: Every 6 months, a formal review will be conducted regarding users' access rights and privileges. At this time, if any changes or modifications are required they will be conducted via formal process.

Doctor's office: Every 6 months, a formal review will be conducted regarding users' access rights and privileges. At this time, if any changes or modifications are required they will be conducted via formal process.

Pharmacy hub: Every 6 months, a formal review will be conducted regarding users' access rights and privileges. At this time, if any changes or modifications are required they will be conducted via formal process.

User Responsibilities

Individuals must exercise good judgment and act in a professional manner when using passwords. Employees are responsible for exercising good judgment regarding the reasonableness of personal use. Individual departments are responsible for creating guidelines concerning personal use of Internet/Intranet/Extranet systems. In the absence of such policies, employees should be guided by departmental policies on personal use, and if there is any uncertainty, employees should consult their supervisor or manager.

The user interface for information contained on Internet/Intranet/Extranet-related systems should be classified as either confidential or not confidential, as defined by corporate confidentiality guidelines, details of which can be found in human resources policies. Examples of confidential information include but are not limited to XYZ private, corporate strategies, competitor sensitive, trade secrets, specifications, customer lists, and research data. Employees should take all necessary steps to prevent unauthorized access to this information.

Network Access Control

Policy on Use of Network Services

- Users will only be given sufficient rights to all systems to enable them to perform their job function. User rights will be kept to a minimum at all times.
- Users requiring access to systems must make a written application on the forms provided by IT services.
- Where possible no one person will have full rights to any system. IT services will control network/server passwords and the system administrator in the end-user department will assign system passwords.
- The system administrator will be responsible for maintaining the data integrity of the end-user department's data and for determining end-user access rights.
- Access to the network/servers and systems will be by individual username and password.
- All users will have an alphanumeric password of at least six characters.
- Passwords will expire every 40 days and must be unique.
- Intruder detection will be implemented where possible. The user account will be locked after three incorrect attempts.
- Users will be given a username and password to log in to the network/servers and another password to login to individual systems.
- IT services will be notified of all employees leaving the XYZ's employment. IT services will then remove the employee's rights to all systems.
- Auditing will be implemented on all systems to record login attempts/failures, successful logins, and changes made to all systems.

Remote Diagnostic Port Protection   Home patients: Out of scope for this project.

Secure remote access must be strictly controlled. Control will be enforced via one-time password authentication or public/private keys with strong pass phrases. Any employees and contractors with remote access privileges to relational database management system (RDBMS) corporate network must not use non-RDBMS e-mail accounts or other external resources to conduct business, thereby ensuring that official business is never confused with personal business.

Network Connection Control   This document describes a required minimal security configuration for all routers and switches connecting to a production network or used in a production capacity at or on behalf of RDBM. All routers and switches connected to RDBMs networks are affected. Every router must meet the following configuration standards:

No local user accounts are configured on the router. Routers must use Terminal Access Controller Access-Control System Plus (TACACS+) for all user authentications.

The enable password on the router must be kept in a secure encrypted form. The router must have the enable password set to the current production router password from the router's support organization.

Disallow the following:

- IP-directed broadcasts
- Incoming packets at the router sourced with invalid addresses such as RFC1918 address
- TCP small services
- UDP small services
- All source routing
- All web services running on router
- Use corporate standardized SNMP community strings
- Access rules are to be added as business needs arise
- The router must be included in the corporate enterprise management system with a designated point of contact

Each router must have the following statement posted in clear view

UNAUTHORIZED ACCESS TO THIS NETWORK DEVICE IS PROHIBITED. You must have explicit permission to access or configure this device. All activities performed on this device may be logged, and violations of this policy may result in disciplinary action, and may be reported to law enforcement. There is no right to privacy on this device.

Operating System Access Control

Automatic Terminal Identification Due to the limited time and resources, we decided not use automatic terminal identification methods at this time, but may consider it for the next release.

Terminal Log-On Procedures Home Patients: Out of scope for this project.

Access to information will only be available via a secure logon process. Every user will be assigned a specific user ID and password. After three unsuccessful tries of the password, system will be locked down. All of this information will be logged using Section 9.7.1.

User Identification and Authentication In order to get access to the systems, all users will have to use their assigned user IDs and passwords.

Password Management System Do not use the same password for internal accounts and, as far as possible, do not use the same password for RDBM and regular Internet access needs.

Do not share your passwords with anyone, including administrative assistants or secretaries. All passwords are to be treated as sensitive, confidential XYZ information. The central server at RDBMS location will manage all the passwords.

Here is a list of "don'ts":

- Do not reveal a password over the phone to ANYONE
- Do not reveal a password in an e-mail message
- Do not reveal a password to the boss
- Do not talk about a password in front of others
- Do not hint at the format of a password (e.g., "my family name")
- Do not reveal a password on questionnaires or security forms
- Do not share a password with family members
- Do not reveal a password to coworkers while on vacation

Use of System Utilities Any unauthorized system utilities will be removed; only RDBMs approved utilities will be allowed.

Duress Alarm to Safeguard Users Out of scope for this release, but we will include in the next release.

Terminal Time-Out

- Home patients: Out of scope for this project.
- Pharmacies: If the systems detect no activity for 15 minutes to the RDBMS database, it will automatically log the terminal out of the system.
- Health plan location: If the systems detect no activity for 15 minutes to the RDBMS database, it will automatically log the terminal out of the system.
- Doctor's office: If the systems detect no activity for 15 minutes to the RDBMS database, it will automatically log the terminal out of the system.
- Pharmacy hub: If the systems detect no activity for 15 minutes to the RDBMS database, it will automatically log the terminal out of the system.

Limitation of Connection Time   Connection will stay active/connected as long as there is an activity between the systems, if no activities it will follow Section 9.5.7.

Application Access Control

Information Access Restriction   This policy is intended to help employees determine what information can be disclosed to nonemployees and the relative sensitivity of information that should not be disclosed outside. All information are categorized into two main classifications:

Public
Confidential

Public information is information that has been declared public knowledge by someone with the authority to do so and can freely be given to anyone without any authorization.

Confidential contains all other information. It is a continuum, in that, it is understood that some information is more sensitive than other information and should be protected in a more secure manner. Included are information that should be protected very closely, such as trade secrets, development programs, potential acquisition targets, and other information integral to the success of our XYZ. Also included as confidential is information that is less critical, such as telephone directories, general corporate information, personnel information, and so on, which does not require as stringent a degree of protection.

Sensitive System Isolation   The sensitivity guidelines provide details on how to protect information at varying sensitivity levels. Use these guidelines as a reference only, as confidential information in each column may necessitate more or less stringent measures of protection depending on the circumstances and the nature of the confidential information in question.

- Minimal sensitivity: General corporate information; some personnel and technical information
- Moderate sensitivity: Business, financial, technical, and most personnel information
- Highest sensitivity: Trade secrets and marketing, operational, personnel, financial, source code, and technical information integral to the success of XYZ company.

Monitoring System Access and Use

Event Logging   We will utilize two different servers for event logging. One server will be dedicated for system logging and it will send alarms to the help desk if it sees any problems. The second systems will be used for user logging and it will send any unusual behavior to the management.

Monitoring System Use   We will also utilize two different servers for event monitoring. One server will be dedicated for system monitoring for up/down status, and it will send alarms to the help desk if it sees any problems. The second systems will be used for user monitoring, and it will send any unusual behavior to the management.

Clock Synchronization   All the routers will be running the network time protocol (NTP), and all network components will be synchronized to each other every night.

Mobile Computing and Teleworking

Mobile Computing

Home patients: Out of scope for this project
Pharmacies: Out of scope for this project

Teleworking

- Home patients: Out of scope for this project
- Pharmacies: Due to the nature of business telecommuting is not permitted
- Health plan location: Due to the nature of business telecommuting is not permitted
- Doctor's office: Due to the nature of business telecommuting is not permitted
- Pharmacy hub: Due to the nature of business telecommuting is not permitted

Security Requirements of Systems

To ensure that security is built into information systems, a security management team has to look into the security on small system responsibilities, access control, data protection and environment, physical equipment, software security, infrastructure, and the networks in the system.

Security in Application Systems

To prevent loss, modification, or misuse of user data in application systems audit trails and controls should be designed into application systems.

Data Validation

The pharmacy Handheld Technology has to validate the data input to ensure that it is correct and appropriate before it is sent, at every point in the system.

- The data have to be checked before sent across the systems.
- The doctor will be responsible for any incorrect information passed to the hub, even if it is accidental.

If the pharmacist has the slightest doubt about the quantity of medicine or its name, he should immediately contact the doctor before sending the data across the systems.

Business Continuity Management

Aspects of Business Continuity Management   This document is the disaster recovery plan for the RDBM XYZ. The information present in this plan guides the XYZ management and technical staff in the recovery of computing and network facilities operated by the XYZ in the event that a disaster (such as fire, flood, tornadoes and high winds, earthquakes, and computer crimes) destroys all or part of the facilities.

The recovery plan is composed of a number of sections that document resources and procedures to be used in the event that a disaster occurs at the XYZ. Each supported computing platform has a section containing specific recovery procedures. There are also sections that document the personnel what will be needed to perform the recovery tasks and an organizational structure for the recovery process.

This plan is available through the XYZ's World Wide Web server in order to make it more generally available to the XYZ staff. But more importantly, a web document format permits it to be published in an online form that can be stored on diskette or CD-ROM media for viewing with a Netscape browser in file browse mode. This plan will be updated on a regular basis as changes to the computing and networking systems are made. Online publishing makes these changes immediately available to all those who are interested.

Primary Focus of the Plan   The primary focus of this document is to provide a plan to respond to a disaster that destroys or severely cripples the XYZ's central computer systems. The intent is to restore operations as quickly as possible with the latest and most up-to-date data available.

All disaster recovery plans assume a certain amount of risk, the primary one being how much data is lost in the event of a disaster. Disaster recovery planning is much like the insurance business in many ways. There are compromises between the amount of time, effort, and money spent in the planning and preparation of a disaster and the amount of data loss you can sustain and still remain operational following a disaster. Time enters the equation too. In order to stay in business, many organizations simply cannot function without the computers. So their recovery efforts may focus on quick recovery, or even zero down time, by duplicating and maintaining their computer systems in separate facilities.

The techniques for backup and recovery used in this plan do not guarantee zero data loss. The XYZ management is willing to assume the risk of data loss and do without computing for a period of time in a disaster situation. To put it in a more fiscal sense, the XYZ is saving dollars in up-front disaster preparation costs and then relying upon business interruption and recovery insurance to help restore computer operations after a disaster.

Data recovery efforts in this plan are targeted at getting the systems up and running with the last available off-site backup tapes. Significant effort will be required after the system operation is restored to (1) restore data integrity to the point of the disaster and (2) to synchronize that data with any new data collected from the point of the disaster forward.

This plan does not attempt to cover either of these two important aspects of data recovery. Instead, individual users and departments will need to develop their own disaster recovery plans to cope with the unavailability of the computer systems during the restoration phase of this plan and to cope with potential data loss and synchronization problems.

Primary Objectives of the Plan   This disaster recovery plan has the following primary objectives:

Present an orderly course of action for restoring critical computing capability to the XYZ premises within 14 days of initiation of the plan

Set criteria for making the decision to recover at a cold site or repair the affected site

Describe an organizational structure for carrying out the plan

Provide information concerning personnel that will be required to carry out the plan and the computing expertise required

Identify the equipment, floor plan, procedures, and other items necessary for the recovery

Plan   This plan uses a "cookbook" approach to recover from a disaster that destroys or severely cripples the computing resources at the XYZ building and possibly at other critical facilities.

Personnel Immediately following the disaster, a planned sequence of events begins. Key personnel are notified, and recovery teams are grouped to implement the plan. However, the plan has been designed to be usable even if some or all of the personnel are unavailable.

In a disaster, it must be remembered that PEOPLE are your most valuable resource. The recovery personnel working to restore the computing systems will likely be working at great personal sacrifice, especially in the early hours and days following the disaster. They may have injuries hampering their physical abilities. The loss or injury of a loved one or coworker may affect their emotional ability. They will have physical needs for food, shelter, and sleep.

The XYZ must take special pains to ensure that the recovery workers are provided with resources to meet their physical and emotional needs. This plan calls for the appointment of a person in the administrative support team whose job will be to secure these resources so they can concentrate on the task at hand.

Salvage Operations at the Disaster Site Early efforts are targeted at protecting and preserving the computer equipment. In particular, any magnetic storage media (servers, hard drives, magnetic tapes, diskettes) are identified and either protected from the elements or removed to a clean, dry environment away from the disaster site.

Designate Recovery Site At the same time, a survey of the disaster scene is done by appropriate personnel to estimate the amount of time required to put the facilities back into working order (in this case the building and utilities). A decision is then made whether to use the cold site, a location some distance away from the scene of the disaster where computing and networking capabilities can be temporarily restored until the primary site is ready. Work begins almost immediately at repairing or rebuilding the primary site.

Purchase New Equipment The recovery process relies heavily upon vendors to quickly provide replacements for the resources that cannot be salvaged. The XYZ will rely upon emergency procurement procedures documented in this plan and approved by the XYZ's purchasing office to quickly place orders for equipment, supplies, software, and any other needs.

Begin Reassembly at the Recovery Site   Salvaged and new components are reassembled at the recovery site. Since all plans of this type are subjected to the inherent changes that occur in the computer industry, it may become necessary for recovery personnel to deviate from the plan, especially if the plan has not been kept up-to-date. If vendors cannot provide a certain piece of equipment on a timely basis, it may be necessary for the recovery personnel to make last-minute substitutions. After the equipment reassembly phase is complete, the work turns to concentrate on the data recovery procedures.

Restore Data from Backups   Data recovery relies entirely upon the use of backups stored in locations off-site from the administration office. Backups can take the form of magnetic tape, CDROMs, disk drives, and other storage media. Early data recovery efforts focus on restoring the operating system(s) for each computer system. Next, first-line recovery of application and user data from the backup tapes is done. Individual application owners may need to be involved at this point so teams are assigned for each major application area to ensure that data is restored properly.

Restore Applications Data   It is at this point that the disaster recovery plans for users (e.g., the application owners) must merge with the completion of the computing services plan. Since some time may have elapsed between the time that the off-site backups were made and the time of the disaster, application owners must have means for restoring each running application database to the point of the disaster. They must also take all new data collected from that point and input it into the application databases. When this process is complete, the XYZ systems can function normally. Some applications may be available only to a limited few key personnel, while others may be available to anyone who can access the computer systems.

Move Back to Restored Permanent Facility   If the recovery process has taken place at the cold site, physical restoration of the administrative services building (or an alternate facility) will have begun. When that facility is ready for occupancy, the systems assembled at the cold site are to be moved back to their permanent home. This plan does not attempt to address the logistics of this move, which should be vastly less complicated than the work done to do the recovery at the cold site.

Compliance

Compliance with Legal Requirements   The company will avoid breaches of any criminal and civil law, statutory, regulatory, or contractual obligations and of any security requirements.

Identification of Applicable Legislation   The specific controls and individual responsibilities to meet statutory, regulatory, and contractual requirements will be defined and documented.

Intellectual Property Rights

Copyright   The company's legal department will take care of the copyrights, design rights, and trademarks. It will take necessary steps to get the permissions and acquisitions and will get the organization legally licensed from the developers of the products.

Software Copyright

- The company will renew the license before it expires from the software organization.
- The company will not go over the system limit prescribed by the application software.
- Nobody can copy or write the software in the organization.
- Backup copy will be kept with the developers' permission.
- Steps will be taken to maintain all the rules and regulations of software copyright.
- Permission to use, copy, and distribute documents and related graphics available on the server will be according to their respective copyright policies.

Safeguarding Organizational Records

1. The doctor will maintain his own database server to keep a record of the patient's history and what he has prescribed.
2. The pharmacy hub will keep the transaction logs, audit logs, and accounting records on the server for a period of 24 months, after which it will be destroyed.
3. The pharmacy hub will maintain patients' history and their prescription information on a separate database and will also make

sure to have it on a magnetic tape and this information will be stored for 5 years so that if for any reason the database loses the information, it can be retrieved from the magnetic tape.

4. The pharmacy hub will have two servers running at a time to store the information so that if for any reason one of the servers goes down, the records can still be stored and retrieved from the other server.

5. The insurance XYZ will have the patient's information on its server as long as he is enrolled. After that the information will be kept on a remote database and will be destroyed after 36 months if he does not re-enroll in that period.

Data Protection and Privacy of Personal Information

We want patients to be assured that their personal information is properly safeguarded.

We use technology that is designed for use with secure web servers. Prescription drug information and patients health history resides in a database behind a firewall where it cannot be accessed without proper authorization. Secure sockets layer (SSL) technology encrypts personal information as well as prescription health history as it is transmitted over the Internet.

Prevention of Misuse of Information Processing Facilities

- Only authorized personnel can have access to the data.
- Only a doctor can change the prescription.
- A manager will be appointed to monitor the information on the systems presently using the information, and any unauthorized activity will be tracked and reported to the management.
- The application software will not give any unwanted data to the user.
- The patient will need a valid ID and password to check his order status.
- Our organization will not share the patient's data with any other XYZ or organization.

Regulations of Cryptographic Controls

1. The company will comply with all agreements, laws, rules, and regulations to control the access to or use of cryptographic controls.
2. A policy will be made to maintain appropriate license and for disposing or transferring software and will comply with terms and conditions for software and information obtained from public networks.

Collection of Evidence   The company will have a policy to collect adequate evidence to support an action against a person or organization. The evidence presented should confirm the rules for evidence laid down in the relevant law of the specific court in which the case will be heard.

- No employee can copy any information on hard disks or in memory until given the permission to do so from the concerned authority.
- Any evidence against any employee of the company will be dealt first in the organization and then will be taken to the court of law.
- Every evidence should be properly documented and stored and depending upon the quality and completeness either in the organization, civil, or criminal court.

Reviews of Security Policy and Technical Compliance

Compliance with Security Policy   The company has a security policy and has set standards to look into information systems, system providers, owners of information, and information assets.

- The policy has standards for users and management so that no data is transferred or copied from the systems.
- The policy will see that only authorized personals can access the data and will be required to have a valid ID and password.
- The management will regularly review, monitor, and change the security policies accordingly.

Technical Compliance Checking   Technical compliance checking will be done on the operational systems to ensure that hardware and software controls have been correctly implemented. The system will be tested for its vulnerabilities; the system has to go through system testing, integration testing, and security. The system will be tested under the technical expertise of the people in the organization.

System Audit Considerations

System audit process will be conducted to maximize the effectiveness and to minimize the interferences from the process.

System Audit Controls   The system audits of the company will be done by an external agency to verify compliance with requirements. Audit requirements and activities to check operational systems will be planned and agreed to minimize the risk of disruptions to business processes at the entry and exit levels. The technical and managerial members will perform the checks; all the procedures, requirements, and responsibilities will be documented.

Protection of System Audit Tools   The company will protect the system audit tools from any misuse and will store the tools with high security. Only privileged members will be able to access the audit tools, that is, the patient's health history and his prescription. All sensitive patient information will be protected and will not be passed to any other external agency.

Part 3: Security Policy Document

Sample Company: XYZ

This sample document is prepared based on ISO 17799, the primary document was prepared by the author as class project for Information Security Class, Master class project at University of Detroit, Mercy.

Title page	
Document Name:	**Security Policy Document** for **XYZ**
Document No:	
Contract No:	
Publication Date:	
Revision Date:	
Project Number:	
Prepared By:	Information Security Team
Approved By:	

Information Security Policy

The security policy document provides management to the organization's approach for managing the information security. Information security is defined as

> ...the process of protecting data from accidental or intentional misuse by individuals inside or outside the organization.

Information security is about balancing risks, with the rewards of doing business electronically. Since risks and vulnerabilities are constantly changing, therefore, security is a never-ending process.

Security policy is about adopting a security process that outlines an organization's expectation for security, which can then demonstrate management's support and commitment to security. The standard ISO 17799 provides a set of recommendations to outline security measures for the organizations.

Security organization—describes the management structure, appointing security coordinators, delegating security responsibilities, and establishing response processes.

Asset classification and control—conducting a detailed assessment and inventory of an organization's information infrastructure and assets to determine an appropriate level of security.

Personnel security—making security a key component of the human resources and business operations. This includes writing security expectations in job responsibilities, background checks on new personnel, use of confidentiality agreements, and having a reporting process for security incidents.

Physical and environmental security—protection of the IT infrastructure, physical plant, and employees. This includes building access, backup power sources, and so on.

Communications and operations management—preventing incidents by the use of preventative measures such as antivirus protection, maintaining logs, securing remote connections, and incident response procedures.

System development and maintenance—ensuring that security is an integral part of system deployment or expansion and that systems are properly maintained. Proper configuration management is a key component.

Business continuity management—planning for natural and man-made disasters and recovering from them.

Compliance—involves complying with any applicable regulatory and legal requirements, such as HIPAA, Gramm–Leach–Bliley Act, and cryptography export controls.

Board and management have several fundamental responsibilities to ensure that information security is appropriately enforced. They should understand why information security needs to be placed at the highest preference. The impacts are

- Risks and threats are real and could have significant impact on the enterprise.
- Effective information security requires coordinated and integrated action from the top to bottom.
- IT investments can be very substantial and easily misdirected.
- Cultural and organizational factors are equally important.
- Rules and priorities need to be established and enforced.
- Security incidents are likely to be exposed to the public.
- Reputational damage can be considerable.

Hence, information security should become an important and integral part of the whole IT framework. Negligence in this regard will render the creation of IT value unsustainable in the long run.

Board-Level Action

- Become informed about information security
- Set direction, that is, drive policy and strategy and define a global risk profile
- Provide resources to information security efforts
- Assign responsibilities to management
- Set priorities
- Support change
- Define cultural values related to risk awareness
- Obtain assurance from internal or external auditors
- Insist management make security investments, security improvements measurable, and monitors reports on program effectiveness

Management-Level Action

- Write the security policy, with business input.
- Ensure that individual roles, responsibilities, and authority are clearly communicated and understood by all. This is imperative for effective security.
- Identify threats, analyze vulnerabilities, and identify industry practices for due care.
- Set up a security infrastructure.
- Develop a security and control framework that consists of standards, measures, practices, and procedures after a policy has been approved by the governing body of the organization and related roles and responsibilities assigned.
- Decide what resources are available, prioritize possible countermeasures, and implement the top priority countermeasures the organization can afford. Solutions should be implemented on a timely basis and then maintained.
- Establish monitoring measures to detect and ensure correction of security breaches so that all actual and suspected breaches are promptly identified, investigated, and acted upon and to ensure ongoing compliance with policy, standards, and minimum acceptable security practices.
- Conduct periodic reviews and tests.
- Implement intrusion detection and incident response.
- Embed awareness of the need to protect information and offer training in the skills needed to operate information systems securely and be responsive to security incidents. Education in security measures and practices is of critical importance for the success of an organization's security program.
- Ensure that security is considered an integral part of the system's development life cycle process and explicitly addressed during each phase of the process.

Organizational Security

Information Security Infrastructure The information security infrastructure framework for XYZ should encompass the necessary roles from the management group to accomplish the goals of information security. These managers will approve or disapprove the policies and roles that will define information security for the organization. For instance, customer records and personal identity information will be privatized according to the established rules.

Management Information Security Forum The management group for XYZ should monitor and review security vulnerabilities and threats to avoid incidents that may harm the overall business goals. The XYZ managers will have defined responsibilities and will report to their proper heads or superiors. At XYZ, there should be one executive manager, the Chief Security Officer (CSO) who be in charge of all security-related activities (both physical and digital aspects of security). This is important because the process of authorizing any security initiatives or changes within the organization will need to be approved. For this approval or disapproval to occur, the CSO will provide a weekly report from the managers under him/her so that a decision can be made.

Information Security Coordination At Handheld Techology, the coordination of information security will be facilitated by putting in place the necessary security controls. These controls will be utilized for the purpose of creating an organizational security discipline. In order for this discipline to take shape in the organization, management from different parts of the organization will need to adhere to their responsibilities, which are coordinated by the security controls.

Allocation of Information Security Responsibilities The information security responsibilities at the organization will be clearly defined. The security managers would adhere to these defined responsibilities, and their roles will reflect the information security policies. The managers will ensure that the employees working underneath them will follow the guidelines that the information security policy dictates.

Authorization Process for Information Processing Facilities In information processing facilities, the authorization process must be documented. The manager must be consulted, and authorization requested. This manager will need to document the request along with the subject matter discussed. After the meeting, if the manager has the authority based on the security policy, then he/she may grant authorization. However, if the manager does not have the authorization, then he/she will need to speak to his/her manager.

Specialist Information Security Advice   It is vital to engage security specialists who can provide the necessary advice to improve the organizational security. The managers along with the CSO will consult with security experts outside the organization. These security consultants will provide up-to-date security trends and assessment methods.

Cooperation between Organizations   Since Handheld Techology has to work with different organizations such as insurance providers, pharmacies, and hospitals, maintaining cooperation between these entities is very important. The information exchange between these organizations makes it essential for managers to maintain a strong level of communication with the managers of other organizations; however, internal security policies that deal with XYZ sensitive information will not be discussed for precautionary reasons.

Independent Review of Information Security   In order to ensure that the XYZ policies and procedure are followed and adhered to by the employees, XYZ will have an internal information security auditor. The auditor will be responsible for reviewing the security policies of the XYZ and for monitoring the organizational practices. If the auditor observes any deviations or XYZ practices that do not adhere to the policies, the necessary changes will be made so that the practices are in accordance with the security policies.

Security of Third-Party Access

Identification of Risks from Third-Party Access   The organization will have various third-party interactions. Security consultants, auditors, and vendors will be given specific accesses.

Types of Access   There will also be a security policy for third-party access to the organization. Third-party access can come in the form of physical access as well as electronic access. Physical access will encompass aspects such as the office cleaning services at Handheld Techology and the vending machine personnel who comes every 2 weeks to service the machines. The electronic access will deal with outside vendors, and the trading partners who have contracts with

XYZ to support certain information technology solutions such as network maintenance and software development and support.

Reasons for Access Software development and maintenance are outsourced to different companies. The outsourced employees will provide their services on-site at the client office (Handheld Technology).

On-Site Contractors As mentioned earlier, there will be on-site contractors who will work with Handheld Technology. There will be specific guidelines that the contractors will need to follow. The guidelines will follow the information security policy of Handheld Technology.

Security Requirements in Third-Party Contracts

In order for both physical and logical access to be granted, specific controls will be put in place so organizational security is not jeopardized. These controls will be formally discussed and documented and contractually agreed upon with the third party. There will also be a risk assessment that will be done by the security managers at Handheld Technology to better understand the implications of granting these accesses.

Outsourcing

Security Requirements in Outsourcing Contracts With outsourcing contracts, there will be a strong need for security requirements to avoid any problems that may occur later. XYZ will have a contract with each contractor. The main reason for this contract is to protect XYZ sensitive data, assets, customer confidentiality, and define the protocols and procedures that are in place if a disastrous event occurs. Also, the client will have the right to audit the work that is related to the contractor.

Asset Classification and Control

Accountability for Assets At XYZ, assets will be accounted for. It is not necessary for each small item to be tracked, but XYZ assets that deal with information systems will be tracked in an inventory database.

Inventory of Assets   Physical assets, such as computer terminals, peripherals, servers, printers, and other office-related machines, would be included in the asset inventory list. Information assets such as XYZ documents, database files, manuals, and other sensitive information will be placed in a secure area. To obtain sensitive information, the requester will follow defined procedures.

Information Classification

Classification Guidelines   The assets will be classified as follows:

1. Highly sensitive—XYZ private information that may not be released to the public
2. Not sensitive—XYZ information that may be released to the public after authorization from the appropriate manager

Depending on the position of the personnel obtaining the information, asset access may be granted from the manager in charge of releasing the information. For certain highly sensitive information, authorization from higher-level managers or executives may be needed.

Information Labeling and Handling

As mentioned earlier, XYZ assets need to be tracked. Information labeling will occur at the same level as the asset classification. The labels to be used are "highly sensitive" and "not sensitive." Whether information processing activity occurs at the copying level, storage level, or the electronic level, these labels should be utilized to properly handle the XYZ assets.

The information security infrastructure framework for Handheld Technology will encompass the needed roles from the management group to accomplish the goals of information security. These managers will approve or disapprove the policies and roles that will define information security for the organization. For instance, patient records and personal identity information will be privatized according to the established rules of HIPAA. These managers will organize the way HIPAA compliancy will occur, and their actions and procedures will be reported to the head of information security. The management group for XYZ will monitor and review security vulnerabilities and threats to avoid incidents that may harm the overall business goals. The XYZ managers will have defined responsibilities and will report to their proper heads or superiors. At XYZ, there will be one executive manager, the CSO, who will be in charge all security-related activities (both physical and digital aspects of security). This is important because the process of authorizing any security initiatives or changes within the organization will need to be approved. For this approval or disapproval to occur, the CSO will be provided a weekly report from the managers under him so that a decision can be made. The managers, along with the CSO, will also consult with the security experts outside the organization. These security consultants will provide to these security managers up-to-date security trends and assessment methods so that proper decisions may take place.

Since XYZ has to work with different organizations such as the insurance providers, pharmacies, and hospitals, maintaining cooperation between these entities is very important. The information exchange between these organizations makes it essential for managers to maintain a strong level of communication with the managers of other organizations; however, internal security policies that deal with XYZ sensitive information will not be discussed for precautionary reasons.

In order to ensure that the XYZ policies and procedure are followed and adhered to by the employees, XYZ will have an internal information security auditor. The auditor will be responsible for reviewing the security policies of the XYZ and for monitoring the organizational practices. If the auditor observes any deviations or XYZ practices that do not adhere to the policies, the necessary changes will be made so that the practices are in accordance with the security policies.

There will also be a security policy for third-party access to the organization. Third party access can come in the form of physical access and logical access. Physical access will encompass aspects such as the office cleaning services at XYZ and the vending machine personnel who comes every 2 weeks to service the machines. The logical access will deal with outside vendors and the trading partners who have contracts with XYZ to support certain information technology solutions such as network maintenance and software development and support. In order for both physical and logical access to be granted, specific controls will be put in place, so organizational security is not jeopardized. These controls will be formally discussed and documented and contractually agreed upon with the third party. There will also be a risk assessment that will be done by the security managers at XYZ, to better understand the implications of granting these accesses.

Personnel Security

Security in Job Definition

Including security in job responsibilities.

Job responsibilities are clearly specified and secured. Each employee has clearly defined job descriptions. Security roles and responsibilities are documented in the organization's manual book.

Personnel Screening Policy

- Previous employment verification
- Education verification
- Personal references check
- Credit history
- Criminal court history
- Civil court history
- Federal court records

Testing Employees

- Medical examinations
- Evaluates important attitudes toward: work ethic, reliability, honesty, drug/alcohol use
- Behavior forecaster

Evaluate Key Job Behaviors

- Three interpersonal skills: friendliness, teamwork, and assertiveness
- Five personality traits: optimism, poise, objectivity, rule-following preferences, and focus on feelings versus facts

- Five motivations: money, power, creativity, knowledge, and customer service
- Evaluates five crucial skills: problem-solving; vocabulary; arithmetic; grammar, spelling and word use and speed; and accuracy in handling small details

Confidentiality Agreements

We shall maintain the confidential information in confidence for a period of 3 years from the date of this agreement and shall use it only for the business purpose. We shall have the right to disclose confidential information to those affiliates who need to know the confidential information pursuant to the business purpose or for corporate management purposes, provided any such individual shall be required to adhere to provisions of nonuse and nondisclosure no less stringent than as agreed to herein.

Terms and Conditions for Employment

The terms and conditions of employment, including compensation and duration of employment, are limited to those written in the employment contract. The department head and human resources collaboratively designate contract positions, decide whether or not recruitment is applicable, and establish the terms and conditions of employment, including salary. The amount of time of all appointments, whether on contract or not, cannot exceed 100%.

- Effective date
- Duration
- Termination date
- Salary
- Benefits/retirement
- Conditions of appointment
- Salary and incremental payments
- Sickness and maternity leave
- Notice of termination of appointments
- Outside work
- Retirement
- Duties
- Removal expenses on appointment

User Training

Information Security Education and Training   Each user must be trained about the system depending upon the user's area of work.

- Employee manual
- Password issue
- Job description

Reporting Security Incidents

- Each incident must be reported immediately
- Reporting security incidents and infractions

Security Incidents Reporting Guideline

- Purpose
- Guidelines
- Possible incidents include
- Confirmed unauthorized access, denial of service, and successful exploits of vulnerabilities

The following incidents should be reported as such:

- Agency name
- Point of contact information including name, telephone, and e-mail address
- Incident category type
- Incident date and time, including time zone
- Source IP, port, and protocol
- Destination IP, port, and protocol
- Operating system, including version, patches, etc.
- System function (e.g., DNS/web server, workstation, etc.)
- Antivirus software installed, including version, and latest updates
- Location of the system(s) involved in the incident (e.g., Washington DC, Los Angeles, CA)

Reporting Security Weaknesses   The security weaknesses identified in the report fell into six categories, including inadequate performance measures, few security education and awareness programs, and virtually no meaningful systems to detect report and share incident information.

Physical and Environmental Security

Physical Security   Most security measures that deal with physical security are designed to protect the computer from climate conditions, although many of them also deal with protecting your computer from intruders who use or attempt to use physical access to the computer to break into it.

- Access control
- Power and electricity
- Climate and environment
- Smoke and fire
- Water
- Food and drinks
- Vibrations
- Backups

Physical Entry Control

- Visitor and unauthorized entrance should be controlled
- Nonworking hour time entrances should be monitored and controlled

Securing Offices, Rooms, and Facilities

Physically Securing the Servers

- Servers must be placed in a locked room.
- If needed, protect the room using electronic card access, thus recording any access to the room.
- Provide temperature and humidity controls to avoid any damage to the equipment.
- If needed, use surveillance cameras.
- Lock CPU case and ensure key is protected. Make a backup key and keep this key in a safety deposit box (outside the office).
- The server room should be arranged in a way that people outside the room cannot see the keyboard (thus seeing users/ admin passwords).
- Only a limited number of people should have access to the server room (no maintenance person should be allowed in these rooms).

- Keep track of your computer inventory (e.g., laptops are often stolen without XYZ knowledge).

Working in Secure Areas

- Do not put your machines behind glass walls where people can watch passwords being typed in. If machines are behind glass walls, avoid having the monitor or keyboard in a location where they can be seen from the outside.
- If you have raised floors or dropped ceilings, make sure that walls extend to the ceilings and floors so that they cannot just be climbed over. Also, this helps to isolate the environment in the room.
- Install a system that monitors the physical environment and warns you of any dangerous changes.
- Have a written disaster recovery plan, which outlines a plan of action in case of natural disaster, which destroys hardware and renders the room, which stores your machine, unusable.

Equipment Security

- Install a UPS on any server and its associated software to allow an automatic server shutdown when there is a power outage.
- If no hardware-based RAID system is installed in servers, there should be at least a software-based RAID system installed.
- Any unused modem must be disabled/removed.
- No password evidence around the system (or under keyboard!).
- Any documentation concerning LAN settings, telecom equipment settings.
- Important user IDs and passwords should be kept in a safe/restricted location.

Protect the System from Undesirable Booting

- Boot sequence in BIOS must be modified. The hard drive must be set up first and the floppy thereafter.
- If possible, modify the BIOS settings so that the key sequence to access the BIOS is not displayed during the boot up sequence.

- On mission-critical servers, floppies and CD-ROM could be disabled or even removed physically to provide the highest level of physical security.
- BIOS password must be set using a hard-to-guess method (good length, mixed letters, and numbers).

Set Up Storage Protection for Backup Tapes

- Backup tape drive and tapes must also be stored in a secured room
- Secure off-site storage system for backup tapes

Note: The information contained on the tapes is crucial information for the XYZ. Therefore, files being backed up can be encrypted on tapes to ensure maximum confidentiality.

Equipment Sitting and Protection   Equipment has to be kept in a secure place to minimize the risk of potential threats, including theft, fire, explosions, smoke, water or power supply failure, dust, chemical effects, and so on.

- No food, drink, or smoking allowed in the electronic equipment area
- Environmental condition will be monitored on a regular basis

Power Supplies   Equipment will be protected from possible power failures and electrical anomalies.

Cabling Security   The following controls would be considered for the cabling security:

- There will be no visible cabling
- Power cables will be segregated from communications cables to prevent interference

Equipment Maintenance   Equipment will be maintained in accordance with the supplier's recommended service intervals and specifications.

General Controls

Clear Desk and Clear Screen Policy   The principle of a "clear desk" each evening when an employee leaves his place of work is used by many corporations. It ensures that confidential data are not made available, for example, to cleaning personnel and encourages methodical management of one's workspace. Confidential information should be kept under lock and key.

Removal of Property   Equipment, information, or software should not be taken off-site without authorization. Where necessary and appropriate, equipment should be logged out and logged back in when returned. Spot checks will be undertaken to detect unauthorized removal of the property.

Communication and Operation Management

Operational Procedure and Responsibilities   The communication and operation management document, an example of health system facility, is provided to make it more meaningful. Information, which is sent by a patient, a doctor, a pharmacy, and insurance XYZ, are stored at XYZ Hub. In order to ensure the correct and secure operation of these information-processing facilities, the following steps will be taken.

Documented Operating Procedures   Operation procedure should be treated as formal documents and changes authorized by the management.

Information Security Certification Procedure (Sample)

PROJECT IDENTIFICATION	
Organization	ABC
Procedure name	Information security certification procedure
Application name	
Version number	1.1
Procedure ID	
Date approved	
Effective date	
Procedure author(s)	
Procedure owner	
Repository	
Approver—1	
Approver—2	
Supporting document	

Document Change Control Log

This log is updated each time this document is updated. The log identifies the version number, the date the revisions were completed, a brief description of the changes, and the author.

VERSION #	DATE	SECTIONS/ PAGE REVISED	DESCRIPTION	REVISED BY NAME AND TITLE	REVIEWED BY NAME AND TITLE
1.0	07/01/2015		Initial draft		
1.1	07/15/2015	All	Security Certification		
1.2	07/30/2015	Section 3.1	Updated project ID		
1.3	08/15/2015	Section 4.2			

Table of Contents

- Statement of purpose
- Scope
- Assignments
- Risks
- Control objectives and control activities
- Role and responsibilities

TITLE	RESPONSIBILITY
Chief information security officer (CISO)	Overall company information security
Director (information security [IS])	Overall direction
Program manager	IS management
Vulnerability and threat manager	Vulnerability and threat assessment, oversight activities
Network team manager	
Physical facility manager	Physical environment, criticality of surrounding networks
Architect	

- Internal and external vulnerability testing
- Physical consideration
- Wireless evaluation
- E-mail filter
- Monitoring
- Documentation
- Conflict resolution and escalations

Security Standards

ISO 15408   ISO 15408, commonly known as common criteria, provides the framework for testing the effectiveness of most security systems. However, it is not intended to measure the effectiveness of an organization's security program.

COBIT   Developed for IT auditors and made available through the ISACA. It provides a framework for assessing a program, developing a performance baseline, and measuring performance over time.

ISO 17799/BS7799   ISO 17799 Information Technology—Code of Practice for Information Security Management began in the United Kingdom as BS 7799 in 1995 as a comprehensive set of controls comprising best practices in information security. It was revised in May 1999 and fast-tracked as an international standard in December 2000. Its chief strength is its flexibility.

Written in an open framework, the standard is a compilation of "best practices" that can be applied by any organization regardless of size or industry.

ISO 17799 is technically a standard, and it reads more like a set of recommendations. It outlines security measures organizations should have but not specifically how to implement them. It simply sets the expectations.

Note: A comprehensive standard is provided at the end of this chapter, which is prepared primarily based on ISO 17799 standard.

OCTAVE   OCTAVE is by Carnegie Mellon's CERT Coordination Center (wwww.cert.org/octave). It provides measures based on accepted best practices for evaluating security programs.

10

INFORMATION AUDIT

Introduction

This chapter contains three parts. Part 1 discusses the basic definition of information audit and different dimensions of audit planning, risk identification, assessment, and details of IT audit, key considerations for IT audit. Part 2 addresses the audit management. Part 3 discusses the audit and information security aspects.

Part 1: Definition and Planning

Definition

IEEE Standard 610 definition of audit is as follows:

> An independent examination of a work product or set of work products to assess compliance with specifications, standards, contractual agreements, or other criteria.*

According to Merriam-Webster, an audit is "A complete and careful examination of the financial records of a business or person" or "A careful check or review of something."

According to dictionary.com:

> Audit is an official examination and verification of accounts and records, especially of financial accounts.
> A report or statement reflecting an audit; a final statement of account.
> The inspection or examination of a building or other facility to evaluate or improve its appropriateness, safety, efficiency, or the like.
> An energy audit can suggest ways to reduce home fuel bills.

---

* IEEE Std 610.12-1990 (Revision and redesignation of IEEE Std7SZ.1983) *IEEE Standard Glossary of Software Engineering Terminology*, p. 11.

The purpose of a software audit is to provide an independent evaluation of conformance of software products and processes to applicable regulations, standards, guidelines, plans, specifications, and procedures.

According to the Wikipedia definition:

The word audit is derived from a Latin word "audire" which means "to hear." During the medieval times when manual book-keeping was prevalent, auditors in Britain used to hear the accounts read out for them and checked that the organization's personnel were not negligent or fraudulent.

Auditing refers to a systematic and independent examination of books, accounts, documents and vouchers of an organization to ascertain how far the financial statements present a true and fair view of the concern. It also attempts to ensure that the books of accounts are properly maintained by the concern as required by law. Auditing has become such an ubiquitous phenomenon in the corporate and the public sector that academics started identifying an "Audit Society." The auditor perceives and recognizes the propositions before him/her for examination, obtains evidence, evaluates the same and formulates an opinion on the basis of his or her judgment, which is communicated through the audit report.[*]

According to IEEE Standard 1028, examples of software products subject to audit include, but are not limited to, the following:[†]

- Backup and recovery plans
- Contingency plans
- Contracts
- Customer or user representative complaints
- Disaster plans
- Hardware performance plans
- Installation plans
- Installation procedures
- Maintenance plans
- Management review reports

---

[*] http://en.wikipedia.org/wiki/Audit

[†] *IEEE Standard for Software Reviews and Audits, IEEE Std 1028™-2008*, IEEE Computer Society, Sponsored by the Software & Systems Engineering Standards Committee, p. 30.

- Operations and user manuals
- Procurement and contracting methods
- Reports and data (e.g., review, audit, project status, anomaly reports, and test data)
- Request for proposal
- Risk management plans
- Standards, regulations, guidelines, plans, specifications, and procedures
- System build procedures
- Technical review reports
- Vendor documents
- Walkthrough reports
- Deliverable media (such as tapes and diskettes)

Audits shall be conducted to ensure

1. As-coded software products (such as a software item) reflect the design documentation.
2. The acceptance review and testing requirements prescribed by the documentation are adequate for the acceptance of the software products.
3. Test data comply with the specification.
4. Software products were successfully tested and meet their specifications.
5. Test reports are correct and discrepancies between actual and expected results have been resolved.
6. User documentation complies with standards as specified.
7. Activities have been conducted according to applicable requirements, plans, and contracts.

Audit Planning

According to ISO 19011-1, the audit team leader should prepare an audit plan to provide the basis for the agreement among the audit client, audit team and the auditee regarding the conduct of the audit. The plan should facilitate scheduling and coordination of the audit activities.

The amount of detail provided in the audit plan should reflect the scope and complexity of the audit. The details may differ, for example, between initial and subsequent audits and also between internal and external audits. The audit plan should be sufficiently flexible to permit changes, such as changes in the audit scope, which can become necessary as the on-site audit activities progress.

According to the document by ISO 19011, the audit plan should cover:*

1. The audit objectives
2. The audit criteria and any reference documents
3. The audit scope, including identification of the organizational and functional units and processes to be audited
4. The dates and places where the on-site audit activities are to be conducted
5. The expected time and duration of on-site audit activities, including meetings with the auditee's management and audit team meetings
6. The roles and responsibilities of the audit team members and accompanying persons
7. The allocation of appropriate resources to critical areas of the audit

The plan should be reviewed and accepted by the audit client and presented to the auditee before starting the on-site audit activities.

Any objections by an auditee should be resolved between the audit team leader, the auditee, and the audit client. Any revised audit plan should be agreed among the parties concerned before continuing the audit.

The audit plan shall describe

- Purpose and scope of the audit
- Audited organization, including location and management
- Software products to be audited
- Evaluation criteria, including applicable regulations, standards, guidelines, plans, specifications, and procedures to be used for evaluation

---

* ISO 19011. *Guidelines for Quality and/or Environmental Management Systems Auditing.* First Edition, 2002, p. 13.

- Auditor's responsibilities
- Examination activities (e.g., interview staff, read and evaluate documents, observe tests)
- Audit activity resource requirements
- Audit activity schedule
- Requirements for confidentiality (e.g., company confidential, restricted information, classified information)
- Checklists
- Report formats
- Report distribution
- Required follow-up activities

Where sampling is used, a statistically valid sampling method shall be used to establish selection criteria and sample size.

The audit plan shall be approved by the initiator. The audit plan should allow for changes based on information gathered during the audit, subject to approval by the initiator.

There are basically four types of participants in an audit:

1. Auditee—The organization being audited
2. Lead Auditor—The chief auditor
3. Auditor—Other auditors on the audit team
4. Recorder

IT Audit Plan Development Process

Role of Supporting Technologies The key supporting technologies, such as the company's network, e-mail application, and encryption software, to business objectives must be identified and represented in the universe of auditable areas (Figure 10.1).

1. Annual business plans
2. Centralized and decentralized IT functions
3. IT support processes
4. Regulatory compliance
5. Define audit subject areas
6. Business applications
7. Assessing risk

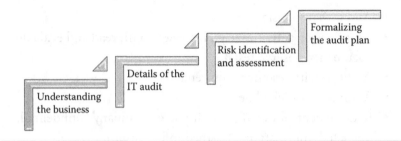

Figure 10.1   The audit development process.

Understanding the Business*

The first step in defining the IT audit plan is to understand the business. As part of this step, auditors need to identify the strategies, company objectives, and business models that will enable them to understand the organization's unique business risks. The audit team must also understand the business operations and IT service functions of the organization to be audited.

Auditors need to become acquainted with the organization's business model as each organization has a distinct mission and set of business goals and objectives.

Auditors can use different internal resources to identify and understand the organization's goals and objectives.

The next step is to identify the key processes that are critical to the objectives' success.

Operating Environment   To become familiar with the organization, auditors first need to understand its objectives and how business processes are structured to achieve objectives.

The degree of customization.
The technologies deployed.
The organization's system architecture diversity.

---

* Kirk Rehage. *Developing the IT Audit Plan*. Chevron Corporation Steve Hunt, Crowe Chizek and Company LLC. Fernando Nikitin, Inter-American Development Bank, July 2008.

Program code, database, operating system, and network infrastructure.

The degree of formalized company policies and standards (i.e., it governance).

Details of the IT Audit

It is very important to define the inclusive collection of audit areas, organizational entities, and locations identifying business functions that could be audited. At this initial phase, the potential audit areas are identified through the risk assessment process. Auditors need to be aware of what audits could be performed before they can assess and rank risks to create the annual audit plan.

Examining the Business Model*

A traditional company may consist of several offices and factories located in different countries, sales, and marketing units, as well as different corporate management and support functions. In decentralized organizations, business units might use different applications for similar business processes, or a common application might be configured differently to the extent it functions like an entirely different application.

Therefore, it is important for auditors to understand the company's IT environment and business model.

Formalizing the IT Audit Plan

Defining the IT audit universe and performing a risk assessment are foundational steps in the IT audit plan.

The IT audit plan should be created as part of the internal audit function's strategic planning process. This planning process should be cyclical and can be understood under the classical management cycle of "Plan-Do-Check-Act."

---

* *Global Technology Audit Guide Management of IT Auditing*, Michael Juergens, Principal, Deloitte & Touche LLP, Authors: David Maberry, Senior Manager, Deloitte & Touche LLP, Contributing Editors, Eric Ringle, Senior Manager, Deloitte & Touche LLP Jeffrey Fisher. Senior Manager, Deloitte & Touche LLP, March 2006, p. 10.

Integration of the IT Audit Plan

One key aspect of the planning process is to determine the integration level of the IT audit plan with non-IT audit activities in the audit department.

A complete business audit, including a review of all IT components, provides the opportunity to evaluate whether there is an appropriate combination of controls to mitigate business risks.

Validating the Audit Plan

The auditors need to establish criteria to evaluate the plan's effectiveness in meeting its objectives. The plan should consist of risk-based audits, mandated audit areas, and management requests for assurance and consulting services. Because one of the objectives of the planning phase is to allocate resources to areas where the department can add the most value to the organization and highest risk IT areas, auditors should determine how the plan reflects this objective.

The IT Audit Plan Should Be Dynamic

As technology is changing every day, it brings new challenges and more complicated potential risks, vulnerabilities, and threats. While designing the audit plan, the important fact to think about is the ongoing changes. Auditors need to consider the speed of the changes in IT.

Part of this dynamism, IT audit plan should be reviewed regularly. The IT audit function also must analyze changes and should have the flexibility to adjust the plan to the new conditions.*

Ten Key IT Considerations for Internal Audit

Ten key IT considerations for internal audit effective IT risk assessment and audit planning[†]

1. Information security
2. Business continuity management
3. Mobile

---

* Ibid, pp. 18–20.
† Ernst and Young. *Ten Key IT Considerations for Internal Audit, Effective IT Risk Assessment and Audit Planning.* Quality In Everything We Do.

4. Cloud
5. IT risk management
6. Program risk
7. Software/IT asset management
8. Social media risk management
9. Segregation of duties/identity and access management
10. Data loss prevention and privacy

Responsibilities of IT Audit Team Members

The following roles shall be established for an audit:

- Lead auditor
- Recorder
- Auditor(s)
- Initiator
- Audited organization

The lead auditor may act as recorder. The initiator should not act as lead auditor. Additional auditors should be included in the audit team; however, audits by a single person are permitted.

Lead Auditor   The lead auditor shall be responsible for the audit. This responsibility includes administrative tasks pertaining to the audit, ensuring that the audit is conducted in an orderly manner, and ensuring that the audit meets its objectives. The lead auditor is responsible for the following:

- Assembling the audit team
- Managing the audit team
- Making decisions regarding the conduct of the audit
- Making decisions regarding any audit observations
- Preparing the audit report (see Section 8.7)
- Reporting on the inability or apparent inability of any of the individuals involved in the audit to fulfill their responsibilities
- Negotiating any discrepancies or inconsistencies with the initiator that could impair the ability to satisfy the exit criteria (see Section 8.6)
- Recommending corrective actions

The lead auditor shall be free from bias and influence that could reduce the ability to make independent, objective evaluations.

Recorder   The recorder shall document anomalies, action items, decisions, and recommendations made by the audit team.

Auditor   The auditors shall examine products as defined in the audit plan. They shall document their observations. All auditors shall be free from bias and influences that could reduce their ability to make independent, objective evaluations, or they shall identify their bias and proceed with acceptance from the initiator.

Initiator   The initiator shall be responsible for the following activities:

   Decide upon the need for an audit
   Decide upon the purpose and scope of the audit
   Decide the software products or processes to be audited
   Decide the evaluation criteria, including the regulations, standards, guidelines, plans, specifications, and procedures, to be used for evaluation
   Decide who will carry out the audit
   Review the audit report
   Decide what follow-up action will be required
   Distribute the audit report

   The initiator may be a manager in the audited organization, a customer or user representative of the audited organization, or a third party.

Audited Organization   The audited organization shall provide a liaison to the auditors and shall provide all information requested by the auditors. When the audit is completed, the audited organization should implement corrective actions and recommendations.

Auditor's Qualifications

Choosing an Auditor   ISO 10011-2 explains how to select a quality auditor.

This guideline lists a number of qualifications that an auditor should possess, which include

- Education
- Skill
- Experience
- Knowledge
- Talent
- Competence

Auditor's Education   Auditors should have at least an education sufficient to acquire the knowledge and skills required to write and speak clearly and effectively. Generic knowledge and skills of quality management system and environmental management system auditors.

Knowledge and Skills

1. Audit principles, procedures, and techniques: To enable the auditor to apply those appropriate to different audits and ensure that audits are conducted in a consistent and systematic manner.
2. Management system and reference documents: To enable the auditor to comprehend the scope of the audit and apply audit criteria.
3. Organizational situations: To enable the auditor to comprehend the organization's operational context.
4. Applicable laws, regulations, and other requirements relevant to the discipline: To enable the auditor to work within, and be aware of, the requirements that apply to the organization being audited.

Auditors should know how to

- Use standards to evaluate quality system performance
- Collect information, evaluate evidence, and make observations
- Plan, organize, and manage an audit
- Prepare and deliver an audit report

Experience The auditors should have

- Four years of work experience, including 2 years in quality assurance (QA)
- Participated in at least four audits covering at least 20 days

Knowledge The auditors should be knowledgeable of

- Quality systems, standards, and audit procedures

Talent

1. Think in abstract terms
2. Make realistic evaluations
3. Analyze complex systems
4. Stay on track and finish the job
5. Respect the feelings of all participants
6. Resist the pressure to change the truth
7. Manage personal and interpersonal stress
8. Draw rational conclusions based on evidence
9. Evaluate evidence in a fair and impartial manner

Competence

1. Auditors should be evaluated at least every 3 years.
2. Confirm that auditors have current knowledge.
3. Make sure that auditors are trained and retrained.
4. Auditors should be selected by an evaluation panel. Set up a panel of judges to review auditor qualifications and to select the best candidates.

Part 2: Audit Process and Procedure

ISO prepared ISO 10011-3 to explain how to manage an audit program. This includes recommendations for how to

1. Organize the process
2. Select personnel
3. Identify relevant standards
4. Support the process
5. Train
6. Monitor the process

It is recommended that the audit process should be conducted separately and entirely independent of the quality system to be audited.

An audit manager should be selected who has practical quality system audit experience.

The quality standards that will be used to perform the audit must be designated.

Steps must be taken to ensure that audit teams are capable of performing quality audits, including selecting auditors and lead auditors.

This selection should be officially approved by a separate auditor evaluation panel.

The audit manager should select auditors who

- Understand the quality system standards that will be applied
- Are generally familiar with the auditee's products and services

The audit manager should select auditors who

- Have studied the regulations that govern the auditee's activities
- Have the technical qualifications needed to carry out a proper audit
- Have the professional qualifications needed to carry out an audit
- Are suitably trained

In addition, audit managers should

- Develop and enforce a code of ethics to govern the audit process
- Monitor and evaluate the performance of the audit teams
- Guarantee consistency—for example, ensure that all auditors make the same observations and draw the same conclusions when confronted with the same evidence

Audit Process

The audit process is a process for determining compliance with the requirements, plans, and contracts as appropriate. This process may be employed by any two parties, where one party (auditing party) audits the software products or activities of another party (audited party).*

---

* *IEEE/EIA 12207.2-1997 Life Cycle Process*, Chapter 6.7, p. 58.

Audit Process Implementation   Process implementation consists of the following tasks:

Auditing personnel shall not have any direct responsibility for the software products and activities they audit.

All resources required to conduct the audits shall be agreed on by the parties. These resources include supporting personnel, location, facilities, hardware, software, and tools.

The parties should agree on the following items at each audit: agenda, software products (and results of an activity) to be reviewed, audit scope and procedures, and entry and exit criteria for the audit.

Problems detected during the audits shall be recorded and entered into the problem resolution process (Section 6.8) as required.

After completing an audit, the audit results shall be documented and provided to the audited party. The audited party shall acknowledge to the auditing party any problems found in the audit and related problem resolutions planned.

The parties shall agree on the outcome of the audit and any action item responsibilities and closure criteria.

Support for the Audit Process   Audit managers should

- Plan and schedule audit activities
- Perform the audit reporting process
- Control the audit follow-up process
- Protect the confidentiality of audit information
- Ensure that auditors have the resources they need

Procedures

Management Preparation   Managers shall ensure that the audit is performed as required by applicable standards and procedures and by requirements mandated by law, contract, or other policy. To this end, managers shall do the following:

Plan time and resources required for audits, including support functions, as required in IEEE Std 1058-1998 [B9], legal or regulatory documents, or other appropriate standards

Provide funding and facilities required to plan, define, execute, and manage the audits

Provide training and orientation on the audit procedures applicable to a given project

Ensure appropriate levels of expertise and knowledge sufficient to comprehend the software product being audited

Ensure that planned audits are conducted

Act on audit team recommendations in a timely manner

Verification of Quality Manual

The manual has to be thorough and convincing. It must provide enough detail for the auditor to see the comprehensiveness of the quality system.

The quality manual is designed to be traceable by paragraph number to each paragraph and section number of the 20 elements within the ISO 9000 Standard.

The latter is a pragmatic consideration that is intended to facilitate the conduct of the compliance audit.

A quality manual enforces the documentation and documentation control elements of the standard. The quality manual discusses how the company will comply with each element, states its quality policy, may include the quality objectives, and an overview of the processes.

The quality manual is an aspect of the production management system. It is that specific element of the documentation system devoted to the control of quality.

It contains all the sample documents used in quality management as well as the procedures.

One advantage of the quality manual is that it selects discrete activities for control.

Verification of Implementation of the Quality Manual

The primary role of the quality manual is to record a formal statement of the organization's quality philosophy. ISO 9000 stipulates that management is responsible for insuring that quality policy and objectives are understood throughout the organization.

The quality manual provides the blue print for doing that while the procedures provide the details. The quality manual states the company's general philosophy. It outlines in general terms how the company will comply with each clause of the standard.

The quality manual is a key element during an audit. All the sample documents are examined in the audit.

A complete set of operating procedures are written to define what has to be done to meet the quality requirements outlined by this manual.

In addition, there is an explicit designation of the people who will be responsible for carrying out each procedure.

A set of work instructions are provided at the third level that explicitly details how the organization will conform to the quality requirements specified at the second level.

The ISO 9000 standard requires that the organization must have a documented quality system (4.2 Quality system).

These documented processes and procedures, together with the quality manual outlined earlier, form the bulk of the audited documentation set.

Process and procedure writing represents most of the formal documentation of the quality system.

Along with the necessary procedure description, the qualifications for the person performing each of these procedures is listed.

Each documented procedure specifies at a minimum the

- Expected input and acceptance criteria
- Expected output criteria
- Interrelationship with other procedures
- Qualifications and skills of the person performing the procedure
- Tools, rules practices, methodologies, and conventions

The ISO 9000 standard requires that the organization must have developed formal procedures for at least 15 of its "must address" clauses such as

1. Document control
2. Purchaser supplied product
3. Product identification and traceability
4. Process control

With respect to the product itself, there have to be formal procedures for

1. Final inspection and testing.
2. Control of nonconforming product.
3. Corrective action.
4. Handling, storage, packing, and delivery.
5. Quality records.
6. Internal quality auditing.
7. Training.
8. Servicing.
9. Statistical techniques.
10. Work instructions.

The third level ensures that the organization "Walks the Talk."

Each of the procedures outlined at the second level have to be accompanied by specific instructions that tell how each will be carried out.

Generally, these work instructions are captured and displayed in the following three common types of plans that detail the typical activities necessary to fulfill each separate requirement:

1. Project plan
2. Build plan
3. Test plan

Sample Work Instructions   The ISO 9000-3 guideline requires plans for each design and development activity.

The project plan fills this requirement by defining the skills required and committing the necessary resources to each task.

Postimplementation Review   A postimplementation review takes place at some predetermined point after the new system has gone live. There are many different variables to consider regarding the target timing for this type of audit, including whether the system needs time to stabilize, how long the project team will be available to correct issues, vendor contractual considerations, and post launch issues raised by the users.

Key Phase Review   A key phase review, undertaken during the course of a project, is a proactive approach often used for high-risk projects. This can include system development life cycle (SDLC) or system design reviews, or participation by the internal auditor in a "gate" or specific project phase review, for example. The key objective is usually associated with assessing how closely the project management or SDLC methodologies are followed. As indicated above, internal auditing can work with project teams to address concerns before the system is moved into the production environment, when it is still relatively inexpensive to make corrections. Through early project involvement, internal auditing can raise questions and suggestions that influence a project in either a formal or informal way. The two IS auditing guidelines from ISACA that can be referenced to guide the IT auditor in carrying out reviews of this nature are discussed in the following sections.

Project Management Methodology Assessment   Auditing the overall project management methodology can identify risks and point out weaknesses in the methodology that could help the entire organization improve. For organizations that have too many projects to audit individually, this type of review utilizes a more holistic approach. In addition, by auditing the methodology, the internal auditor will be better prepared to audit individual projects because the Project Management Office (PMO) audit will provide a strong basis for understanding the organization's practices.

Possible objectives of auditing project methodologies include the following:

Assessing the adequacy of project management methodologies.
Determining whether the methodology supports the full range of IT projects in the organization from very small to very large.
Determining whether the PMO policies, standards, methodologies, and processes are implemented and executed consistently across all projects in the organization.
Assessing the ability of the PMO to add the intended level of value.
PMO should have a complete inventory of all projects in the organization.
Determining whether the project portfolio management processes are working effectively.

The project plan is developed at the beginning of the project and is updated as the project progresses.

Because unknowns are given in software projects this plan must be a "living" document.

Since the plan is subject to change it has to be under control, which means that it has to be associated with an organizational stakeholder.

In addition, it has to provide a complete set of procedures for review, approval, change, distribution, withdrawal, and tracking.

Privacy and Audit Management

The IIA's International Professional Practices Framework reminds auditors to take privacy regulations and risks into account when planning, performing, and reporting assurance and consulting assignments. Professional bodies, legislators, and supervisory authorities issue a broad variety of guidance and regulations.

When hiring auditors, there is even a greater need for due diligence to ensure that newly hired auditors act in accordance with relevant laws and policies when using personal information during assurance or consulting engagements.*

Five Key Focus Areas for Project Audits

GTAG focuses on five key areas of projects around which we recommend building an audit approach. The following five categories were chosen as the logical areas around which to focus based on a variety of research and the authors' past experience with using various project risk assessment methodologies.†

1. Business and IT alignment
2. Project management
3. IT solution readiness
4. Organizational and process change management
5. Postimplementation

---

* Ulrich Hahn. *Global Technology Audit Guide 5: Managing and Auditing Privacy Risks*. Switzerland/Germany Ken Askelson, JCPenney, USA, Robert Stiles, Texas Guaranteed (TG), USA, June 2006, pp. 19–22.

† Karine Wegrzynowicz, Lafarge SA Steven Stein. *Global Technology Audit Guide (GTAG®)12, Auditing IT Projects*. Hewlett-Packard, March 2009, p. 7.

The next sections provide considerations for each of the five key focus areas.

Business and IT Alignment   Business and IT alignment means that the vision and objectives of both the business and IT are understood, are in agreement with each other, and that the project is in line with the strategy of the organization.

The audit team should verify the plan and process of regular meetings with all stakeholders present and ensure that channels for an open flow of communication are available.

Project Management   Internal auditors will have to invest time to study and better understand project management processes and terminology.

In order to plan, scope, and assess projects and programs, the auditors must understand the concepts of project management, project governance, project management methodology within the context of their business and organization, and the discipline of organizing and managing resources within defined scope, quality, time, and cost constraints.

Project Management Methodologies   The auditor should know about the integrated policies, standards, methodologies, life cycles, procedures, tools, techniques, stakeholders, and organizations that are used to guide the planning and execution of a project.

Before even performing audits, the team should have a better understanding of the organization's project management methodology and SDLC.

Project Stakeholders   Internal auditors must understand how the organization identifies and includes stakeholders in IT projects. Stakeholders must provide strategic guidance, as well as financial, political, and emotional support to the audit team.

PMO may play a key role during project audits and may serve as a valuable liaison between internal auditing and project managers. Auditors can play an advisory role to the PMO by sharing their perspective on IT project risk and by setting auditing expectations for the PMO and individual projects.

Maturity Models   If the audited organization uses maturity model, auditors can use maturity models as a basis for assessing an organization's project management and/or systems development processes.

Auditors should view the use of maturity models by the organization as a very positive step in terms of improving the organization's IT project management approach. However, there is no requirement for an organization to use a maturity model.

IT Solution Readiness   The IT audit team should focus and check the full IT solution readiness. Different companies may use their own SDLC methodology. It may differ by the type of technology being developed.

The internal auditors should verify the existence of some type of development life cycle and will need to determine whether it is appropriately followed. Then, they will use the phases in the life cycle to determine when to perform the project audit and what controls to test.

Solution Design   Auditors should look to ensure that business requirements and both the existing and future business processes are taken into consideration. At the end of the solution design phase, the project scope should be frozen, and all functionalities should be prioritized in terms of what is required for the system launch.

Organizational and Process Change Management   The audit team should ensure that the organizational and process change management are assessed with the right level of skills and all documented. The audit team verifies that the change management is well communicated, cleared, and the impact of the change is well documented.

These points should be stated clearly at the beginning of the project and must be managed well beyond postimplementation.

An assessment should be made on the skill set of existing staff members compared to changing to new roles and determine whether processes or workflows are clearly defined to gauge the readiness of the organization to accept the change.

The audit team should also evaluate whether the training is complete, timely, and includes user guides that are not generic. In addition, training provided to the IT team and/or helpdesk *personnel should be reviewed to determine whether it is adequate to support the new system.*

Documenting Audit Conclusions   At the end of the audit, the auditors make a list of key nonconformities based on the evidence obtained.

Then, the auditors draw conclusions about how well the quality system is applying its policies and achieving its objectives, they should discuss their evidence, observations, conclusions, and nonconformities with the auditee's senior managers before they prepare a final audit report.

The Audit Report   The lead auditor should prepare the audit report and send it to the client, and the client sends it to the auditee. The auditee is expected to take whatever actions are necessary to correct or prevent quality system nonconformities. Follow-up audits might be scheduled in order to verify that corrective and preventive actions were taken.

Postlaunch Support   It is essential for auditors to ensure that a post go-live support plan is defined in terms of the support team organization for both functional and technical issues. The support team should be analyzed to determine whether it is correctly sized for the go-live and postlaunch workload, which is usually much higher than normal. Additionally, contingency plans should be established in the event something goes wrong during the go-live period.

Postimplementation   During postimplementation phase, an audit team ensures the key risks to watch for many of which might be related to the change management aspects. The auditors must determine whether the new system is being used correctly and the functionality is meeting the requirements as intended. A key consideration is to determine whether there is any prolonged resistance to change.*

Problem Resolution Process   The objective is to provide a timely, responsible, and documented means to ensure that all discovered problems are analyzed and resolved and trends are recognized.

List of activities: This process consists of the following activities:

---

* David Coderre. *Continuous Auditing: Implications for Assurance, Monitoring, and Risk Assessment.* Royal Canadian Mounted Police (RCMP), Global Technology Audit Guide, (GTAG 3).

1. Process implementation
2. Problem resolution

Part 3: Auditing and Information Security

This section offers a practical and comprehensive understanding of the body of knowledge in audit-based information security.

Defined and Planned Strategy

From an execution standpoint, the first provision implies that the organization has to actively define and deliberately plan a systematic security strategy.

The second implies that the organization must define substantive policies, assign roles and responsibilities, educate employees, and describe and enforce accountability.

Effective realization of both of these principles requires time and resources.

Auditing Privacy Risks

An audit team should audit the organization's privacy practices and risk assessment plans and procedures. There are some specific areas where an audit team needs to focus on, as follows:

- Laws and regulations in all jurisdictions in which business is conducted
- Internal privacy policies and guidelines
- Privacy policies intended for the customers and the public
- Liaising with in-house legal counsel to understand the legal implications
- Liaising with information technology specialists and business process owners to understand information security implications
- The maturity of the organization's privacy controls

The auditors should also conduct privacy risk assessments and provide assurance over privacy controls across the organization including

- Management oversight
- Privacy policies and controls
- Applicable privacy notices
- Types and appropriateness of information collected
- Systems that process personal information
- Collection methodologies
- Use of personal information according to stated intent, applicable laws, and other regulations
- Security practices covering personal information

The independence of internal auditors may be impaired, when they assume a portion of the responsibility for developing and implementing a privacy program. For this reason and due to the possible need for sufficient technical and legal expertise, third-party experts may be required.*

Auditing Data Categorization

Prioritizing and classification of data are very important. The IT audit team needs to ensure that data are prioritized and classified. For example, data need to be assigned based on sensitivity level—such as proprietary, confidential, or public. The auditor verifies the following aspects:

- What are the regulatory penalties for mishandling privacy protected data?
- How has data ownership been assigned and what appropriate controls have been established in handling the data?
- Has the data been classified? Are the levels of classification appropriate for ensuring adequate privacy controls?
- How widely would a privacy breach be disclosed? Who would need to be notified? How will they be notified?
- How costly would it be to remediate various types of unauthorized privacy disclosures?
- How would a privacy breach impact customer, citizen (in case of a public entity), or investor confidence? How much would it cost to recover trust and confidence?

---

* Ibid, p. 19.

Auditing Law and Regulation Aspects

Compliance with applicable laws and regulations is the foundation of most privacy programs. An attorney who is well versed in privacy can champion privacy compliance, assisting in the design of a compliant privacy program, review of contracts with third parties to ensure appropriate privacy controls, and counsel in response to a privacy disclosure incident. Because privacy laws and regulations continue to evolve through the actions of courts and regulators on an almost daily basis, an organization may seek to obtain services from a legal professional with specialization in the organization's industry.

Organization Threats

The basic rule of information security is to provide confidentiality, integrity, and availability of data, which in other words covers many of the goals of a privacy plan. Privacy relies on the information security, even though not all information security addresses privacy; however, audit of a privacy program comprises information security controls.

Application Risks

After the auditor identifies the automated processes, very basic security questions need to be addressed regarding any application that handles private information:*

- Confidential issues need to be identified in the requirements defining the application.
- Data with categorization standards should be implemented in the application.
- Requirement should be validated in the development and deployment of the application.
- Application authorization and authentication process and procedure should be specified.
- Enterprise single sign on should be specified.
- The user access to the data and logging procedure should be tracked.
- External interfaces of other application procedure.

---

* Ibid, p. 18.

Business Process Risks

The IT audit team must be aware of the business process and their risks, and how the data are being used. Measures to protect printed information should follow the same principles used to classify and protect electronic data. At the minimum, the desks should be clean, and the draws and filing cabinets should be locked. Discretion should be used in areas open to the public.

Auditors should identify the threats to the organization's data through research, benchmarking, and brainstorming and categorize them according to the likelihood of occurrence and impact.

Vulnerability assessments and penetration test methods are often cited as assurance methods for network accessible applications and infrastructure.

Vulnerability assessments generally focus on the identification of potential vulnerabilities in information systems. The assessments identify and prioritize vulnerabilities in the configuration, administration, and architecture of information systems.

The auditor can verify aspects such as

- Private information is prepared according to the policy and procedures
- Documents are stored securely prior to the disposal or shredding
- Working documents with private data are stored securely
- Confidential information should not be viewable by unauthorized personnel
- All workstations are locked when unattended
- The application of privacy controls is consistent across various departments

Auditing IT Vulnerabilities

Identifying Insignificant Vulnerability Management The Global Technology Audit Guide (GTAG 6) managing and auditing IT vulnerabilities has recommended the top six indicators of poor vulnerability management processes, which are as follows:

- A higher than acceptable five number of security incidents during a given period of time.

- Being unable to identify vulnerabilities that may result in critical assets.
- Being unable to assess risk and vulnerabilities and lack of mitigation plan.
- Poor working relationships between IT management and IT security.
- Lack of an asset management system.
- Lack of a configuration management process that is integrated with vulnerability mitigation efforts.

The Internal Auditor's Role on Information Security   Internal auditors provide guidance and value to the business in many ways. They can assess the effectiveness of preventive, detective, and mitigation measures against past attacks, as deemed appropriate, and future attempts or incidents deemed likely to occur. Internal auditors should confirm that the board of directors has been appropriately informed of threats, incidents, vulnerabilities exploited, and corrective measures.

Vulnerability and Risk

Risk management has been defined as "the process of identifying risk, assessing risk, and taking steps to reduce risk to an acceptable level" and typically involves the following steps:

- Asset evaluation: Identifying the overall value an organization places on an asset.
- Threat assessment: Identifying the likelihood of harmful events that could affect an asset.
- Vulnerability assessment: Identifying all the weaknesses of an asset and their severity.
- Risk determination: Evaluating and prioritizing the risks posed to an asset.
- Risk decision: Deciding whether to accept, transfer, or mitigate the risk posed to an asset.*

---

* *Managing and Auditing IT Vulnerabilities (GTAG 6)* Sasha Romanosky, Heinz School of Public Policy and Management, Carnegie Mellon University Gene Kim, Tripwire, Inc. and IT Process Institute Bridget Kravchenko, General Motors Corp., October 2006, p. 13.

Persistent Auditing and Monitoring

Persistent auditing is a method used by auditors to perform audit-related activities on a more continuous or continual basis. It is the continuum of activities ranging from continuous control assessment to continuous risk assessment—all activities on the control-risk continuum. Technology plays a key role in automating the identification of exceptions and/or anomalies, analysis of patterns within the digits of key numeric fields, analysis of trends, detailed transaction analysis against cutoffs and thresholds, testing of controls, and the comparison of the process or system over time and/or against other similar entities.

Constant auditing helps auditors to evaluate the adequacy of management's monitoring function. Continuous auditing also identifies and assesses areas of risk and provides information to auditors that can be communicated to the management to support its efforts to mitigate the risk. Additionally, it can be used when developing the annual audit plan by focusing audit attention and resources on areas of higher risk.

Understanding the terminology surrounding continuous auditing is a key in understanding the fact that control and risk both represent opposite sides of the same coin. Controls exist to help mitigate risk, and identification of control deficiencies highlights the areas of potential risk. Conversely, by examining risk, auditors can identify areas where controls are needed and/or are not working.

Constant risk assessment refers to the activities used by auditors to identify and assess the levels of risk. Constant risk assessment identifies and assesses risks by examining trends and comparisons—within a single process or system, as compared to its own past performance, and against other processes or systems operating within the enterprise.

Continuous monitoring is a process that management puts in place to ensure that its policies, procedures, and business processes are operating effectively. Management identifies critical control points and implements automated tests to determine if these controls are working properly.*

---

* David Coderre. *Continuous Auditing: Implications for Assurance, Monitoring, and Risk Assessment.* Royal Canadian Mounted Police (RCMP), Global Technology Audit Guide (GTAG 3), p. 5.

Suggested Readings

Software configuration management plans (see IEEE Std 828-2005 [B3])

Software design descriptions (see IEEE Std 1016-1998 [B7])

Unit development folders

Software project management plans (see IEEE Std 1058-1998 [B9])

Software quality assurance plans (see IEEE Std 730-2002 [B2])

Software requirement specifications (see IEEE Std 830-1998 [B5])

Software safety plans (see IEEE Std 1228-1994 [B13])

Software test documentation (see IEEE Std 829-2008 [B4])

Software user documentation (see IEEE Std 1063-2001 [B10])

Software verification and validation plans (see IEEE Std 1012-2004 [B6])

Software architectural descriptions (see IEEE Std 1471-2000 [B14])

11

SOFTWARE RELIABILITY AND PROCESS IMPROVEMENT

Introduction

This chapter contains two parts. Part 1 discusses definition and measurement and metrics of reliability based on standards. Part 2 discusses ISO 15504 standard, capability maturity models (CMMs), personal software process (PSP), and team software process (TSP). This chapter also provides an appendix that contains a software process improvement sample document.

Part 1: Definition and Measurement

What Is Reliability?

According to IEEE 610 (p. 62) "Reliability is the ability of a system or component to perform its required functions under stated conditions for a specified period of time."

In a very basic understanding, reliability means that confidence in a given piece of software can be assured through measurement.

What Are Reliability Metrics?

A metric is the term for a mathematical definition, algorithm, or function that is used to obtain a quantitative assessment of a product or process.

Classifications   There are two general classes of metrics:

1. **Management metrics** assist in the management of the software development process
2. **Quality metrics** are predictors or indicators of the product qualities

Management metrics can be used for controlling any industrial production or manufacturing activity.

They are used to assess resources, cost, and task completion.

Quality metrics are used to estimate the characteristics or qualities of a software product.

Some metrics can serve both management and quality purposes, that is, they can be used for both project control and quality assessment.

This is particularly true of metrics for software quality (e.g., maintainability, reliability, and usability).

These measures must be interpreted by comparison with plans, similar projects, or similar components within the current project.

There is a standard for ISO 9126, which we have discussed in detail in Chapter 1, Part 2.

Since there are an infinite number of possible metrics, users need to adopt a criteria to decide which metrics best fit the needs of their project.

Standards Defining Reliability Measurement

The IEEE 1045: *Standard for Software Productivity Metrics* (1992), IEEE 982.1 *Standard Dictionary of Measures to Produce Reliable Software* (1988), and IEEE *982.2 Guide for the Use of IEEE Standard Dictionary of Measures to Produce Reliable Software* (1988).

Selection of Measures

Application of the measures in IEEE 982.1 requires an intelligent selection process.

There are 39 measures defined that are not intended to be applied as a whole to any given project.

The measures selected the need to reflect the project goals that can be implemented within the project constraints.

Thus, the 982.2 Guideline is provided to offer a basis for the project managers to consider and discuss which measures best fit the project requirements.

Measures from IEEE 982.2

Fault density—faults per thousand source/software lines of code (KSLOC).

Defect density—used after design and code inspections. If this defect density is outside the norm after several inspections, it is an indication that there may be problems in the inspection process.

Cumulative failure profile—a profile is used to predict the reliability of a given artifact after testing—based on the profile recommendations that can be made for additional testing of the artifact or a subset.

Error distributions—plots error information to provide the distribution of errors according to different criteria—can identify causes of failure and predict failure against a profile.

Measurement-Based Assurance

Basically, reliability means that the confidence in a given piece of software can be assured through measurement.

This is based on the organization having a range of standardized metrics that allow it to assess the performance of

- A given piece of software
- At a given point in time
- In a given situation

Criteria for Selection

Ideally, a metric should possess the following five characteristics:

1. Simple—definition and use of the metric is simple
2. Objective—different people will give same value
3. Easily collected—the cost and effort are reasonable
4. Robust—metric is insensitive to irrelevant changes
5. Valid—*metric measures what it is supposed to*

Sample Primitive Metrics

1. Age of open real problem reports
2. Age of unevaluated problem reports
3. Age of real closed problem reports
4. Time when errors are discovered
5. Rate of error discovery

Primitive Cost and Effort Metrics

1. Time spent
2. Elapsed time
3. Staff hours
4. Staff months
5. Staff years

Primitive Change Metrics

1. Number of revisions, additions, deletions, or modifications
2. Number of requests to change the software requirements specification
3. Number of requests to change the software design

Software Requirements Metrics

1. The main reasons to measure software requirements specifications are to
   a. Provide early warnings of quality problems
   b. Enable more accurate project predictions
   c. Improve the specifications

Requirements Size Metrics

This involves a simple count.

In that process, large components are assumed to have a larger number of residual errors.

- That is because they are more difficult to understand than smaller components.

As a result, their reliability may be affected based on the following:

- Number of pages or words
- Number of requirements
- Number of functions

Requirements Traceability

- This is used to assess the degree of requirements traceability (RT) by measuring percent of requirements that have been implemented in the software design.

- It is also used to identify requirements that are either missing in addition to the original requirements.
- The measure is computed using the equation: $RT = R1/R2 \times 100\%$, where R1 is the number of requirements met by the design, and R2 is the number of original requirements.

Completeness

This metric is used to determine the completeness (CM) of the specification.

This metric references the following:

- Number of functions not satisfactorily defined
- Number of functions
- Number of defined functions
- Number of defined functions not used
- Number of referenced functions (and number of decision points)

Fault-Days Number

This metric specifies the number of days that faults spend in the software product from their creation to their removal.

This measure uses two primitives:

- Activity, date, or time the fault was introduced.
- Activity, date, or time the fault was removed.
- The fault days are the number of days from the creation of the fault to its removal.

Software Design Metrics

The main reasons for computing metrics during software design are as follows:

- Provide an early indication of project status
- Enable selection of alternative designs
- Identify potential problems early in the software development process
- Limit complexity

- Help in deciding how to modularize so that the resulting modules are both testable and maintainable

Primitive Size Metrics

These metrics are used to estimate the size of the software design or software design documents.

- Number of pages or words
- DLOC (lines of program design language)
- Number of modules
- Number of functions
- Number of inputs and outputs
- Number of interfaces

Primitive Fault Metrics

These metrics identify potentially fault-prone modules.

- Number of faults associated with each module
- Number of requirements faults detected during detailed design
- Number of structural design faults detected during detailed design
- Number of unresolved faults at planned end of activity
- Number of faults that have not been corrected
- Number of outstanding change requests
- Number of software requirements and design faults detected during reviews and walkthrough

Primitive Complexity Metrics

These metrics identify modules that are complex or hard to test.

- Number of parameters per module
- Number of states or data partitions per parameter
- Number of branches in each module

Defect Density

Used after design inspections or large block modifications to assess the inspection process.

The following primitives are used:

- Total number of unique defects detected during the inspection or during the software development activity
- Total number of inspections to date
- Number of source lines of design statements in thousands (KSLOD)

Test-Related Primitives

These metrics check whether each module is, or has been, adequately tested.

They also assess the effectiveness of early testing

- Number of software integration test cases planned/executed involving each module
- Number of black box test cases planned/executed per module
- Number of requirements faults detected (which also reassesses the quality of the specification)

Code Metrics

Lines of code (LOC)—although LOC is one of the most popular metrics,

- It has no standard definition.
- The predominant definition for LOC is any line of a program text that is not a comment or blank line.
- It is an indication of size that allows for estimation of effort, time scale, and total number of faults for the application.

Cyclomatic Complexity (C)

Used to determine the structural complexity of a coded module in order to limit its complexity, thus, promoting understandability.

- In general, high complexity leads to a high number of defects and maintenance costs.
- Also used to identify minimum number of test paths to assure test coverage.

- The primitives for this measure include number of nodes and the number of edges (which can be determined from a graph representing the module).

Amount of Data

This measure can be determined by primitive metrics such as

- Number of inputs/outputs
- Number of variables

These primitive metrics can be obtained from a compiler cross-reference.

Live Variables

- For each line in a section of code, determine the number of live variables (i.e., variables whose values could change during execution of that section of code).
- The average number of live variables per line of code is the sum of the number of live variables for each line, divided by the number of LOC.

Test Metrics

Sample metrics are

- Number of faults detected in each module
- Number of requirements, design, and coding faults found during unit and integration

Testing

- Number of errors by type (e.g., logic, computational, interface, and documentation)
- Number of errors by cause or origin
- Number of errors by severity (e.g., critical, major, and cosmetic)

Fault Density

This measure is computed by dividing the number of faults by the size (usually in KLOC).

Fault-days number can be used to perform the following:

- Predict remaining faults by comparison with expected fault days
- Determine if sufficient testing has been completed based on predetermined goals
- Establish standard fault densities for comparison and prediction

Defect Age

- Defect age is the time interval between when a defect is introduced and when it is detected or fixed.
- Assign the numbers 1–6 to each of the software development activities from requirements to operation and maintenance.
- The defect age is computed as:

$$\text{Average Defect Age} = \frac{\left(\text{Activity Detected} - \text{Activity Introduced}\right)}{\text{Number of Defects}}$$

Defect Response Time

This measure is the time from when a defect is detected to when it is fixed or closed.

Defect Cost

The cost of a defect may be a sum of the cost to analyze the defect, the cost to fix it, and the cost of failures already incurred due to the defect.

Defect Removal Efficiency

The defect removal efficiency (DRE) is the percentage of defects that have been removed during an activity.

The DRE can also be computed for each software development activity and plotted on a bar graph to show the relative DREs for each activity.

Or, the DRE may be computed for a specific task or technique (e.g., design inspection, code walkthrough, unit test, 6-month operation, etc.).

Primitive Test Case Metrics

Total number of planned white/black box test cases run to completion

Number of planned software integration tests run to completion

Number of unplanned test cases required during test activity

Statement Coverage

Measures the percentage of statements executed (to assure that each statement has been tested at least once).

Branch Coverage

Measures the percentage of branches executed.

Path Coverage

- Measures the percentage of program paths executed.
- It is generally impractical and inefficient to test all the paths in a program.
- The count of the number of paths may be reduced by treating all possible loop iterations as one path.
- Path coverage may be used to ensure 100% coverage of critical (safety or security related) paths.

Data Flow Coverage

Measures the definition and use of variables and data structures.

Test Coverage

Measures the CM of the testing activity.

Test coverage is the percentage of requirements implemented (in the form of defined test cases or functional capabilities) multiplied by the percentage of the software structure (in units, segments, statements, branches, or path test results) tested.

Mean Time to Failure

Mean time to failure (MTTF) describes the expected time to failure for a nonrepairable system.

For example, assume that you tested three identical systems starting from time 0 until all of them failed. The first system failed at 10 hours, the second failed at 12 hours, and the third failed at 13 hours.

The MTTF is the average of the three failure times, which is 11.6667 hours.

This metric is the basic parameter required by most software reliability models.

High values imply good reliability.

Failure Rate

> Used to indicate the growth in the software reliability as a function of test time.

> Usually used with reliability models.

> This metric requires two primitives: t_i is the observed time between failures for a given severity level i and f_i is the number of failures of a given severity level in the ith time interval.

Cumulative Failure Profile

Uses a graphical technique to

- Predict reliability
- Estimate additional testing time needed to reach an acceptable reliability level
- Identify modules and subsystems that require additional testing

This metric requires one primitive for the total number of failures of a given severity level I in a given time interval.

Cumulative failures are plotted on a time scale. The shape of the curve is used to project when testing will be complete and to assess reliability.

It can provide an indication of clustering of faults in modules, suggesting further testing for these modules.

Customer Ratings

- These metrics are based on results of customer surveys, which ask customers to provide a rating or a satisfaction score (e.g., on a scale of 1–10) of a vendor's product or customer services (e.g., hotlines, fixes, and user manual).
- Ratings and scores can be tabulated and plotted in bar graphs.

Customer Service Metrics

- Number of hotline calls received
- Number of fixes for each type of product
- Number of hours required for fixes
- Number of hours for training (for each type of product)

Making Reliability Metrics Meaningful

There are three conditions that apply to all data associated with software reliability measurement.

- Primitives—measures must be constructed that are directly observable (such as temperature) versus inferred (such as comfort)
- Flexibility—primitive-based measures are available that fit the given life cycle situation
- Understandability—measures must be able to be converted into information understandable to the business side of the organization (graphs)

Standards Defining Software Measurement

There are two IEEE standards sets that define metrics for software.

IEEE 1045: IEEE Standard for Software Productivity Metrics (1992)

IEEE 982.1 Standard Dictionary of Measures to Produce Reliable Software (1988) and IEEE 982.2 Guide for the Use of IEEE Standard Dictionary of Measures to Produce Reliable Software (1988)

Productivity Metrics: IEEE 1045   As we said, this standard defines the measurement primitives for computing software productivity.

- It categorizes these primitives by attributes
  - An attribute is a measurable characteristic of a primitive.
- This standard does NOT claim to improve productivity but only to measure it.
- It provides a consistent and measurement based way to characterize the software productivity.
- Software productivity metrics terminology is meant to ensure an understanding of the basis for measuring both code and document production in a project.
- It should be noted that although this standard describes measurements to characterize the software process it does NOT measure the quality of software.

Software Reliability: IEEE 982   The objective of this standard is to provide the software community with defined measures currently used as indicators of reliability.

The predictive nature of these measures is dependent on the correct application of a valid model.

This standard presents

- A selection of applicable measures
- The proper conditions for using each measure
- The methods of computation
- A framework for a common language among users

In addition, it provides

- The means for continual assessment of the process and product
- The stipulation of a teaching phase in the life cycle

By emphasizing early reliability assessment, this standard also supports measurement-based methods for improving product reliability.

Quality Metrics Methodology

Application of quality metrics implies the need for a methodology, which is specified in IEEE 1061–1992 Software Quality Metrics Methodology as

> Some people feel that the word "quality" is misapplied in the title since the methodology outlined in it is applicable to any aspect of measurement of a software product.

This standard provides a methodology for establishing quality requirements and identifying analyzing and validating the process and product using metrics.

This methodology spans the entire life cycle of software.

It may be appropriately applied by acquirers, developers, user's maintainers, or independent assessors.

The basic approach is to establish a metrics framework that is a three-level hierarchy.

- This starts with the definition of a set of top level quality requirements and their attributes.
- Factors representing user and management views are associated with these attributes and characterized by direct metrics.

IEEE 1061–1992

- For example, MTTF might serve as a direct measure of reliability.
- These direct metrics are intended to be measured in the completed system.
  - But they probably cannot be measured during the development phase of the life cycle.
- Each factor is decomposed into subfactors representing concrete attributes of the software elements of the system.
  - These must always be meaningful to the development staff.
- For example, reliability at this level might be expressed as the system's ability to detect and recover from execution faults.
- The subfactors are further decomposed into metrics that are used to make measurements during the development process itself.

- These in effect serve as a baseline for predicting the overall quality of the system as it is being built.
  - They permit estimating the eventual outcome of the top level desired attributes of the system.

Software Reliability Measurement

Software reliability measurement consists of three interrelated technical areas:

1. Models
2. Metrics
3. Data

None of these areas can advance very far without the support from and progress in the other areas.

What Is a Model?

- A model is an abstract (usually mathematical) representation of the relationships among two or more variable attributes of an entity.

Qualities of a Good Model

- A good model will incorporate the influence of all variables that affect the outcome.
- A good model will have predictive capabilities.
  - That is, given the values, it will determine the future values of other attributes with an acceptable degree of uncertainty.

The Importance of Data

- Models require data because an essential step in the development of useful models is validation.
- Validation of this involves applying the model to a set of historical data and comparing the model's predicted results to the actual results recorded.

Metrics and Models

- Applying a metric to a product results in a data item.
- Applying a set of metrics to a product and applying them throughout the course of the development results in a data set.
- A model uses metric data as input and produces another metric as output.

Model Development and Independent Metrics

- Model development research drives metric definition in this sense.
- But work in the development of generic software metrics has progressed independently and comprehensively.
- Such that now model developers can design their models to incorporate existing metrics.

The Issue of Availability

- As software metrics become standardized, the software engineering community has access to more complete and consistent data for validating models.
  - Yet the availability of software data remains a problem for several reasons.

To get data, you need

- Metrics
- Samples
- Sufficient justification for collecting it to outweigh the added costs that data collection adds to a development effort

Data Retention and Use

- Once data have been collected, it needs to be stored so that it retains its usefulness.
- The data must be retrievable, understandable, and relevant.
- Storage of software measurement data has not posed a significant hurdle because the amount of data that has been collected is not large in relation to existing storage capacities.

Validity

The validity of the data itself needs to be established as well. That is, when data collected by different people or at different times are compared or combined, care must be taken to standardize the data items with respect to each other so that the numbers retain their meaning.

Software Reliability Estimation

The measures included

- Execution time
- Speed
- Parallel efficiency
- Overhead ratio
- Processor utilization
- Redundancy
- Cost-effectiveness
- Speed up of the parallel algorithm over the corresponding serial algorithm
- An additive measure called "price" that assigns a weighted value to computations and processors

CMMs: The Software Engineering Institute's Capability Maturity Model

The CMM is an assessment of the capability of a given software organization based on key practices.

Maturity Levels

There are five levels of maturity in the CMM

1. Initial
2. Repeatable
3. Defined
4. Managed
5. Optimizing

Initial

- This is the level of chaos.
- There are no defined processes, therefore, everything is ad hoc.
- Because nothing is defined, nothing is repeatable.
- Organizations at this level spend a lot of time fighting fires.

Repeatable   This is the first level where a set of reliable key processes exist.

- Software quality administrator (SQA)
- Software configuration management
- Requirements management
- Project planning
- Project tracking and oversight
- Subcontractor management

Since they are defined, they can be improved.

Defined   Key processes at this level serve to improve the overall process.

- Organization process focus (software process improvement guide [SPIG])
- Organization process definition
- Training
- Integrated software management
- Software product engineering
- Intergroup coordination
- Peer reviews

Managed   This level uses organizationally standard measures to control and improve the process.

- Quantitative process management
- Software quality measurement

Optimized   This level creates a self-sustaining organization.

Key process areas (KPAs) at this level lead to an "intelligent" organization.

- Defect prevention
- Technology change management
- Process change management

Common Features

Besides KPAs, the following are common features that represent the institutionalization factors:

- Ability to perform
- Commitment to perform
- Activities performed
- Measurement and analysis
- Verifying implementation

CMMI

The official title of this CMM is actually CMMI-SE/SW/IPPD v1.02.

There are two types as follows:

- Staged
- Continuous

One of these must be selected along with the disciplines to be included in the assessment

Staged Representation   This model will

- Provide a sequence of improvements like CMM beginning from basic to advanced
- Permit comparisons across and among based on maturity levels
- Easily integrate with other CMMs

This model does not organize process areas in the same way as ISO 15504.

Continuous Representation   This model is intended to allow the organization to

Select the order of improvement that best meets the organization's business objectives

Enable comparisons across and among organizations on a
process area by process area basis

Provide an easy integration with ISO 15504 because the organization of process areas is derived from that model

Disciplines and Environments

Currently there are two disciplines and one development environment
included in CMMI:

- System engineering discipline
- Software engineering discipline
- Integrated product and process development environment

CMMI Application

- CMMI provides guidance for improving development, acquisition, and maintenance of products and services
- From CMMI the organization can

  - Set process improvement objectives and priorities
  - Improve processes
  - Provide guidance for assuring stable processes

Maturity Levels

The maturity levels of CMMI are slightly different from SW-CMM:

- Initial
- Managed
- Defined
- Quantitatively managed
- Optimizing

Process Areas

The level two process areas are also slightly different:

- Requirements management
- Project planning

- Project monitoring and control
- Supplier agreement management
- Measurement and analysis
- Process and product quality assurance
- Configuration management

Level Three Process Areas

- Requirements development
- Technical solution (design)
- Product integration
- Verification
- Validation
- Organizational process focus
- Organizational process definition
- Organizational training

Level Four Process Areas

- Integrated project management
- Risk management
- Decision analysis and resolution
- Organizational environment for integration
- Integrated teaming
- Quantitative organizational process performance understanding
- Quantitative project management

Level Five Process Areas

- Organizational innovation and deployment
- Causal analysis and resolution

IDEAL

- SEI recommends its IDEAL (initiating, diagnosing, establishing, acting, leveraging) approach to software process improvement.
- These assessments are done by lead assessors.

- They also require trained and qualified individuals to conduct the assessment.
- IDEAL embodies the (CBA IPI) V1.1 assessment method [Dunaway 96b] and the
- Electronic Industries Alliance/Interim Standard (EIA/IS) 731.2 Appraisal Method [EIA 98b].
- Assessment is the diagnostic tool that supports, enables, and encourages an organization's commitment to process improvement.
- The method helps an organization gain insight into its process capability or organizational maturity by identifying strengths and weaknesses of its current processes.

Part 2: Software Process Improvement and Capability Determination (SPICE)

ISO 15504 and Management

ISO 15504, in effect, identifies the potential risks associated with a given unit's capability; this enables managers to put in place appropriate controls for risk containment. It also establishes a quantified basis for evaluating project requirements against the unit's capability.

The Assessment Process   The assessment process compares an organizational unit's processes against a common reference contained in 15504 part 2.

That common reference model describes the set of base practices that are considered essential for good software engineering in each instance.

- Base practices are provided in part 2 for each process instance.

The Reference Model   The reference model defines a process in terms of its

- Purpose
- Practices
- Capability

The reference model is made up of two dimensions. The process dimension that is characterized by process purpose statements and the base practices that address that purpose.

The capability dimension is characterized by a generic set of attributes that describes a given level of capability.

The Capability Dimension

- In addition, 15504 specifies a generic set of management practices (e.g., this set applies to all processes).

These are grouped by capability level.

- The assessment output consists of a set of adequacy ratings and/or process capability level ratings for each process instance.

The generic management practice adequacy ratings are the foundation of the capability dimension.

- Each process instance can potentially be rated at one of five capability levels.
- The rating is dependent on how many of the generic practices characteristics of a given level of maturity are embodied in that process in each instance.
- There are two elements that are involved in the capability determination:
  - Base practices—which describe the performance of the process.
  - Common features—which describe progressively more capable states of the management process.

The Engineering Process Category

The processes belonging to the engineering process category are as follows:
- Develop system requirements and design
- Develop software requirements
- Develop software design
- Implement software design
- Integrate and test software
- Integrate and test system
- Maintain system and software

The Project Process Category   The project category consists of processes that establish the project and manage its resources.

Processes belonging to this category are as follows:

- Plan project life cycle
- Establish project plan
- Build project teams
- Manage requirements
- Manage quality
- Manage risks
- Manage resources and schedule
- Manage subcontractors

The Support Process Category   The support process category consists of processes that may be employed by other processes.

The processes belonging to support are as follows:

- Develop documentation
- Perform configuration management
- Perform quality assurance
- Perform problem resolution
- Perform peer reviews

The Organization Process Category   The organization process category consists of processes that establish the business goals:

- Engineer the business
- Define the process
- Improve the process
- Perform training
- Enable reuse
- Provide software engineering environment
- Provide work facilities

ISO/IEC 15288 Processes

The processes and their groupings are as follows:

- *Agreement processes*
  - Acquisition
  - Supply

- *Enterprise processes*
  - Enterprise environment management
  - Investment management
  - System life cycle process management
  - Resource management
  - Quality management

- *Project Processes*
  - Project planning
  - Project assessment
  - Project control
  - Decision making
  - Risk management
  - Configuration management
  - Information management

- *Technical Processes*
  - Stakeholder requirements definition
  - Requirements analysis
  - Architectural design
  - Implementation
  - Integration
  - Verification
  - Transition
  - Systems analysis
  - Validation
  - Operation
  - Maintenance
  - Disposal

ISO 15288 Relation to Other Frameworks   ISO/IEC 15288 uses two standards as normative references and these are as follows:

- ISO 9001:2000
- ISO/IEC 12207:1995

A committee resolution has been passed to initiate the harmonization of ISO/IEC 15288 with ISO/IEC 15504 and the replacement for ISO 9000-3.

Personal and Team Approaches

PSP and TSP to CMM

Personal Software Process   The PSP is a structured software development process that is intended to help software engineers to better understand and improve their performance by tracking their predicted and actual development of code. The PSP was created by Watts Humphrey to apply the underlying principles of the Software Engineering Institute's (SEI) CMM to the software development practices of a single developer. It claims to give software engineers the process skills necessary to work on a TSP team.*

According to Carnegie Mellon, SEI, PSP document and PSP provide engineers with a disciplined personal framework for doing software work. The PSP process consists of a set of methods, forms, and scripts that show software engineers how to plan, measure, and manage their work. The PSP is designed for use with any programming language or design methodology, and it can be used for most aspects of software work, including writing requirements, running tests, defining processes, and repairing defects. When engineers use the PSP, the recommended process goal is to produce zero-defect products on schedule and within planned costs.

The document also claims that the PSP is the improvement process to the people who actually do the work—the practicing engineers. The PSP concentrates on the work practices of the individual engineers. The principle behind the PSP is that to produce quality software systems, every engineer who works on the system must do quality work.

The PSP is meant to help software professionals consistently use comprehensive engineering practices. It guides them on how to plan and track their work, use a defined and measured process, establish measurable goals, and track performance against these goals. The PSP shows engineers how to manage quality from the beginning of the job, how to analyze the results of each job, and how to use the results to improve the process for the next project.†

---

* https://en.wikipedia.org/wiki/Personal_software_process

† Watts S. Humphrey. *The Personal Software ProcessSM (PSPSM)*. Carnegie Mellon Software Engineering Institute, November 2000, Team Software Process Initiative.

The PSP Process Structure

Planning
Design
Design review
Code
Code review
Compile
Test
Postmortem

PSP Quality Management

One of the most important aspects in PSP is data collection and analysis. In each phases, PSP engineers need to analyze the size of their work, how much time they spent, how many LOC they produced, and the quality of those products.

They record the starting time and end time of the task and any interruption time in between.

PSP maintains its own method of quality management. In the PSP framework, all engineers must manage the quality of their personal work. To help them do this, the PSP guides engineers in tracking and managing every defect.

Engineers must fix all defects they are aware of. Thus, while there are many aspects to software quality, the engineer's first quality concern must necessarily be on finding and fixing defects.

Simple coding mistakes can produce very destructive or hard-to-find defects. PSP training shows engineers how to track and manage all of the defects they find in their programs.

The first PSP quality principle is that the engineers are personally responsible for the quality of the programs they produce. The PSP provides a series of practices and measures to help engineers assess the quality.

Early Defect Removal The principal PSP quality objective is to find and fix defects before the first compile or unit test. The PSP process initiates design and code review steps in which engineers personally review their work products before they are inspected, compiled, or tested.

Defect Prevention   Like the old saying, prevention is better than the cure, the PSP advocates this ethic. There are three different methods that PSP recommends to prevent defects, as follows:

1. Root cause analysis: Record and review data to find out the root cause related to each defect they find and fix.
2. Clear and complete design: The second prevention approach is to use an effective design method and notation to produce complete designs. To completely record a design, engineers must thoroughly understand it.
3. Simple and systematic design: The third defect prevention method is a direct consequence of the second: with a more systematic design, coding time is reduced, thus reducing defect injection.

PSP Project Plan Summary

• Name	
• Project	
• Language	
• Summary (LOC/hour)	
• Planned—actual—to date	
PSP project plan summary	
• Program size (LOC):	
• Base (B)	
• Deleted (D)	
• Modified (M)	
• Added (A)	
• Reused (R)	
• Total new and changed (N)	
• Total LOC (T)	
• Total new reused	
• Total object LOC (E)	
PSP project plan summary	
• Time in phase (minutes) (as planned—actual–to date)	
• Planning	
• Design	
• Code	
• Compile	
• Test	

• Postmortem	
• Total	
PSP project plan summary	
• Defects injected (as actual–to date)	
• Planning	
• Design	
• Code	
• Compile	
• Test	
• Total development	
PSP project plan summary	
• Defects removed (as actual–to date)	
• Planning	
• Design	
• Code	
• Compile	
• Test	
• Total development	

Outcomes of the Process At the conclusion of the application of this discipline, engineers

- Know how to measure their work
- Have observed the effectiveness of various software engineering methods
- Have defined and used a special process for their own use

The Team Software Process

Definition The TSP provides a defined operational process framework that is designed to help teams of managers and engineers organize projects and produce software products that range in size from small projects to very large projects. The TSP is intended to improve the levels of quality and productivity of a team's software development project in order to help them better meet the cost and schedule commitments of developing a software system.*

The initial version of the TSP was developed and piloted by Watts Humphrey in the late 1990s and the technical report for TSP sponsored

---

* https://en.wikipedia.org/wiki/Team_software_process

by the U.S. Department of Defense was published in November 2000. The book by Watts Humphrey, Introduction to the TSP, presents a view the TSP intended for use in academic settings, that focuses on the process of building a software production team, establishing team goals, distributing team roles, and other teamwork-related activities.

According to Carnegie Mellon SEI, TSP document,

> The Team Software Process (TSP) guides engineering teams in developing software-intensive products. Early experience with the TSP shows that its use improves the quality and productivity of engineering teams while helping them to more precisely meet cost and schedule commitments. The TSP is designed for use with teams of 2 to 20 members, and the larger multi-team TSP process is designed for teams of up to about 150 members. While TSP versions are planned for larger projects, they are not available at the time of this writing.[*]

The TSP is a fully defined and measured process that teams can use to plan their work, execute their plans and continuously improve their software development processes. The TSP process is defined by a series of process scripts that describe all aspects of project planning and product development.

That makes the TSP method a legitimate documentation process, which includes documenting team roles, defining measures, and postmortem reports. The TSP technology is an implementation strategy for teams that are attempting to apply disciplined software process methods.

Watts Humphrey developed the PSP and the TSP as a follow-up to his work with the CMM.

TSP development follows the quality strategy that was originated by W. Edwards Deming and Joseph Moses Juran and it was further extended with the introduction of the CMM in 1987 and the PSP in 1995.[†]

The TSP Team Working Process

1. Leading the team
2. Communication
3. Maintaining the plan
4. Rebalancing team workload

---

[*] Ibid, p. 1.
[†] Ibid, p. 1.

Once the TSP team is launched, the principal need is to ensure that all team members follow the plan. This includes the following major topics:

1. Leading the team
2. Process discipline
3. Issue tracking
4. Communication
5. Management reporting
6. Maintaining the plan
7. Estimating project completion
8. Rebalancing team workload
9. Relaunching the project
10. TSP quality management

What Does TSP Do for Software?   The level of maturity of the software processes significantly affects their ability to succeed.

In a study of its implementation (conducted by SEI) in four different organizational settings, it was found that it significantly reduced defect densities in system-level test activities, the actual duration of system-level tests. In addition, it produced improved accuracy of software estimates, while variation in estimation accuracy was significantly reduced.

Measurement   The TSP is designed to address cost, schedule, and quality problems by instilling disciplined quality methods in the process and by quantitatively measuring the results. There are operational definitions within the TSP scripts of the measures to be used.

TSP measurement also includes the following:

- Basic size of the product such as (thousands of lines of code [KLOC])
- How much time (minutes and hours)
- Quality (defects)
- Derived productivity measures (KLOC/hour)
- Process yield (percentage of defects removed)
- Defect densities (defects/KLOC)

The TSP process establishes how these measures are defined, estimated, collected, reported, and analyzed. The TSP process also makes use of the team's historical data, as well as industry planning and quality guidelines.

Application   The TSP was designed to provide both a strategy and a set of operational procedures for deploying disciplined methods at the team level.

The purpose of the TSP is to help engineering teams efficiently and effectively build software products.

It targets many of the current problems in the development process and shows teams and managers explicitly how to address them.

The TSP provides explicit guidance on questions that teams typically struggle with such as the following:

- What are our goals?
- What are the team roles and who will fill them?
- What are the responsibilities associated with these roles?
- How will the team make decisions and settle issues?
- What standards and procedures does the team need and how do we establish them?
- What are our quality objectives?
- How will we track quality and performance?
- What should we do if they fall short of our goals?
- What processes should we use to develop the product?
- What should be our development strategy?
- How should we produce the design?
- How should we integrate and test the product?
- How do we produce our development plan?
- How can we minimize the development schedule?
- How can we determine project status?
- How do we assess, track, and manage risks?
- What do we do if our plan does not meet management's objectives?
- How do we report status to management and the customer?

TSP Quality Management

The Quality Plan   During the team launch, TSP teams make a quality plan. Based on the estimated size of the product and historical data on defect injection rates, they estimate how many defects they will inject in each phase. The team examines the quality plan to see if the quality parameters are reasonable and if they meet the team's quality goals. If not, the engineers adjust the estimates and generate a new quality plan.

Once the team members have generated the quality plan, the quality manager helps them to track performance against it.

Identifying Quality Problems In the TSP, there are several ways to identify quality problems. One can quickly see where defect densities, review rates, yields, or other measures deviate significantly for the team's goals.

Finding and Preventing Quality Problems One of the most important and comprehensive aspects of the PSP and TSP processes is that they are designed to prevent problems before they occur. In PSP training, engineers typically learn how to reduce their defect injection rates by 40%–50%. In the TSP, the design manager can further reduce defect injection rates by ensuring that the team produces a complete and high-quality design. The quality plan and process tracking make the engineers more sensitive to quality issues so that they are more careful, reducing defects even further. Finally, the TSP introduces a defect review where every postdevelopment defect is analyzed to identify potential process changes that will find or prevent similar defects in the future.*

Relationship of PSP and TSP to CMM

The PSP is a defined process for individuals, and it is the foundation from which the TSP was developed for teams. It defined the practices used at the individual level, as if that individual were trying to operate at SW-CMM Level 5.

It is like concentric circles where PSP works in an individual level, TSP works as a team, and CMM works as a whole. PSP addresses the engineering disciplines and TSP addresses the team building and disciplines management discipline.

---

* Ibid.

Appendix

*Software Process Improvement**

Process improvement team

> *Project leader*
> *Project administrator*
> *SQA administrator*
> *Process engineers*

Introduction

Purpose   The purpose of this plan is to accomplish and complete a common and understandable framework for the software life cycle process of MY COMPANY. MY COMPANY is considering to have a large portion of the budget allocated for the process engineering project. In this plan, we employ the "best practices" for the software process improvement for MY COMPANY, therefore, the industry's one of the best standard 12207 for Software life cycle processes will be the template used to guide the implementation of software processes throughout the organization.

The document is also expected to assist with the decision making within the organization on software projects.

Scope

The scope of this document is to provide a detailed analysis by evaluating the current processes and operational structure of MY COMPANY and provide process improvement based on the "best practices." It can be seen that there are quite some gaps between the current processes at the MY COMPANY and the processes given by the 12207 Standard. This document is intended to focus on software improvement processes of MY COMPANY, which is failing in many areas. The intended use

---

* This Software Process Improvement, sample document was prepared for Masters in Information Systems Class project by the author.

of this document is specifically intended for internal use at MY COMPANY. The analysis that follows will be helpful in developing the plan according to the organizational and operational structure at MY COMPANY.

Assumptions

There is an assumption from the process improvement team that management is fully behind the improvement initiative.

Constraints

The organizational unit responsible for implementing the new processes will have the ability to increase resources depending on the outcome of the improvements.

Compliance

The process improvement initiative at MY COMPANY will use the IEEE 12207 standard as its guide and template to implement the process improvements. The standard will be used throughout the organization and every level of the organization will follow the standard.

Acronyms and References

Acronyms   The following alphabetical contractions appear within the text of this guide:

CCB	Configuration control board
CDR	Critical design review
CI	Configuration item
CM	Configuration management
CML	Change management ledger
COTS	Commercial-off-the-shelf
ICD	Interface control document
PDR	Preliminary design review
QA	Quality assurance
RVTM	Requirements verification traceability matrix

SCM	Software configuration management
SCMP	Software configuration management plan
SCMP	Software configuration management plan review
SDD	Software design description
SDP	Software development plan
SMM	Software maintenance manual
SPMP	Software project management plan
SQA	Software quality assurance
SQAP	Software quality assurance plan
SRR	Software requirements review
SRS	Software requirements specifications
SVVP	Software verification and validation plan
SVVPR	Software verification and validation report
SVVR	Software verification and validation report
TQM	Total quality management
UDR	User documentation review
V & V	Verification & validation

Organization and References

- Organizational structure
- Organizational perspective
- Supporting processes

The supporting life cycle processes consist of eight processes. A supporting process supports another process as an integral part with a distinct purpose and contributes to the success and quality of the software project.

Index

Printed in the United States
by Baker & Taylor Publisher Services